BESTSELLING
BOOK SERIES

Handspring™ Visor™ For Dummies®

W9-AVJ-351

Sheet

Graffiti Letter Guide

Here's how to make all the letter characters in Graffiti:

Character	Stroke		Character	Stroke
A	∧		G	G
B	B		H	h
C	C		I	l
D	D		J	J
E	E		K	⅄
F	Γ		L	L

(continued)

Alternative Graffiti Strokes

There are easier ways to write several Graffiti characters. Cut out this card and carry it with you along with the Graffiti card that comes with your Palm device.

Character	Stroke	Description
B	3	Draw the number 3 on the letter side of the Graffiti area.
D	∂	Draw a reverse cursive L.
F	Γ	Start from the bottom.
G	6	Draw the number 6 on the letter side of the Graffiti area.
K	∝	This Graffiti character is the trickiest. Just draw the "legs" on the side of the K, joined by a little loop. Leave out the vertical bar. To me, this character looks like a fish swimming from right to left.

Graffiti Letter Guide (continued)

Here's how to make all the letter characters in Graffiti:

Character	Stroke		Character	Stroke
M	M		T	T
N	N		U	U
O	O		V	V
P	P		W	W
Q	Q		X	X
R	R		Y	Y
S	S		Z	Z

Alternative Graffiti Strokes (continued)

Character	Stroke	Description
V	V	Draw the V backward (that is, start from the top right)
X		A reversed Graffiti letter *K*
Y		Just draw the lower loop of a cursive capital Y. It's just a loop, just like the letter K except that the fish is swimming downward.

When You're in a Bind

When all else fails, go here for help.

Product support (U.S): (716)-871-6448   Web site: www.handspring.com

E-mail: www.handspring.com/support/form_techsupport.asp

The IDG Books Worldwide logo is a registered trademark under exclusive license to IDG Books Worldwide, Inc., from International Data Group, Inc. The ...For Dummies logo is a trademark, and For Dummies is a registered trademark of IDG Books Worldwide, Inc. All other trademarks are the property of their respective owners.

Copyright © 2000 IDG Books Worldwide, Inc.
All rights reserved.

Cheat Sheet $2.95 value. Item 0724-9.
For more information about IDG Books,
call 1-800-762-2974.

For Dummies®: Bestselling Book Series for Beginners

TM

References for the Rest of Us! ®

BESTSELLING BOOK SERIES

Are you intimidated and confused by computers? Do you find that traditional manuals are overloaded with technical details you'll never use? Do your friends and family always call you to fix simple problems on their PCs? Then the *...For Dummies*® computer book series from IDG Books Worldwide is for you.

...For Dummies books are written for those frustrated computer users who know they aren't really dumb but find that PC hardware, software, and indeed the unique vocabulary of computing make them feel helpless. *...For Dummies* books use a lighthearted approach, a down-to-earth style, and even cartoons and humorous icons to dispel computer novices' fears and build their confidence. Lighthearted but not lightweight, these books are a perfect survival guide for anyone forced to use a computer.

> *"I like my copy so much I told friends; now they bought copies."*
>
> — Irene C., Orwell, Ohio

> *"Quick, concise, nontechnical, and humorous."*
>
> — Jay A., Elburn, Illinois

> *"Thanks, I needed this book. Now I can sleep at night."*
>
> — Robin F., British Columbia, Canada

Already, millions of satisfied readers agree. They have made *...For Dummies* books the #1 introductory level computer book series and have written asking for more. So, if you're looking for the most fun and easy way to learn about computers, look to *...For Dummies* books to give you a helping hand.

IDG BOOKS WORLDWIDE ®

Handspring™
Visor™
FOR
DUMMIES®

Handspring™ Visor™ FOR DUMMIES®

by Bill Dyszel

IDG Books Worldwide, Inc.
An International Data Group Company

Foster City, CA ◆ Chicago, IL ◆ Indianapolis, IN ◆ New York, NY

Handspring™ Visor™ For Dummies®

Published by
IDG Books Worldwide, Inc.
An International Data Group Company
919 E. Hillsdale Blvd.
Suite 400
Foster City, CA 94404
www.idgbooks.com (IDG Books Worldwide Web site)
www.dummies.com (Dummies Press Web site)

Copyright © 2000 IDG Books Worldwide, Inc. All rights reserved. No part of this book, including interior design, cover design, and icons, may be reproduced or transmitted in any form, by any means (electronic, photocopying, recording, or otherwise) without the prior written permission of the publisher.

Library of Congress Control Number: 00-102509

ISBN: 0-7645-0724-9

Printed in the United States of America

10 9 8 7 6 5 4 3 2 1

1Q/RQ/QX/QQ/IN

Distributed in the United States by IDG Books Worldwide, Inc.

Distributed by CDG Books Canada Inc. for Canada; by Transworld Publishers Limited in the United Kingdom; by IDG Norge Books for Norway; by IDG Sweden Books for Sweden; by IDG Books Australia Publishing Corporation Pty. Ltd. for Australia and New Zealand; by TransQuest Publishers Pte Ltd. for Singapore, Malaysia, Thailand, Indonesia, and Hong Kong; by Gotop Information Inc. for Taiwan; by ICG Muse, Inc. for Japan; by Intersoft for South Africa; by Eyrolles for France; by International Thomson Publishing for Germany, Austria and Switzerland; by Distribuidora Cuspide for Argentina; by LR International for Brazil; by Galileo Libros for Chile; by Ediciones ZETA S.C.R. Ltda. for Peru; by WS Computer Publishing Corporation, Inc., for the Philippines; by Contemporanea de Ediciones for Venezuela; by Express Computer Distributors for the Caribbean and West Indies; by Micronesia Media Distributor, Inc. for Micronesia; by Chips Computadoras S.A. de C.V. for Mexico; by Editorial Norma de Panama S.A. for Panama; by American Bookshops for Finland.

For general information on IDG Books Worldwide's books in the U.S., please call our Consumer Customer Service department at 800-762-2974. For reseller information, including discounts and premium sales, please call our Reseller Customer Service department at 800-434-3422.

For information on where to purchase IDG Books Worldwide's books outside the U.S., please contact our International Sales department at 317-596-5530 or fax 317-572-4002.

For consumer information on foreign language translations, please contact our Customer Service department at 1-800-434-3422, fax 317-572-4002, or e-mail rights@idgbooks.com.

For information on licensing foreign or domestic rights, please phone +1-650-653-7098.

For sales inquiries and special prices for bulk quantities, please contact our Order Services department at 800-434-3422 or write to the address above.

For information on using IDG Books Worldwide's books in the classroom or for ordering examination copies, please contact our Educational Sales department at 800-434-2086 or fax 317-572-4005.

For press review copies, author interviews, or other publicity information, please contact our Public Relations department at 650-653-7000 or fax 650-653-7500.

For authorization to photocopy items for corporate, personal, or educational use, please contact Copyright Clearance Center, 222 Rosewood Drive, Danvers, MA 01923, or fax 978-750-4470.

LIMIT OF LIABILITY/DISCLAIMER OF WARRANTY: THE PUBLISHER AND AUTHOR HAVE USED THEIR BEST EFFORTS IN PREPARING THIS BOOK. THE PUBLISHER AND AUTHOR MAKE NO REPRESENTATIONS OR WARRANTIES WITH RESPECT TO THE ACCURACY OR COMPLETENESS OF THE CONTENTS OF THIS BOOK AND SPECIFICALLY DISCLAIM ANY IMPLIED WARRANTIES OF MERCHANTABILITY OR FITNESS FOR A PARTICULAR PURPOSE. THERE ARE NO WARRANTIES WHICH EXTEND BEYOND THE DESCRIPTIONS CONTAINED IN THIS PARAGRAPH. NO WARRANTY MAY BE CREATED OR EXTENDED BY SALES REPRESENTATIVES OR WRITTEN SALES MATERIALS. THE ACCURACY AND COMPLETENESS OF THE INFORMATION PROVIDED HEREIN AND THE OPINIONS STATED HEREIN ARE NOT GUARANTEED OR WARRANTED TO PRODUCE ANY PARTICULAR RESULTS, AND THE ADVICE AND STRATEGIES CONTAINED HEREIN MAY NOT BE SUITABLE FOR EVERY INDIVIDUAL. NEITHER THE PUBLISHER NOR AUTHOR SHALL BE LIABLE FOR ANY LOSS OF PROFIT OR ANY OTHER COMMERCIAL DAMAGES, INCLUDING BUT NOT LIMITED TO SPECIAL, INCIDENTAL, CONSEQUENTIAL, OR OTHER DAMAGES. FULLFILLMENT OF EACH COUPON IS THE RESPONSIBILITY OF THE OFFEROR.

Trademarks: Handspring and Visor are trademarks of Handspring, Inc. For Dummies, Dummies Man, A Reference for the Rest of Us!, The Dummies Way, Dummies Daily, and related trade dress are registered trademarks or trademarks of IDG Books Worldwide, Inc. in the United States and other countries, and may not be used without written permission. All other trademarks are the property of their respective owners. IDG Books Worldwide is not associated with any product or vendor mentioned in this book.

is a registered trademark under exclusive license to IDG Books Worldwide, Inc. from International Data Group, Inc.

About the Author

Bill Dyszel writes frequently for such leading publications as *Chief Executive* magazine, *Success* magazine, *PC* magazine, and *Computer Shopper* while also working as a consultant to many of New York City's leading firms in the securities, advertising, and publishing businesses. His list of current and former clients includes Salomon Brothers, First Boston, Goldman Sachs, Ogilvy & Mather, KMPG Peat Marwick, and many others. As a public speaker, he regularly entertains audiences across the United States in his programs about using technology to keep life simple. He is also the author of *Microsoft Outlook 2000 For Dummies* and *PalmPilot For Dummies.*

The world of high technology has led Bill to grapple with such subjects as multimedia (or how to make your $2,000 computer do the work of a $20 radio), personal information managers (how to make your $3,000 laptop computer do the work of a $3 date book), and graphics programs (how to make your $5,000 package of computers and peripheral devices do the work of a 50-cent box of crayons). All joking aside, he has found that after you've figured out the process, most of this stuff can be useful, helpful, and, yes, even cool.

Like many public figures with skeletons in their closets, this author has a secret past. Before entering the computer industry, Bill sang with the New York City Opera and worked regularly on the New York stage as a singer and an actor in numerous plays, musicals, and operas. He also wrote the opera spoof *99% ARTFREE!,* which won critical praise from *The New York Times,* the *New York Daily News,* and the Associated Press when he performed the show off-Broadway.

ABOUT IDG BOOKS WORLDWIDE

Welcome to the world of IDG Books Worldwide.

IDG Books Worldwide, Inc., is a subsidiary of International Data Group, the world's largest publisher of computer-related information and the leading global provider of information services on information technology. IDG was founded more than 30 years ago by Patrick J. McGovern and now employs more than 9,000 people worldwide. IDG publishes more than 290 computer publications in over 75 countries. More than 90 million people read one or more IDG publications each month.

Launched in 1990, IDG Books Worldwide is today the #1 publisher of best-selling computer books in the United States. We are proud to have received eight awards from the Computer Press Association in recognition of editorial excellence and three from Computer Currents' First Annual Readers' Choice Awards. Our best-selling ...*For Dummies*® series has more than 50 million copies in print with translations in 31 languages. IDG Books Worldwide, through a joint venture with IDG's Hi-Tech Beijing, became the first U.S. publisher to publish a computer book in the People's Republic of China. In record time, IDG Books Worldwide has become the first choice for millions of readers around the world who want to learn how to better manage their businesses.

Our mission is simple: Every one of our books is designed to bring extra value and skill-building instructions to the reader. Our books are written by experts who understand and care about our readers. The knowledge base of our editorial staff comes from years of experience in publishing, education, and journalism — experience we use to produce books to carry us into the new millennium. In short, we care about books, so we attract the best people. We devote special attention to details such as audience, interior design, use of icons, and illustrations. And because we use an efficient process of authoring, editing, and desktop publishing our books electronically, we can spend more time ensuring superior content and less time on the technicalities of making books.

You can count on our commitment to deliver high-quality books at competitive prices on topics you want to read about. At IDG Books Worldwide, we continue in the IDG tradition of delivering quality for more than 30 years. You'll find no better book on a subject than one from IDG Books Worldwide.

John Kilcullen
Chairman and CEO
IDG Books Worldwide, Inc.

VIII WINNER
Eighth Annual Computer Press Awards ≥1992

IX WINNER
Ninth Annual Computer Press Awards ≥1993

1995 COMPUTER CURRENTS READERS' CHOICE

X WINNER
Tenth Annual Computer Press Awards ≥1994

XI WINNER
Eleventh Annual Computer Press Awards ≥1995

IDG is the world's leading IT media, research and exposition company. Founded in 1964, IDG had 1997 revenues of $2.05 billion and has more than 9,000 employees worldwide. IDG offers the widest range of media options that reach IT buyers in 75 countries representing 95% of worldwide IT spending. IDG's diverse product and services portfolio spans six key areas including print publishing, online publishing, expositions and conferences, market research, education and training, and global marketing services. More than 90 million people read one or more of IDG's 290 magazines and newspapers, including IDG's leading global brands — Computerworld, PC World, Network World, Macworld and the Channel World family of publications. IDG Books Worldwide is one of the fastest-growing computer book publishers in the world, with more than 700 titles in 36 languages. The "...For Dummies®" series alone has more than 50 million copies in print. IDG offers online users the largest network of technology-specific Web sites around the world through IDG.net (http://www.idg.net), which comprises more than 225 targeted Web sites in 55 countries worldwide. International Data Corporation (IDC) is the world's largest provider of information technology data, analysis and consulting, with research centers in over 41 countries and more than 400 research analysts worldwide. IDG World Expo is a leading producer of more than 168 globally branded conferences and expositions in 35 countries including E3 (Electronic Entertainment Expo), Macworld Expo, ComNet, Windows World Expo, ICE (Internet Commerce Expo), Agenda, DEMO, and Spotlight. IDG's training subsidiary, ExecuTrain, is the world's largest computer training company, with more than 230 locations worldwide and 785 training courses. IDG Marketing Services helps industry-leading IT companies build international brand recognition by developing global integrated marketing programs via IDG's print, online and exposition products worldwide. Further information about the company can be found at www.idg.com.   1/26/00

Author's Acknowledgments

Thanks to the many people who have made this book possible, especially Senior Project Editor Kyle Looper, Acquisitions Editor Ed Adams, and Technical Editor Gayle Ehrenman. Special thanks also to Diane Steele, Mary Bednarek, Andy Cummings, and everyone else at IDG Books. And special thanks to the good folks at Handspring, Inc., for lending a Visor to IDG Books during the development and production of this book.

Publisher's Acknowledgments

We're proud of this book; please register your comments through our IDG Books Worldwide Online Registration Form located at http://my2cents.dummies.com.

Some of the people who helped bring this book to market include the following:

Acquisitions, Editorial, and Media Development

Project Editors: Nate Holdread, Kyle Looper

    (Previous Edition: Rebecca Whitney)

Acquisitions Editor: Ed Adams

Copy Editors: Marla Reece-Hall, Paula Lowell

Proof Editors: Teresa Artman, Dwight Ramsey

Technical Editor: Gayle Ehrenman

Permissions Editor: Carmen Krikorian

Associate Media Development Specialist: Megan Decraene

Editorial Manager: Leah P. Cameron

Media Development Manager: Heather Heath Dismore

Editorial Assistant: Beth Parlon

Production

Project Coordinator: Maridee Ennis

Layout and Graphics: Joe Bucki, Barry Offringa, Tracy K. Oliver Brent Savage, Jacque Schneider, Janet Seib, Erin Zeltner

Proofreaders: Laura Albert, John Greenough, Susan Moritz, Carl Pierce, Marianne Santy, Charles Spencer

Indexer: York Production Services, Inc.

Special Help

Amanda M. Foxworth, Maureen Spears, Jeremy Zucker

General and Administrative

IDG Books Worldwide, Inc.: John Kilcullen, CEO

IDG Books Technology Publishing Group: Richard Swadley, Senior Vice President and Publisher; Walter R. Bruce III, Vice President and Publisher; Joseph Wikert, Vice President and Publisher; Mary Bednarek, Vice President and Director, Product Development; Andy Cummings, Publishing Director, General User Group; Mary C. Corder, Editorial Director; Barry Pruett, Publishing Director

IDG Books Consumer Publishing Group: Roland Elgey, Senior Vice President and Publisher; Kathleen A. Welton, Vice President and Publisher; Kevin Thornton, Acquisitions Manager; Kristin A. Cocks, Editorial Director

IDG Books Internet Publishing Group: Brenda McLaughlin, Senior Vice President and Publisher; Sofia Marchant, Online Marketing Manager

IDG Books Production for Branded Press: Debbie Stailey, Director of Production; Cindy L. Phipps, Manager of Project Coordination, Production Proofreading, and Indexing; Tony Augsburger, Manager of Prepress, Reprints, and Systems; Laura Carpenter, Production Control Manager; Shelley Lea, Supervisor of Graphics and Design; Debbie J. Gates, Production Systems Specialist; Robert Springer, Supervisor of Proofreading; Trudy Coler, Page Layout Manager; Troy Barnes, Page Layout Supervisor, Kathie Schutte, Senior Page Layout Supervisor; Michael Sullivan, Production Supervisor

Packaging and Book Design: Patty Page, Manager, Promotions Marketing

◆

The publisher would like to give special thanks to Patrick J. McGovern, without whom this book would not have been possible.

◆

Contents at a Glance

Cartoons at a Glance

By Rich Tennant

"These are the handheld devices you recommended our employees use to communicate with?!"

page 7

"Let's see if I can get a menu any faster from their web site than I can from the waiter."

page 171

page 67

"OH, WELL SHOOT! MUST BE THAT NEW PAINT PROGRAM ON MY HPC."

page 233

"It's a Weber PalmPit Pro handheld barbeque with 24 btu, rechargeable battery pack, and applications for roasting, smoking, and open-flame cooking."

page 291

Fax: 978-546-7747
E-mail: richtennant@the5thwave.com
World Wide Web: www.the5thwave.com

Table of Contents

Introduction

· ·

Welcome to the leading edge of technology. The Visor is currently the coolest personal organizer you can own. It's so cool that many people don't even know what a Visor is yet! That's the coolest thing of all. Of course you do, because you're reading this book – congratulations!

I discovered that busy people like using a Visor, but those people are often too busy to learn how to use it effectively. That's understandable; it's part of the territory, really. It only takes a few minutes to learn each feature of your Visor, so I put this book together in independent chunks for busy people who only want to read a few pages at a time while they jet from place to place.

If you're like me, using a Visor may make you impatient with your regular desktop computer. The Visor pops right on and does what you want without a lot of "booting up" and waiting around. Perhaps those bigger computers can take the Visor's example and get down to business.

Sadly, I can't dispense with my regular computer just yet. The Visor isn't meant to replace conventional computers; it's intended to give you a handy and portable window for accessing information, much of which you keep on your computer. But don't be fooled – the Visor is a really powerful little machine in itself.

Who Should Buy This Book

The Visor is the brainchild of Jeff Hawkins and Donna Dubinsky, the parents of the original PalmPilot. That would make the Visor and the PalmPilot siblings, wouldn't it? Well, sort of, but not exactly. I could write an entire soap opera about the Visor family tree, but I may save that for a later edition. The PalmPilot and the Visor use the same software and do most of the same things the same way, so you could call them very very close cousins. If you know how to use a PalmPilot, you know how to use a Visor, too.

The Visor takes advantage of all the benefits of being a member of the PalmPilot family. PalmPilot was the most successful new electronic product in history. In the first two years following the PalmPilot's introduction, nearly two million units were sold. That's hot. No gadget has ever sold so quickly, including hit products like the VCR, the Sony Walkman, and the answering machine. In 1997, the sales for handheld units using the Palm system were greater than the sales for handhelds using the Macintosh system.

Chances are strong that if you don't have a Visor or PalmPilot yourself, someone you know either has one or wants one. As you read this book, you'll find out how a Visor works and what it can do for you. You'll also get a taste of what peripherals you can add to Visor to make it suit your needs better. If you fit into any of the following categories, this book is meant for you:

✔ You're planning to buy a Visor, and you want to know what you can do with it and especially what it can do for you.

✔ You already own a Visor, and you want to get the most from it quickly.

✔ You're looking for a gift for someone who already owns a Visor. Visors are very popular gifts. You can send me one anytime.

✔ You own one of those Windows CE machines and realize the error of your ways (say it ain't so!).

Even if you're just curious about the Palm phenomenon, this book aims at showing you what all the excitement's about. Anyone can receive some benefit from a Visor, even if all that person wants is a little fun.

Visor, PalmPilot, Whatever — Make Up Your Mind

It's exciting to be a Visor owner because improvements for Visor and other Palm computers come along so quickly. But the rapid pace can be confusing because some of the features that are available for the current models weren't available on products sold only six or eight months ago.

The Visor is only one brand of organizer that uses the Palm operating system. You may also be using another product that's based on Palm Computing technology but has a different name; perhaps a regular Palm Computing product like the Palm III, Palm V, or Palm VII. I wrote a whole book for those models, called *Palm Computing For Dummies*, but never fear – most of the basics of PalmPilot and Visor are so close that either this book or that book would be helpful. You may also be using an IBM WorkPad (Sheesh! What a drab name! I wish they'd call it IBM FunPad.). The information in this book applies to the WorkPad, too. Other products based on the Palm Computing design are in the pipeline as well; companies like Sony, Apple, Nokia, and Qualcomm are planning new products that work just like the PalmPilot and Visor. The general principles in this book should work for those products, too.

How This Book Is Organized

To help you more easily find out how to do what you want to do, I divided this book into parts. Each part covers a different aspect of using Visor. The first couple of parts focus on Visor itself – what you can do if you just have that. In later parts, I discuss add-ons for Visor and the desktop computer program that comes with PalmPilot. Yes, PalmPilot can actually talk to your desktop computer. Let's hear it for Computer Détente!

Here's a quick-and-dirty outline of this book – just enough to whet your whistle and make you want to buy it!

Part I: Getting to Know Your Visor

"Getting to know you, getting to know all about you. . . ." Ahem, sorry – I can't resist a little show tune every now and again. Anyway, nothing about using the Visor is difficult, but many features and options aren't exactly obvious. The first part of this book describes what you have to work with on your Visor and how you work with what you have. I explain all those funny-looking buttons and other doodads on the outside of your Visor, and I give you a lesson in Graffiti – and no, not so you can join a gang and practice spray-can art. *Graffiti* is the special alphabet that you can use to enter information into your Visor. And if you're in the secret agent biz (or if you're just security-minded), you can find out how to keep confidential information on your Visor safe from prying eyes.

Part II: Getting Down to Business

Yes, Virginia, the Visor is a computer. It doesn't act grouchy and forbidding like other computers, but it can do many of the jobs that are typically performed by enormous desktop units (ironically called microcomputers, of all things). The Visor comes with a set of pre-installed programs when you buy it. These programs act as a personal information manager (PIM) to help you keep track of your schedule, address book, and to-do list. If you've ever used a computer for personal organizing, the methods of Visor may seem familiar. There's also a Memo Pad for jotting down random notes to yourself or others, and you can even copy your e-mail to your Visor and read it while you sit by the pool. (Sorry, the pool isn't included.) Your Visor also features *infrared beaming*, a method for sending information between two Visors or PalmPilots through the air using an invisible beam of light. How cool is that?

Part III: Visor and the Outside World

No computer is an island, especially the tiny Visor. If it were, you'd be in trouble at high tide. The people who invented the Visor and PalmPilot figured that folks would use Visors in conjunction with some other computer, simply because there's no denying the physical limitations of a tiny computer when entering data and connecting to other resources, such as the Internet or a CD-ROM. Part III tells you all that you need to know about *HotSyncing* (the process through which your Visor and your Windows PC or Macintosh talk to each other) and walks you through installing and operating the desktop programs that come with your PalmPilot. And when you're out and about and you want to use the Handspring Modem to HotSync to your computer . . . well, I show you how to do that, too. How's that for a bargain?

Part IV: Going "Outside the Box" with Your Visor

Like any appliance, the day may come when you need more from your Visor, and the Maytag repairman is nowhere in sight. Or perhaps you need to make your Visor do something new. In Part IV, I show you some options for making your little Visor do big things. I cover some software add-ons that may impress your coworkers. Whether you're a doctor or a bartender, there's add-on software out there for you.

Part V: The Part of Tens

Why ten? Beats me! All the other *For Dummies* books get a Part of Tens, so I'll be darned if mine doesn't have one, too! Here, you find out what your Visor *can't* do and how to stylishly accessorize your Visor without having to call Calvin Klein for wardrobe advice.

Conventions Used in This Book

You may be a die-hard reader of *For Dummies* books, living in a beautiful black-and-yellow home filled with black-and-yellow books. You may be familiar with the approach, and this book works a lot like all the other books in this series.

If you've never read a *For Dummies* book, welcome. Buying and reading this book proves that you're one smart cookie who doesn't want to deal with those overgrown paperweights that litter the shelves of your local bookstore's computer section. Instead, you want a clear, no-nonsense explanation of the things that you really need to know, and nothing else. That's what you get here.

How much do you need to know?

I figure that you know how to push a button. This skill will get you far with a Visor because it's so simple to use. Although you can use a Visor without HotSyncing it with a desktop computer, I assume that you will use your Visor with a desktop machine at some point and that you already know how to use it. If you're still a little iffy on using your desktop computer, I suggest you pick up a copy of the *For Dummies* book that covers the system you use. A few helpful titles include *Macs For Dummies*, *PCs For Dummies*, *Windows 98 For Dummies*, and *Mac OS 8 For Dummies* (all published by IDG Books Worldwide, Inc.).

Some helpful terms

To reduce confusion as you read this book, here are a few tidbits and terms that you need to understand:

- When I refer to a desktop computer, I mean a conventional computer running either Microsoft Windows or Mac OS. If your main computer is a laptop, that's fine. Please forgive me if I always say "desktop" – they all look so big compared to a Visor.

- Although Visor is made to work as an extension of more than one type of computer system, the terms that I use to describe what you should do on your desktop machine assume that you're using the Windows platform. I cover the Macintosh platform in my other book, *Palm Computing For Dummies*. Because Visor and PalmPilot are so similar, those directions should suit Mac users to a "T."

- *Tapping* means touching your Visor stylus to a named area on the PalmPilot display.

- *Clicking* means pressing the left-mouse button on an item.

- *Choosing* means to either tap a menu choice on your Visor or click a given menu choice with your desktop computer's mouse.

- *Right-clicking* means to press the right-mouse button.

- *Double-clicking* means quickly clicking the left-mouse button (or the only mouse button) twice.

- *Dragging* (on the Visor) means touching an item with your stylus and sliding the point of the stylus from one spot on the display to another.

- *Dragging* (on a Windows PC or a Mac) means holding down the mouse button while moving the mouse.

- *Selecting* or *highlighting* means either tapping a choice on a list or sliding your stylus across a specific area of text, which prepares the PalmPilot for you to do something to that piece of text.

All the tasks I describe in the preceding list are much easier to do than they sound. You'll catch on in no time. Here are a few items that you may see me mention from time to time:

- ✔ *Dialog boxes* are rectangles that pop up on the screen and can include messages for you to read, buttons for you to tap or click, lists for you to choose from, blanks for you to fill in, and check boxes for you to tap. Don't worry, I tell you what to do with each dialog box as you encounter it.

- ✔ *Buttons* are real, physical buttons on the front of your Visor case. I normally call each button by the name of the application it runs. Your Visor comes with two types of buttons: hard and soft. The *hard buttons* are at the bottom of your Visor below the screen. The *soft buttons* are just above the hard buttons but are actually part of the screen. You can find more about all this button stuff in Chapter 1.

I normally simplify menu commands by saying something like Go⇨Cubs, which means "Choose Go from the menu bar and then choose Cubs."

Icons Used in This Book

Sometimes the fastest way to find information in a book is to look at the pictures. In this case, icons draw your attention to specific types of information that are useful to know. Here are the icons I use in this book:

The Cross-Reference icon alerts you to when you can seek out other *For Dummies* books for further in-depth detail on a topic.

I use this icon for important information that you shouldn't forget.

As if the Visor weren't easy enough to use, I've found even shorter ways of doing things. The Shortcut icon points out super-speedy methods for performing a task. But don't confuse this with official Palm ShortCuts – I cover those in their own section in Chapter 3.

The Tip icon notes a hint or trick for saving time and effort, or highlights text that makes the Visor easier to understand.

The Warning icon alerts you to something that you should be careful about to prevent problems.

Part I
Getting to Know Your Visor

The 5th Wave   By Rich Tennant

"These are the handheld devices you recommended our employees use to communicate with?!"

In this part . . .

You can do lots with the Palm organizer's few tiny buttons and little plastic stylus. Although you may figure out a great deal by just fiddling around, this part's quick tour gives you a head start. I also show you how to customize your Palm device to your specific needs.

Chapter 1

What Can a Visor Do?

*Y*our tiny Handspring Visor is a full-fledged computer. Although easy to mistake for a toy, and despite being no bigger than a stack of index cards, that friendly little package is a real-live computer, standing by to serve you at any time, anywhere.

It seems that as a computer gets smaller, the number of things you can do with it increases. When every computer was the size of a house, it made sense to use one to shoot a rocket to the moon — but not to shoot a joke to your friend in the next cubicle. Even today, a laptop computer is too bulky to carry around 24 hours a day. You certainly wouldn't use a laptop to check your shopping list at the grocery store.

You can, however, keep your trusty Handspring Visor with you at all times. You can put your shopping list on a Visor. You may think of things to do with it that nobody has ever thought of before. After a while, you'll forget that it's a computer and think of your Visor as a little electronic companion.

If you don't have the time to figure out cool new things to do with your Visor, other people are ready to do that for you. Over 5,000 programs already exist for use on your Visor, dealing with everything from blackjack to biochemistry. You can also clip on a springboard cartridge, which enables you to read novels, almanacs, or the great works of philosophy on your Visor screen.

But this chapter starts simple. Most people use their Visor to keep track of what they plan to do, when they plan to do it, and whom they plan to do it with. This chapter covers the basic uses of the Handspring Visor. I get into the finer points later in the book.

What Is This Thing, Anyway?

The Visor is a simple little contraption with almost no moving parts. Sometimes it's hard to believe that it's a computer at all. After all, computers are supposed to have zillions of buttons and lights and make scary sounds when they start up, right? Well, you don't have to think of your Visor as a computer at all; think of it as your little electronic friend that helps you keep track of your real friends. If you have imaginary friends, your Visor can help you keep track of them too, along with all those nice people in the white coats. (I can't get my publisher to let me write *Delusions For Dummies,* so you're on your own for now.)

The Visor really has only three elements — the buttons, the screen, and the stylus. No mouse, no cables, no disks, none of it. You'll probably want to use your Visor along with a normal computer that has all those annoying gizmos, but as long as you're just using your Visor, you can keep things simple. Figure 1-1 shows you what the Visor looks like, and the following sections tell you what all those funny little doodads do.

Figure 1-1:
The buttons at the bottom of the Visor case are called hard buttons.

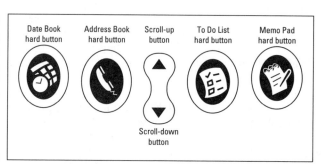

Does my Visor do Windows?

Don't make me WinCE! The Visor doesn't run Windows, and for that you should be glad. The Palm Desktop Software does connect your Visor to the world of Windows quite nicely, but the Visor itself isn't running the Windows operating system. The Visor uses the Palm Operating System, which is the same system that runs all those PalmPilots and lots of other popular hand-held computers.

Some handheld computers don't use the Palm system. Those handheld computers use a system from Microsoft called Windows CE (usually called "WinCE," a word that sounds like the face you make when you smell something bad) that's specially made for palm-sized computers. WinCE looks a tiny bit like the version of Windows that you may be running on your desktop, including a Start button and some of the old menus. WinCE also has a feature from the desktop that we could all do without — an hourglass that shows up regularly when the system is too slow to do any work for you. Your Visor won't make you wait like that; it gets right to work.

On the whole, Windows CE isn't any more compatible with your desktop machine than your Visor is. Virtually all Palm software runs on all Visors as well as on all Palm products. Also, more software is being written for computers like the Visor than is being written for those WinCE devices. You can currently find over 5,000 programs available for the Visor, compared to a mere fraction of that number for Windows CE machines. What can I say? Figures don't lie.

One way or another, you'll probably want to synchronize your palm-sized computer to a desktop or laptop computer, and a Visor synchronizes every bit as well as a WinCE palmtop. My recommendation; enjoy your Visor. It's the real thing.

What's on the Outside of Your Visor

The case of your Visor has a bunch of little buttons on it that do all sorts of cool stuff. I explain in this section what those buttons do.

Application hard buttons

The *application hard buttons* are easy. I use the word *hard* to mean real, actual, physical buttons that you can push with your finger to make something happen. Figure 1-1 shows you what those buttons look like.

The application buttons are the four round buttons at the bottom of the Visor case (as shown in Figure 1-2). Push any of these buttons at any time and the Visor shows you the application (or program) that is assigned to that button. Applications are just jobs that the Visor is ready to do for you.

You can even push an application button when the Visor is turned off. When you do, your Visor automatically turns on and opens the application assigned to that button. A Visor is a little like a microwave oven in that way; you don't have to turn on your microwave and then tell it to start cooking — just push the button and you're cooking. Unlike your microwave oven, your Visor needs very little cleaning, and it won't make your breakfast eggs explode.

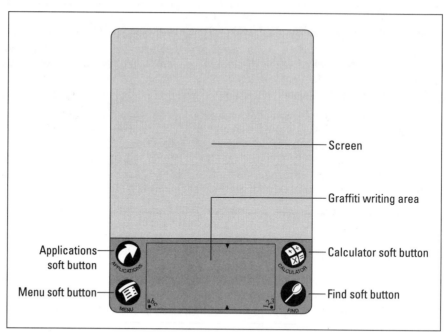

Figure 1-2:
The Palm
Organizer
screen.

Here's what those buttons do:

- **Date Book:** The far-left application button. The Date Book button is easy to identify by the little icon that looks like a page from a day calendar. You don't need to get bent out of shape when you use the Date Book, which shows you dates and appointments. (See Chapter 8 for more on the Date Book.)

- **Address Book:** The second button from the left with the little telephone icon. Pressing this button helps you find names, addresses, and (naturally) phone numbers. (See Chapter 5 for more on the Address Book.)

- **To Do List:** The third application button (second from the right side of the case), which is decorated with a checklist. The To Do List button opens the application that tracks your tasks. (See Chapter 6 for more on the To Do List.) Scroll buttons, which I describe later in this chapter, separate the two applications on the right side of the Visor from the ones on the left.

- **Memo Pad:** The far-right button, with the picture of an itty-bitty notebook. The Memo Pad is the place where you enter and store text. (See Chapter 7 for more on the Memo Pad.)

You can assign different programs to the four applications buttons than the ones that come installed on your Visor. For example, if you don't use the To Do List or the Memo Pad much, you can reassign those buttons to other programs. Check out Chapter 3 to find more about how it's done.

Visor — a real computer

Don't be fooled — the Visor is a real computer. It may look like those little electronic organizers that have been around for years, but it contains the same Motorola computer chip that powered the first Macintosh. Yes, you can manage addresses and appointments on a Visor, just like you can on those old organizers. But you can also run and load software, just like you can on a conventional computer.

The biggest difference between a Visor and a regular computer is what computer geeks call the *user interface*. The Visor has no keyboard; you write and tap on the Visor's touch-sensitive screen. Many types of programs that people commonly use on conventional computers are being developed for the Visor, including spreadsheets, database managers, and Web browsers. The software on the CD accompanying this book gives you a taste of how far you can go with the power of the Visor handheld computer.

Scroll buttons

At the bottom center of your Visor case are the *scroll buttons*. The scroll buttons work like the power window buttons in a car. If you want to move down through a screen to see what doesn't fit, press the bottom button. If you want to go back to the top of the screen, use the top button. Sometimes the scroll buttons change the way that they act in different applications. Sometimes pressing a scroll button makes the information on the display leap to the next screen instead of crawling gradually. Sometimes a scroll button does nothing, especially when there's no next screen to see.

Power button

The black button with the little green dot on at the left edge of the Visor case is the power button.

The power button has a second job; it turns the Visor backlight on and off. To turn the backlight on, hold the power button down for at least two seconds. (You can also customize your Visor so that the backlight goes on with a certain stroke of your stylus. I discuss that topic in Chapter 3.) The backlight makes text on the screen of the Visor much easier to read in the dark.

Although the backlight makes reading the Visor screen easier in dim light, the light itself drains the batteries like crazy. The best time to use your backlight is when you can't read text on-screen without it.

One nice thing about the way the Visor works is a quality called a *persistent state*. No, that's not the feeling you get after you meet all the salesmen in Utah; it means that whatever is happening on the Visor screen when you turn the power off will be happening when you turn the Visor on again. It's like sleep mode on your desktop computer. Persistent state is a very handy feature when you get interrupted in the middle of doing something and want to get right back to it, even if you get a call from a long-winded salesman from Utah.

Reset button

Sometimes you need to tell your Visor to stop what it's doing and start all over again. That's called *resetting* your Visor. Occasionally, a program that you've installed on your Visor misbehaves and makes the Visor hang up or act crazy. That happens rarely, and resetting the Visor usually fixes the problem.

You can reset your Visor two different ways: the hard way and the kinder, gentler soft way. A *soft* reset just makes the Visor stop everything and start again. You can perform a soft reset on your Visor by pushing the end of a bent paper clip into the little hole labeled Reset on the back.

A *hard* reset erases all your data and your username. Needless to say, you don't want to do a hard reset without a pretty good reason. If you're selling your Visor to someone else, you could do a hard reset to make the unit act like it did when it was brand new. (I wish I could do that to myself now and then.) To perform a hard reset, hold the power button down and then press the end of a paper clip into the hole marked Reset on the back of your Visor. When you do, a prompt appears on the Visor screen, asking you if you really want to erase all your data. Think hard again whether you want to do that — then either press the scroll-up hard button if you do or the scroll-down button if you don't.

The Screen

You can't miss the most important part of the Visor — the screen, which you can see in Figure 1-3. It shows you the information that you've stored in your applications and lets you know what the applications are ready to do for you next.

An equally important function of the Visor screen is to take information from you. Two parts of the screen, the display and the Graffiti area, take information from you in different ways. The soft buttons (not to be confused with the hard buttons described earlier in this chapter) let you do all sorts of other neat things.

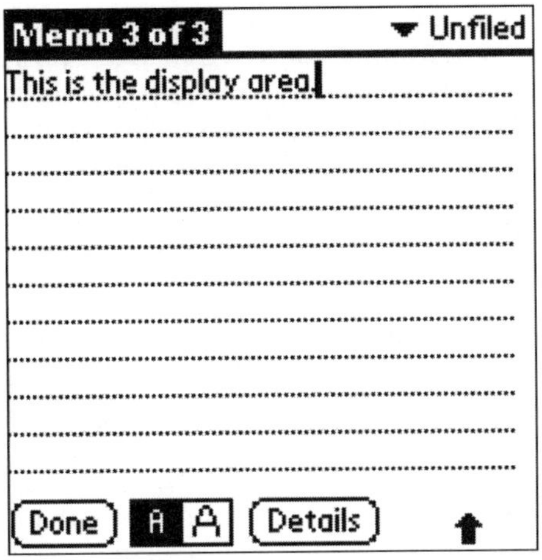

```
┌─────────────────────────────────────────┐
│ Memo 3 of 3              ▼ Unfiled        │
│ This is the display area.................. │
│ ........................................ │
│ ........................................ │
│ ........................................ │
│ ........................................ │
│ ........................................ │
│ ........................................ │
│ ........................................ │
│ ........................................ │
│ ........................................ │
│ ........................................ │
│ (Done)  🅰 🅰  (Details)          ⬆       │
└─────────────────────────────────────────┘
```

Figure 1-3:
Your Visor
screen.

The display

The largest part of the Visor screen is the main *display area,* as shown in
Figure 1-4. The display area not only shows the text that you're working with,
but also contains a number of active areas upon which you can tap your
stylus to make something happen, such as display the contents of a memo or
mark a task complete. You can also slide your stylus across the surface of the
screen to select (or highlight) the text that's displayed in some applications.

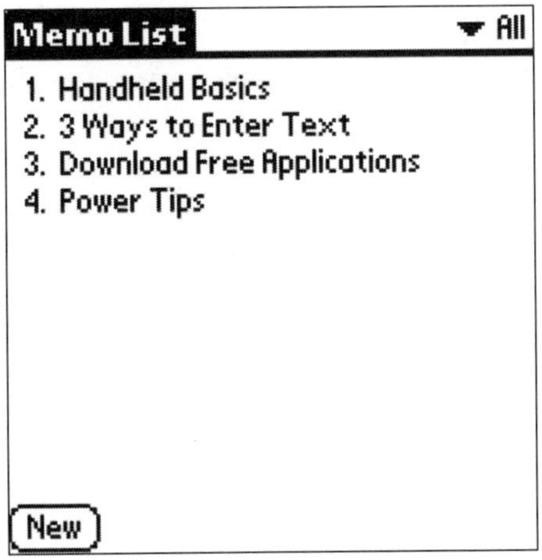

```
┌─────────────────────────────────────────┐
│ Memo List                      ▼ All      │
│ 1. Handheld Basics                        │
│ 2. 3 Ways to Enter Text                   │
│ 3. Download Free Applications             │
│ 4. Power Tips                             │
│                                           │
│                                           │
│                                           │
│                                           │
│                                           │
│ (New)                                     │
└─────────────────────────────────────────┘
```

Figure 1-4:
The display
area.

Most standard Visor applications organize the display into areas that do pretty much the same job from one application to the next. The upper-left corner of the screen displays a tab that shows the name of the application that you're using, such as Address List, To Do List, or Memo Pad. The upper-right corner usually tells you the category of the item that you're viewing. The bottom of the display usually contains buttons that you can tap to create, find, or edit items in the application that you're using. The main, central part of the display is the part that shows the bulk of your information. Some applications offer a scroll bar on the right edge of the screen that enables you to scroll the display to show information that's higher or lower on the list of items that you're viewing. This scroll bar does the same thing as the scroll buttons at the bottom of your Visor (see "Scroll buttons" earlier in this chapter).

I frequently use the words *sometimes* and *usually* when describing the display because every program works a bit differently. Every element doesn't work the same way all the time, but the preceding description is how most well-designed Visor programs tend to work.

Soft buttons

Soft buttons aren't really soft, like a pillow; they're more like pictures of buttons painted on to the Visor screen. Unlike hard buttons, soft buttons have no moving parts, and they don't do anything until your Visor is powered on. Figure 1-5 shows what the soft buttons look like.

To use one of the soft buttons, just tap it with your stylus. The four jobs that are assigned to the four soft buttons are Applications, Menu, Calculator, and Find. The following sections outline what each soft button does.

Applications

The *Applications* soft button calls up a list of all the applications on your Visor, showing their icons. Figure 1-6 shows the icons that you should see on your Visor.

Figure 1-5:
The soft buttons work only when the Visor is powered on.

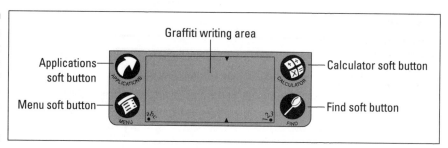

Figure 1-6:
Every program on your Visor has an icon in the list of applications.

Several applications come already installed on your Visor, including the following:

- ✔ **Expense:** Use this application to keep track of what you spend.

- ✔ **HotSync:** The program that makes your Visor communicate with your desktop computer.

- ✔ **Mail:** Exchanges messages with the e-mail program on your desktop.

- ✔ **DateBook+:** A special souped up version of the Date Book that gives you a more powerful set of organizing tools than the basic datebook program.

- ✔ **Preferences:** Use this application to configure your Visor to suit your needs.

- ✔ **Security:** Set up passwords and hide or show private items.

Any applications that you install on your Visor also show up in this list. I tell you more about the applications that come with your Visor later in this chapter (see "What Do the Standard Applications Do?"), and I show you how to install other applications in Chapter 12. You can start any application that you see in the applications list by tapping the icon for that program. The little battery icon in the applications list tells you how much power is left in your batteries.

Menu

The *Menu* button activates the menus in any application that you're running. Most Visor programs have a set of menus that enable you to cut, copy, or paste text, as well as create new items or delete old ones (these menus are similar to those you find in the applications for your desktop computer — except they're not as involved). To use the menus in any application, start the application, and then tap the Menu button and tap the menu that you want to use. Figure 1-7 shows a sample menu.

Record	Edit	Options

- Delete Item... ⁄D
- Attach Note ⁄A
- Delete Note... ⁄O
- Purge... ⁄E
- Beam Item ⁄B
- Beam Category

■ 1 Find Stranger in Paradise

(New) (Details...) (Show...)   ↑

Figure 1-7:
If you don't like the specials, you can always order from the Menu.

Calculator

The *Calculator* button contains no mysteries; it starts up the on-screen calculator, as shown in Figure 1-8. Tap the numbers just like you would with a handheld calculator. You can even press the on-screen calculator buttons with your finger. Naturally, it's not a good idea to put your fingers on the screen if you have gooey stuff like chocolate on your hands, because it leaves a mess on your screen, which makes your calculations hard to read. I don't know what happens if you try to lick chocolate off your Visor screen (or worse, somebody else's Visor screen). I wouldn't try it.

Figure 1-8:
You can perform simple calculations on your Visor calculator.

Find

The *Find* button starts up a little program that searches your entire Visor for a certain string of text. If you want to find every item on your Visor that contains the word *chocolate,* tap the Find button and enter the word **chocolate** by using either the on-screen keyboard or Graffiti (see Chapter 2 for more about entering text), and then tap OK (see Figure 1-9). The Find program then finds all the *chocolate* on your Visor, which is faster and healthier than finding all the chocolate in your grocery store.

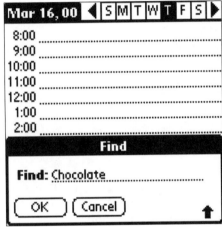

Figure 1-9:
You can find
a word that
occurs in
any Visor
application
by using the
Find tool.

I'll tell you one odd thing about the Find tool; if you enter only the first part of a word, it finds the word that you're looking for. But if you enter only the last part of the word, your word won't turn up. If you enter *choco,* you still find chocolate, but if you enter *late,* you come up with *late, later,* and *latest,* but not *chocolate.*

Contrast control

The contrast control isn't really a button; it's a little dot at the lower-left corner of the Visor screen. When you tap the contrast button, a box Adjust Contrast appears at the bottom of your screen. Just use your stylus to slide the button toward the right side of the screen to darken the display, or to the left to make the display lighter. When the screen is as bright or dark as you like, tap the Done button.

The Graffiti area

A large box between the soft buttons called the *Graffiti area* occupies most of the bottom part of the screen, as shown in Figure 1-10. A pair of tiny triangles at the top and bottom of the Graffiti area separate the part for entering letters from the part for entering numbers. You can use the Visor stylus to write letters on the left side in a special alphabet, called Graffiti. You can enter Graffiti-style numbers on the right side. Graffiti is a lot like plain block printing that you were taught in kindergarten, but a few letters are written a little differently. (For more about using Graffiti to enter text, see Chapter 2.)

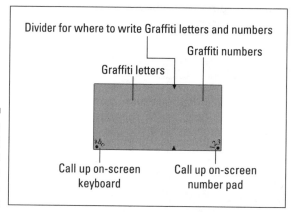

Figure 1-10: The Graffiti area is the place to enter text.

The letters *abc* appear in the lower-left corner of the Graffiti area, and the numbers *123* appear in the lower-right corner. As you may have guessed, tapping *abc* calls up an on-screen keyboard, and tapping *123* calls up a number pad. (For more information on entering text via the on-screen keyboard and number pad, see Chapter 2.)

What Do the Standard Applications Do?

The Visor wasn't designed just to be a cool little computer, although it's definitely a cool little computer. It was designed to do useful things for you as soon as you take it out of the box. I like nothing better than instant gratification, and that's what you get with the Visor. (I do, anyway.)

The standard Visor applications don't have to be installed, configured, or fussed with in any way; they're ready to use with one press of a button. You can, of course, configure the preferences for the applications to get them exactly the way you want them (for more on preferences, see Chapter 3). To get started, just press the button assigned to that application or tap the Applications soft button for a list of your Visor programs and pick the one you want to use.

The programs that you can use as soon as you take your Visor out of the box include the following:

- ✔ **Address Book:** This is your "little black book" of names, addresses, and phone numbers. You can keep a detailed description about everything that you need to know about the people in your list by attaching a note to each record. You can also keep track of everyone's e-mail address and use the Address Book as the Personal Address Book for e-mail that you compose on your Visor. (For more about e-mail on the Visor, see Chapter 10; for more on the Address Book, see Chapter 5.)

- ✔ **Calculator:** The calculator is a simple tool for punching in numbers and performing arithmetic. The Visor calculator does one trick that a hand-held calculator can't handle — it shows a list of recent calculations. After performing a series of calculations, tap Menu and then choose Options⇨Recent Calculations to see a recap of your last few calculations, as shown in Figure 1-11.

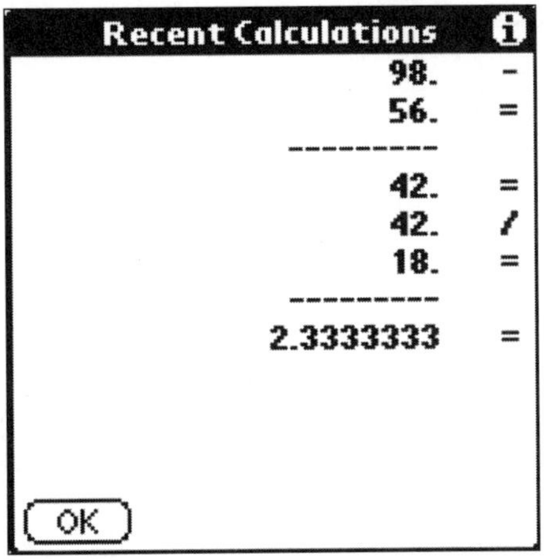

Figure 1-11:
You can see a series of calculations on your list of recent calculations.

Recent Calculations	
98.	−
56.	=

42.	=
42.	/
18.	=

2.3333333	=

(OK)

- ✔ **Date Book:** Think of this as your calendar of appointments and events. The Date Book, as shown in Figure 1-12, lets you set appointments and alarms to remind yourself of those appointments. You can also add notes to any appointment to keep details about each appointment handy. (For more on the Date Book, see Chapter 8.)

- ✔ **Expense:** Here's a handy application for keeping track of what you spend. The Expense program, as shown in Figure 1-13, synchronizes to special Microsoft Excel spreadsheets on your desktop to enable you to collect expense figures on the road and then pull them together when you get home. (See Chapter 12 for more on Expense.)

Figure 1-12:
Keep up to
date with
your Date
Book.

Figure 1-13:
You can
save data
about what
you've spent
in the
Expense
application.

✔ **Welcome:** This is the program that you see when you first start up your Visor. Welcome asks you to tap a target on the screen to set up your Visor properly, and then invites you to play a Graffiti learning game. The game is a great way to sharpen your skills at Graffiti, which makes your Visor that much more useful. Figure 1-14 shows a sample screen from the game.

✔ **HotSync:** This program links your Visor to your desktop computer. The HotSync program has two parts: the part on the Visor and the part on the desktop. Either a PC or a Mac can synchronize data with the same Visor, but the PC and the Mac need different desktop software. (See Chapter 11 for more information on using HotSync.)

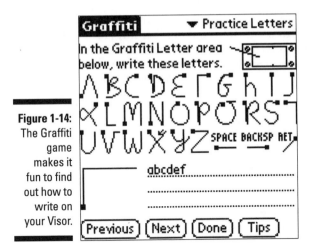

Figure 1-14:
The Graffiti game makes it fun to find out how to write on your Visor.

✔ **Mail:** This simple e-mail program enables you to HotSync your e-mail with your desktop computer so that you can read e-mail, compose replies, and create messages to be sent through your desktop e-mail system. (For more on the Mail program, see Chapter 10.)

✔ **Memo Pad:** This is your collection of plain old text notes that you can keep around for future reference. Figure 1-15 shows the memos that exist in your Visor when you buy it. You can either create notes on your desktop computer and transfer them to your Visor to keep critical information handy, or you can create memos on your Visor for later transfer to desktop computer programs, such as your word processor. (For more on the Memo Pad, see Chapter 7.)

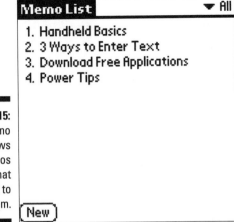

Figure 1-15:
The Memo List shows your memos anytime that you want to read them.

✔ **Preferences:** This program lets you customize your Visor by changing application button assignments, time and number formats, modem setup, and shortcuts. Figure 1-16 shows the General Preferences screen; for other preferences screens, choose from the pull-down menu in the upper-right corner. (For more on setting preferences, see Chapter 3.)

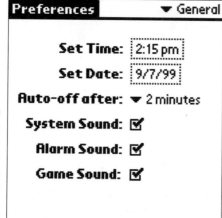

Figure 1-16:
Make your
Visor your
own by
setting your
Preferences.

✔ **Security:** This program lets you hide or show all the items on your Visor that you've marked private. You can also set, remove, or change a password to protect your information. Figure 1-17 shows you what to expect from the Security screen. (For more on using the security features, see Chapter 3.)

✔ **To Do List:** Here's a list of tasks that you need to remember, sorted in order of priority, due date, or by the name of the task. You can also keep track of tasks that you've completed in the To Do List for future reference. (For more on the To Do List, see Chapter 6.)

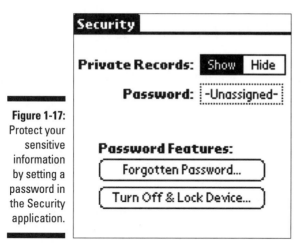

Figure 1-17:
Protect your
sensitive
information
by setting a
password in
the Security
application.

HotSyncing Is Definitely Hot Stuff

HotSyncing, put simply, is when you have your desktop computer and Visor talk to each other — sort of like when you get together with a friend at happy hour. You compare your days, talk about what you did, and maybe exchange notes. HotSyncing does the same thing — only more efficiently.

During a HotSync, the two machines compare data and then match up that data exactly, keeping each other current on who you know, what you've done, when you did it, and what you gotta do tomorrow. HotSyncing also enables you to install additional applications onto your Visor, as well as back up (or *archive*) all your data on your desktop computer so that your data is safe. (Your Visor does this automatically, so you don't even have to think about it.)

For more on HotSyncing and using your Visor with your desktop computer, see Chapters 11 and 12.

Batteries Are Included, But. . . .

In case you haven't noticed, your Visor doesn't plug into the wall. And though the cradle may look like it can recharge your Visor, it doesn't. Instead, your Visor runs on a pair of ordinary AAA batteries, which should last you nearly a month in normal use. If you use the backlight a lot, you'll drain the batteries faster.

When you change batteries, HotSyncing first is a good idea, just in case something goes wrong. When you take out a set of batteries, you have 30 seconds to insert a new set before the Visor starts forgetting things.

If you press the Applications soft button, you can see how much power remains in your batteries on the applications screen. The remaining battery power is indicated by a silhouette of a battery at the top of the applications screen. When your batteries are at maximum power, the battery is completely black. As the batteries drain, the black part of the battery indicator gets smaller and smaller.

Sure, rechargeable batteries are cool, but . . .

You may like to be environmentally conscious by using rechargeable batteries, but you need to know two things about using rechargeables in your Visor. First, rechargeables don't recharge when you leave the Visor in its cradle. The cradle would have to draw power from the PC that it's connected to, and it doesn't do that.

The second thing is that when rechargeable batteries lose their power, they usually go dead all at once. Nonrechargeable batteries usually drain a little at a time and die slowly. Your Visor pops a warning on-screen when you need to replace your batteries. But if you use rechargeables, that warning may come too late. I'm not saying that you shouldn't use rechargeable batteries in your Visor, but if you do, you need to watch your battery power more closely than you would if you used regular batteries.

Chapter 2

Going in Stylus

● ●

In This Chapter

▶ Understanding Graffiti letters and numbers

▶ Moving the Graffiti cursor

▶ Making capital letters without a Shift key

▶ Graffiti whiz secrets and shortcuts

▶ Using the on-screen keyboard

▶ Exploring other text-entry options

● ●

*G*etting information out of your Visor is a cinch, but putting information into your Visor is a bit more challenging. You won't find a keyboard to tap information into, which is a good thing. If the Visor had a keyboard, you would either be stuck with a set of teeny-weeny keys that you can barely read (let alone press with your fingers) or you would have a laptop computer: portable, sure, but not nearly portable enough.

The people who make the Visor recommend that you enter most of your data to the Visor via the Visor desktop program. (I describe how to install the Visor desktop program in Chapter 11 and how to use it in Chapter 12.) The Visor desktop program is, without doubt, the clearest way to deal with data entry. You don't have to guess what you entered, and full-size computer screens are usually easier to see.

But I think being able to jot down a memo while riding on a train or sitting by a pool is half the fun of having a Visor, so I like to use either Graffiti or the on-screen keyboard that's built into the Visor. Some programmers are creating products that offer interesting new ways to enter text into your Visor, but those products cost extra. I discuss them at the end of the chapter in the section titled "Other Text-Entry Tricks." However, most of this chapter focuses on using Graffiti.

Spraying Graffiti All Around

Using words to explain *Graffiti* on your Visor is like trying to describe a spiral staircase without using your hands. But even though a spiral staircase is tricky to describe, it's easy to use; the same goes for Graffiti. After you use Graffiti for even a little while, it begins to come naturally. Graffiti is the special alphabet the Visor understands. You'll understand it pretty quickly, too. It's really just kindergarten block lettering with a few pieces missing. If you got through the first grade you should be able to handle Graffiti.

To write in Graffiti, you need to use a stylus. A *stylus* is a special pen with no ink. You can use the stylus that comes with your Visor, which you can find stored in a holder on the right side of your Visor. You can also go out and buy a fancy, expensive stylus from people who also sell fancy, expensive writing pens, but the cheap plastic stylus that comes with your Visor does the job just as well.

Your Visor will probably work perfectly for a long time with little or no trouble, but if you accidentally scratch the screen, you'll start having problems. Don't use a sharp object as a stylus. Always use the stylus that comes with your Visor.

You can use the stylus to tap on-screen buttons and to select text, but to write text in Graffiti, you need to write in the box at the bottom of the screen, cleverly named the Graffiti area, as shown in Figure 2-1.

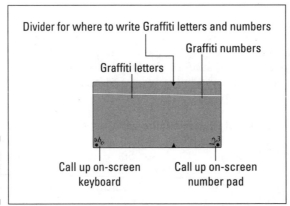

Figure 2-1:
The Graffiti
writing area.

Divider for where to write Graffiti letters and numbers

Graffiti numbers

Graffiti letters

Call up on-screen
keyboard

Call up on-screen
number pad

Graffiti letters and numbers

You need to write letters and numbers in different parts of the Graffiti area. You can see the letters *abc* in the lower-left corner of the Graffiti area. That's to remind you that you need to write letters on the left side of the box. The numbers 123 are printed in the lower-right corner, to remind you that, you guessed it, you can only write numbers on the right side of the screen. Two tiny triangles separate the letter writing area from the number writing area.

Remember that Graffiti is a special alphabet that you have to learn; it's not handwriting recognition software that learns your handwriting style. Most of the letters and numbers in the Graffiti alphabet are the same as the plain block letters that you learned in the first grade, with one important adjustment: *Graffiti letters must be written with a single stroke of the stylus.* If you remember that one rule, Graffiti seems pretty simple.

For example, Figure 2-2 shows the letter *A* in Graffiti.

Figure 2-2:
The letter *A*.

The Graffiti letter *A* looks just like a normal capital *A* without the crossbar. (That dot on the lower-left end of the *A* shows where you start the stroke — it's the same place that most people start writing a capital A.) You don't write a crossbar because writing the crossbar requires a second stroke of the stylus. Picking up the stylus is the way you tell Graffiti that you've moved on to the next letter. So for the letter *A,* just draw the upper, triangular part of the A, and then move on to your next letter.

Your Visor comes with a program that teaches you the basics of Graffiti in about 15 minutes. The program runs automatically the first time you start your Visor. If you skip that part or just want to practice Graffiti, you can run the lesson again. Just tap the Applications icon on the Visor screen and then tap the Graffiti icon in the list of applications. You also receive with your Visor a little sticker that shows you the whole Graffiti alphabet. Put the sticker on the cover of your Visor so that you can use it as a reference.

Nearly all Graffiti charts display the alphabet as little squiggles with a dot at one end. The dot tells you where to begin drawing the Graffiti stroke. Think of it like those connect-the-dot games, except that you only connect one dot. After you lift the stylus, the Visor assumes that you've moved on to another letter.

In case you've lost the little sticker, Figure 2-3 shows the whole Graffiti alphabet.

As you can see, the Graffiti alphabet is easy to understand. The trick is remembering the tiny differences between regular writing in block letters and writing Graffiti.

Figure 2-3:
The whole Graffiti alphabet.

Entering spaces — the final frontier

Without spaces, your entries quicklybeginstolooklikethis, which makes them a bit difficult to understand. So being spacey is a good thing.

To create a space, draw the Graffiti space character in the Graffiti area, as shown in Figure 2-4. To enter a space character, simply draw a horizontal line from left to right.

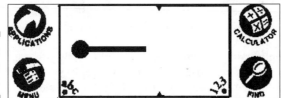

Figure 2-4:
The space character.

Getting spotted for your handspring

Gonna try with a little help from my Visor, yeah . . . Sorry. If you need some help with Graffiti while using your Visor, you can bring up a Graffiti Help screen from within most Visor programs, as follows:

1. **Tap the Menu soft button.**

   The menu bar appears.

2. **Choose Edit⇨Graffiti Help.**

   The Graffiti Help screen appears.

After you find the Graffiti letter that you want to use, tap the Done button to return to your program and write the letter.

The Graffiti Help screen only appears when you can enter text. If you're looking at your To Do List, for example, then you can't access the Graffiti Help screen; you need to select a To Do item or create a new To Do (or some other function that allows you to enter text) before you can access the Help screen.

You may find that it takes a bit of time to get used to writing Graffiti. Don't despair — that's normal. Like most computers, your Visor can be a bit finicky about stuff like which humans' handwriting it deems good enough to interpret accurately. My handwriting is actually pretty awful, so I generally write slowly and carefully when I enter Graffiti into my Visor. When I write text on paper, however, it still looks like hieroglyphics. Maybe I should've become a doctor.

If you know how to type beyond hunting and pecking, then you won't be able to achieve the same speed when you enter text in Graffiti as you can when you type. The point of Graffiti isn't so much speed as convenience; you can use Graffiti anytime without having to tuck a keyboard under your coat.

Moving the Graffiti cursor

When you're creating text in Graffiti, you always see a little blinking line in the display, called the *insertion point* or the cursor, which shows you where the next letter that you type will appear. Sometimes, you want to make the cursor move without entering a letter. The easiest way to move the cursor is to simply tap the spot on the screen where you want the cursor to be. Your cursor moves right to that spot.

After you finish with a line of text and want to start entering text on a new line, use the Graffiti return character. The return character works a little bit like the Enter key on a regular desktop computer, although you use the return character a lot less on the Visor than you would on a regular computer.

To insert a new line, draw the return character in the Graffiti area, as shown in Figure 2-5. It's a slanted line drawn from the upper-right to the lower-left part of the Graffiti area.

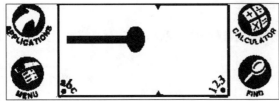

Figure 2-5:
The return
character.

Backing out of a mistake

If you make a mistake, you may want to backspace to erase the last letter
that you wrote. The backspace character works just like the backspace key
on a regular desktop computer. To backspace, draw the Graffiti backspace
character in the Graffiti area, as shown in Figure 2-6. It's just a horizontal line
drawn from right to left, the opposite of the space character. Although some
characters need to be entered either in the letters or numbers area of the
Graffiti box, you can enter spaces and backspaces in either area.

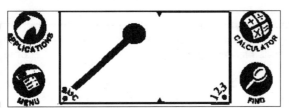

Figure 2-6:
The
backspace
character.

When you want to delete a whole word or a larger block of text, selecting
the text before drawing the backspace character to delete everything that
you've selected is quicker than writing a backspace for each letter. To select
text, draw an imaginary line through the text that you want to select in the
display area (not in the Graffiti area). You can see which text you've selected
because the text you select is highlighted. Backspacing after highlighting text
erases the text. You can also just start writing again after selecting text; the
new text replaces the old.

Making capital letters without a Shift key

When you type a capital letter on a regular keyboard, you hold down the Shift
key while pressing the letter's key. You can't hold a key while entering a
Graffiti letter, so you have to enter the Shift character before you enter the
letter that you want capitalized.

The shift character is simply an upward, vertical stroke in the Graffiti text area, as shown in Figure 2-7. To enter a capital *A,* draw a vertical line upwards in the Graffiti text area, followed by the letter A. After you draw the shift character, an upward-pointing arrow appears in the lower-right corner of the screen to show that your next letter will be capitalized.

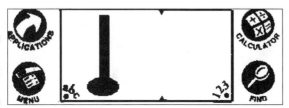

Figure 2-7:
The shift character.

On a regular keyboard, if you want to capitalize a whole string of letters, you press the Caps Lock key and type away. After you finish typing capital letters, you press the Shift key to return to regular lowercase text.

Entering two shift characters in a row in Graffiti, as shown in Figure 2-8, is the same as pressing the Caps Lock key. After you enter the shift character twice, you see an arrow with a dotted tail in the lower-right corner of the display, which tells you that all the text you enter will be capitalized. You can cancel the Caps Lock by entering the shift command again.

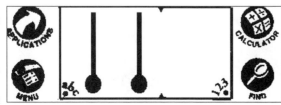

Figure 2-8:
The Caps Lock command.

In quite a few cases, Visor applications assume that the first letter of a sentence or proper name should be capitalized, so the shift arrow automatically shows up in the lower-right corner of the screen to indicate that the next letter will be capitalized. If you don't want to capitalize the beginning of a sentence, enter the shift character twice to return to lowercase text.

Using other shift functions

Graffiti has another type of shift character called the extended shift, entered as a downward, diagonal line starting from the top-left, as shown in Figure 2-9. The extended shift character offers a way to enter special characters, such as the copyright symbol and the trademark symbol. You can also use the extended shift to create certain punctuation characters, such as the upside-down question marks and exclamation points that you need to enter text in Spanish, as well as some mathematical symbols like plus signs. When you enter the extended shift stroke, a little diagonal line appears in the lower-right corner of the screen.

Figure 2-9:
The
extended
shift stroke.

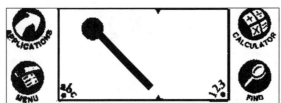

Another shift character that you may use is the command shift, an upward, diagonal line starting in the lower-left part of the Graffiti screen, as shown in Figure 2-10. You can perform quite a few common tasks in many Visor programs by entering the command shift followed by a letter. For example, to delete a To Do item, tap the item and then enter the command shift stroke followed by the letter *D*. Doing so opens the Delete dialog box, just as if you had chosen Record ⇨Delete Item from the menu. You can see what the command shift can do in any program by tapping the Menu soft button and looking at the list of commands at the right side of each menu.

Figure 2-10:
The
command
shift stroke.

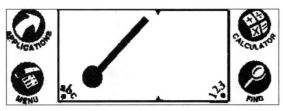

Punctuating your text

Although Graffiti letters and numbers look pretty normal, Graffiti punctuation is pretty strange. You may not want to punctuate at all when you're entering Graffiti text except for the occasional period and dash.

To enter punctuation characters such as periods, dashes, and commas, you need to tap your stylus once in the Graffiti area before entering the character. Many punctuation characters have different meanings if you don't tap first before drawing them. When you tap once, a little dot appears in the lower-right corner of the display to show that you've tapped.

The simplest punctuation character is the period. Tap twice in the Graffiti area to create a period. Figure 2-11 shows a dot where I'm making a period.

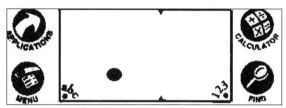

Figure 2-11:
The Graffiti
period.

The second simplest punctuation character is the dash. Tap once in the Graffiti area, and then draw a horizontal line from left to right. After you've used Graffiti for a while, you'll think of this as tapping, then drawing the space character.

TIP

If you need to enter e-mail addresses in your Address Book, you'll almost certainly need to be able to enter the @ sign, for e-mail addresses like somebody @something.com. The @ sign is simply a tap followed by the letter O.

Graffiti whiz secrets

I think that most people can get a pretty good handle on Graffiti within a few hours, except for people under 15 years of age, who usually pick it up in about five minutes. I've heard stories of kids in junior high school who write notes to each other in Graffiti. That's pretty clever. I hope they don't write naughty words on walls in Graffiti; that would be redundant.

REMEMBER

But even with some experience, certain Graffiti letters tend to stay finicky and hard to enter accurately. One thing to remember is that you need to make your Graffiti characters as large, square, and vertical as possible.

Another trick is to learn which letters can actually be entered by writing a number on the letter side of the Graffiti area and a letter on the number side of the Graffiti area. For example, if you write the number 3 on the letter side of the Graffiti area, the letter B turns up more reliably than it does if you draw the actual Graffiti letter B. Table 2-1 shows a list of letters that are often a problem and how to get your Visor to recognize them more reliably.

Table 2-1	Tricks of the Graffiti Trade
To Get This Character . . .	*Perform This Stroke*
B	Draw the number 3 on the letter side of the Graffiti area.
G	Draw the number 6 on the letter side of the Graffiti area.
K	This is the trickiest Graffiti character. Just draw the "legs" on the side of the K, joined by a little loop. Leave out the vertical bar. To me it looks a little bit like a fish swimming from right to left. I describe this character in greater detail later in this chapter.
P	Start at the bottom of the P and make the loop at the top pretty small.
Q	Draw an O with a really long tail at the top.
R	Make this character just like the P that I describe, but make the tail of the R extra long.
V	Draw the V backwards; that is, start from the top right.
Y	Just draw the lower loop of a cursive capital Y. It's just a loop, like the letter K, except the fish is swimming down.
2	Draw the letter Z on the number side of the Graffiti writing area.
4	Draw the letter C on the number side of the Graffiti area.
5	Draw the letter S on the number side of the Graffiti area.
7	Draw a backwards letter C on the number side of the Graffiti area.

The amazing Graffiti fish loop

One Graffiti character has no counterpart in the normal alphabet, but knowing how to draw this character can help you enormously when you use Graffiti. It doesn't have an official name, so I just call it the *fish loop*.

I know that my fish story is a pretty dopey explanation, but I bring it up for two reasons. First, Graffiti seems to recognize this loop symbol more reliably than most other letters or numbers, so learning to use it will certainly make you a quicker and slicker Graffitist.

The second reason for my fish story is that I find stupid explanations the easiest to remember. By that measure, you'll NEVER forget this explanation.

So, if you draw a little loop that looks like a fish swimming from right to left, as shown in Figure 2-12, Graffiti translates that loop as the letter K.

Figure 2-12:
Did you
have your
Special K
today?

If you make the fish look like he's swimming downward, as shown in Figure 2-13, Graffiti translates that loop as the letter Y.

Figure 2-13:
No YMCA
here; just Y.

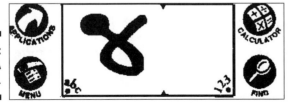

If you make the fish look like he's swimming from left to right, as shown in Figure 2-14, Graffiti translates that loop as the letter X.

Figure 2-14:
X marks the
spot,
sometimes.

If you make the fish look like he's swimming upward and you start drawing from the left, as shown in Figure 2-15, Graffiti translates that loop as the ShortCut symbol, a very useful tool that I discuss in the next section, "The Graffiti ShortCut symbol."

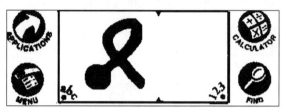

Figure 2-15:
Little Red
Riding Hood
should've
had a
shortcut
like this!

By the way, I apologize for referring to the fish as a male in all instances, but because the fish has no eyes, he appears to have no idea where he's going, a situation in which I find myself regularly. That makes me assume that the fish is male, like me. Feel free to draw your own conclusions. About the fish, that is.

The Graffiti ShortCut symbol

Another compelling reason to use Graffiti is that you can create and use ShortCuts. *ShortCuts* are abbreviations that automatically expand themselves into longer blocks of text or automated entries, such as the current date and time.

When you buy your Visor, a few ShortCuts are already built in. Some of the preprogrammed ShortCuts are for useful words such as *meeting, breakfast, lunch,* and *dinner.* You also get some useful time stamp ShortCuts for entering the current date and time.

To add a time stamp to a memo or note, write the Graffiti ShortCut symbol, (a lowercase, cursive letter *L*)followed by the letters TS, as shown in Figure 2-16.

As soon as you finish writing the letter S, the three characters you entered disappear, and the current time appears.

The three preprogrammed time stamp ShortCuts are

- **TS** for time stamp — enters the current time
- **DS** for date stamp — enters the current date
- **DTS** for date time stamp — enters the current date and time

Figure 2-16:
It's Greek to
me, you
say? Nope,
it's a time
stamp!

Other preprogrammed ShortCuts include

- ✔ **ME** for the word *meeting*
- ✔ **BR** for the word *breakfast*
- ✔ **LU** for the word *lunch*
- ✔ **DI** for the word *dinner*

In Chapter 4, I show you how to create ShortCuts of your own.

The On-Screen Keyboard

Perhaps you don't want to spend time learning Graffiti. You may just want to get down to business. That's fine. You can call up the on-screen keyboard to enter letters by tapping on a tiny picture of a keyboard, as shown in Figure 2-17.

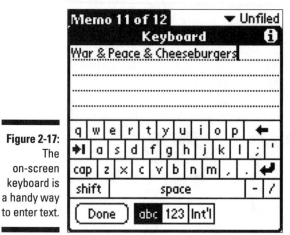

Figure 2-17:
The
on-screen
keyboard is
a handy way
to enter text.

The on-screen keyboard is too small for touch typing. You'll definitely need the stylus to pick out those tiny little keys. I use the on-screen keyboard as little as possible because I think I type more slowly when I'm trying to find those tiny little keys. But I know plenty of people who stick exclusively with the on-screen keyboard and they do just fine.

To make the on-screen keyboard appear, tap the dot in one of the two lower corners of the Graffiti area. When you tap the dot on the letter side of the Graffiti area, the alphabet keyboard appears. When you tap the dot on the number side, a numeric keypad appears, as shown in Figure 2-18. After you enter the text that you want, tap Done to make the on-screen keyboard go away.

Figure 2-18:
Enter
numbers
with the
numeric
keypad if
you don't
like Graffiti.

Remember that the on-screen keyboard only appears when it's possible for you to enter text. If you're looking at your list of memos, for example, the on-screen keyboard won't appear, because you need to open a memo or create a new memo before you can enter text.

On the on-screen keyboard, you can also see a button labeled Int'l that unlocks a special set of keys for entering those festive international characters that English sadly lacks.

Other Text-Entry Tricks

For a few dollars more, you can take advantage of some other ways of entering text into your Visor by buying a new piece of hardware or software. Here are some favorites.

JOT writing system

Graffiti isn't the only way to enter written information into your Visor. You can also buy Jot, a piece of software that uses a different, but equally simple set of letters for entering text. Some people prefer Jot to Graffiti the way others might prefer Pepsi to Coke. Personally, I stick with Graffiti because it's free, but if you're not satisfied, check out Jot by visiting the manufacturer's Web site at www.cic.com.

Keyboards

I love having a real, physical keyboard to go with my handheld computer. Even if you're pretty quick with Graffiti, you can just fly through text when you have a keyboard attached.

My very favorite keyboard at the moment is the folding Stowaway keyboard, distributed by Targus. It's an amazing James-Bond-style gadget that folds out from a pocket-sized case to form a full-sized keyboard. People literally gasp when they see you unfold the Stowaway, so even if you don't type much, it's a great conversation starter. Because the Stowaway fits in a coat pocket (or even in a shirt pocket sometimes), you can carry it everywhere you take your Visor.

Before the Stowaway appeared, my favorite keyboard for handheld computers was the GoType keyboard from Landware. It doesn't fold up into your pocket, but it opens like a clam to reveal a slightly miniaturized keyboard. Because the GoType doesn't fold the way the Stowaway does, you can rest it on your lap while typing, which makes it handy for taking notes in lectures and other situations when you're not sitting at a table.

Chapter 3

Making Your Visor Your Own

Millions of people own Visors and PalmPilots, and you can be sure that everyone uses their handheld computers a little differently. Some people think of their Visors as glorified datebooks, and they're happy with that. Other people install programs that do things you'd never guess, such as track their location by satellite, send e-mail messages by radio, and heaven knows what else.

Because everyone uses a Visor a little differently, many people want to personalize the way theirs work. In this chapter, I show you some of the easier ways to make your Visor work the way that you do, by using the preference and security settings that are standard on the Visor.

Setting General Preferences

When you start up your Visor for the very first time, the General Preferences screen appears automatically as an invitation to set the time and date accurately. You may also want to reset the time, if you travel frequently to different time zones. If you've already started Visor at least once, follow these steps to access the General Preferences screen:

1. **Tap the Applications soft button.**

    The list of applications appears on your screen.

2. **Tap the Prefs icon.**

    The Preferences application launches, as shown in Figure 3-1.

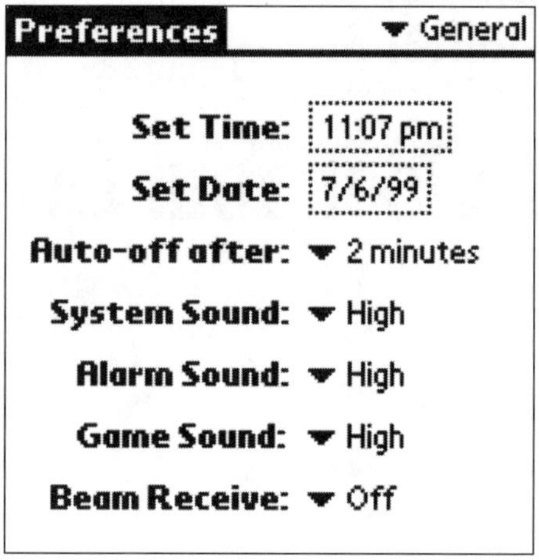

```
Preferences              ▼ General

        Set Time:  ┊11:07 pm┊
        Set Date:  ┊7/6/99┊
   Auto-off after:  ▼ 2 minutes
   System Sound:  ▼ High
    Alarm Sound:  ▼ High
    Game Sound:  ▼ High
   Beam Receive:  ▼ Off
```

Figure 3-1:
Customizing
Visor to suit
your
preference.

3. **Tap whatever word is displayed in the upper-right corner of the screen. In Figure 3-1, for example, tap General.**

   The Preferences program has eight sections of different preferences: Buttons, Digitizer, Formats, General, Modem, Network, Owner, and ShortCuts. The name of the section that you're looking at appears in the upper-right corner of the screen. The triangle next to the name of the section means that you can tap the name of the section to see a pull-down list of its available sub-sections.

4. **Choose General.**

   The General Preferences screen appears. Use this dialog to change the time, date, Auto-off feature, various sounds, and beaming reception.

To change the individual settings of the General Preferences screen, continue with the following sections.

Setting the time

I like having my Visor remind me of my appointments shortly before they occur, just to avoid missing anything that I've scheduled. But the Visor is a bit like an alarm clock; alarms can't go off at the right time if you don't set the Visor to the right time in the first place.

Follow these steps to set the time on your Visor:

1. **With the General Preferences screen visible, tap the time shown in the Set Time box.**

The Set Time dialog box opens, showing Visor's current time setting, along with a pair of triangles for changing the time. The top triangle sets the time later, and the bottom triangle sets the time earlier, as shown in Figure 3-2.

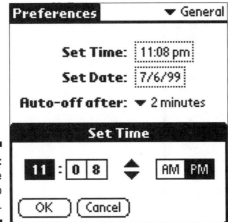

Figure 3-2:
Tap the triangles to set the time.

2. **Tap the hour in the Set Time dialog box.**

   Visor highlights the hour.

3. **Tap the triangles repeatedly until the hour you want appears.**

   The hour changes as you tap the triangles.

4. **Set the minutes by following Steps 2 and 3 for each of the two minutes boxes.**

   The minutes change as you tap the triangles.

5. **Tap the AM or PM box to choose the appropriate setting and make sure it's highlighted.**

6. **Tap OK.**

   The Set Time dialog box closes.

If you like to show the time in a different format than the standard 1:35 PM format, I show you how to change the time format in the section "Setting Format Preferences" later in this chapter.

Setting the date

If you use the calendar frequently or if you enter lots of tasks with due dates assigned, you may want your Visor to know what day it is.

Follow these steps to set the date on your Visor:

1. **With the General Preferences screen visible, tap the date shown in the Set Date box.**

   The Set Date dialog box opens, as shown in Figure 3-3.

Figure 3-3:
Finding the
current
date on a
calendar in
the Set Date
dialog box.

			Set Date			
		◀	1999	▶		
Jan	Feb	Mar	Apr	May	Jun	
Jul	Aug	Sep	Oct	Nov	Dec	

S	M	T	W	T	F	S
				1	2	3
4	5	6	7	8	9	10
11	12	13	14	15	16	17
18	19	20	21	22	23	24
25	26	27	28	29	30	31

[Cancel] [Today]

2. **Tap one of the triangles on either side of the year to set the current year.**

   After you tap the triangle on the left, the year shown moves one year earlier. Tapping the triangle on the right moves the year shown to the next year. Keep tapping until the current year appears.

3. **Tap the month that you want.**

   Visor displays a calendar for the highlighted month.

4. **Tap the day of the month that you want to set.**

   The Set Date dialog box closes, and the date that you chose appears in the Preferences screen.

After you've set the date, your Visor remembers and keeps track of the date automatically, unless you let the batteries go dead for a month or more. If you go around the world for 80 days and come home to a dead Visor, just change the batteries and reset the date and time. For more on batteries, see Chapter 1.

Setting the Auto-off interval

Your Visor goes a long way on a pair of AAA batteries; mine usually runs for the better part of a month before I need to replace the batteries. One method that the Visor uses to stretch battery life is to turn off automatically when you haven't pressed a button for a few minutes. You don't have many choices about how long the Visor waits before shutting off, but these steps show how you can choose from what's available:

1. **With the General Preferences screen visible, tap the triangle next to the words Auto-Off After.**

   The pull-down list of Auto-off intervals appears. You can choose either one-, two-, or three-minute Auto-off intervals, as shown in Figure 3-4.

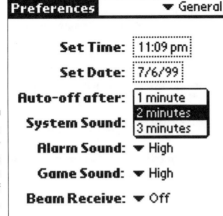

Figure 3-4: Save your batteries with the Auto-off feature.

2. **Choose the Auto-off interval that you want.**

   The interval that you tap appears in the Auto-Off After box.

You don't need to worry too much about having the Visor turn off too fast; you only need to press the green power button to switch right back to the program that you were working on when the Visor turned off.

Setting the sound volume

A tiny little speaker that's inside your Visor makes little chirping sounds when you tap the screen and plays a squeaky little fanfare when you run the HotSync program. If you think a Visor should be seen and not heard, you can turn the sound off or change the volume.

You have three volume settings that you can adjust:

✔ **System:** System sounds are those that the system is programmed to make in certain events. For example, when you want to do something specific that your Visor can't do at that moment, you may get an error beep, just like when your desktop PC protests one of your actions.

✔ **Alarm:** An alarm sounds when you set a reminder for an appointment. You can also get some third-party Visor programs that use the alarm sound.

✔ **Game:** Game sounds work only with games that are programmed to use them. Most games are more fun with sounds, but those game-like boinks and bleeps are a dead giveaway that you're not using your Visor for serious work. If you plan to secretly play a shoot-'em-up game on your Visor at the weekly staff meeting, a good career move may be to turn off your game sounds.

If your Visor goes off when you're at the movies, you may get some dirty looks, so be a good sport and turn off the sounds when you go to the MegaMultiplex.

Here's how to adjust the volume for all three types of sounds:

1. **With the General Preferences screen visible, tap the triangle next to the type of sound that you want to change.**

   A pull-down list of volume choices appears. You can choose either Off, Low, Medium, or High, as shown in Figure 3-5.

Figure 3-5:
Adjusting
system
sound
volume.

2. **Choose the volume level that you want.**

   The volume level that you tap appears in the System Sound box.

The tiny little speaker in your Visor won't exactly wake the neighbors no matter how loud you make it, but it's nice to have a choice.

Turning off beam reception

Your Visor can send or receive all sorts of things by *beaming*, which is the rather neat process of sending data between handheld computers via an invisible light beam across the air. (Sounds kind of magical, doesn't it? To demystify beaming, see Chapter 9.) The Visor doesn't distinguish between truly useful information and useless junk when it sends stuff out over the air; it's a little like television that way. If you'd like to avoid having unwanted junk beamed to your Visor, you can elect not to receive beamed items by following these steps:

1. **With the General Preferences screen visible, tap the triangle next to Beam Receive.**

   The pull-down list of choices appears.

2. **Choose either On or Off.**

   The choice that you tap appears in the Beam Receive box.

Turning off beam receiving doesn't stop you from beaming items to others. If you've turned off beam receiving and you try to beam something, though, a dialog box opens up to ask you if you want to turn beam receiving back on. Switching beam receiving back on, in order to exchange business cards with another Visor user, makes sense. You don't want to be unsociable, do you?

Setting Button Preferences

You may use some programs more than others. As a result, you may want to assign a different program to one of the hard buttons at the bottom of your Visor case. Switch the programs assigned to the Applications buttons by following these steps:

1. **Tap the Applications soft button.**

   The list of applications appears, showing icons for all the programs installed on your Visor.

2. **Tap the Prefs icon.**

   The Preferences screen appears.

3. **Tap the word displayed in the upper-right corner of the screen.**

   A pull-down list of preferences appears.

4. **Choose Buttons.**

   The Buttons Preferences screen appears and displays five icons: one for each of the four buttons at the bottom of your Visor screen and one for the Calculator soft button (the other soft buttons aren't up for grabs). The name of the assigned program appears next to each icon.

5. **Tap the triangle next to the button whose program you wish to change.**

   A pull-down list of all the applications installed on your Visor appears in alphabetical order, as shown in Figure 3-6. Your applications list may be long. When the list gets too long to fit on the Visor screen, scroll-type arrows appear at the top and bottom of the list to indicate that more programs are available. Use the on-screen arrows or the up and down buttons to view the list.

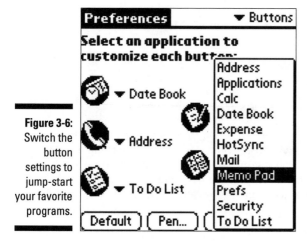

Figure 3-6: Switch the button settings to jump-start your favorite programs.

6. **Choose the name of the application that you want to assign to that button.**

   The name of the application that you tap appears in the Buttons Preferences screen next to the button you've assigned to it.

Now when you press that particular button, your Visor runs the newly assigned program. All your programs still appear after you tap the Applications soft button, but only the assigned programs run from the hard buttons.

Setting Format Preferences

People express time and numbers differently in different places, so your Visor has settings to suit a variety of local customs. Follow these steps to change the way that dates and numbers appear:

1. **Tap the Applications soft button.**

   The list of applications appears, showing icons for all the programs installed on your Visor.

2. **Tap the Prefs icon.**

   The Preferences screen appears.

3. **Tap the word displayed in the upper-right corner of the screen.**

   A pull-down list of preferences appears.

4. **Tap Formats.**

   The Format Preferences screen appears.

5. **Tap the triangle next to Preset To.**

   A pull-down list of countries appears, as shown in Figure 3-7.

Figure 3-7:
Use the
schema of
your favorite
country by
choosing
from the
Preset To
list.

6. **Choose the country whose presets you want to use.**

   The name of the country that you tap appears in the Preset To box, and all the number formats on the Format Preferences screen change to the formats common to the country that you chose.

7. **If you wish to change an individual type of formatting, tap the triangle next to the example of that type.**

   A pull-down list of formatting choices appears. For example, if you choose the United States, the entry in the Time box says HH:MM am/pm, which means that all time entries on your Visor appear the way that people write them in the United States, for example, 11:13 am. If you want the time to appear the way they display time in Italy — for example, 11.13 — choose the entry named HH.MM.

The format that you tap appears in the Format Preferences screen, as shown in Figure 3-8.

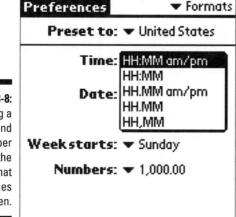

Figure 3-8:
Picking a
time and
number
format in the
Format
Preferences
screen.

Changing your format preferences changes the way that numbers appear in all Visor applications. If you want to use one format in one application and another format in a different application, you're out of luck. One format per customer, please.

Using the Security Application

If you keep very much sensitive business data on your Visor, it's wise to take advantage of the security features that are already built in. You can hide items that you want to protect from unauthorized eyes, and you can even assign a password to lock your Visor from any unauthorized use.

Follow these steps to access the Security screen:

1. **Tap the Applications soft button.**

   The list of applications appears on your screen.

2. **Tap Security.**

   The Security screen appears, as shown in Figure 3-9.

To change the individual settings in the Security Preferences screen, read the following sections.

Security

Private Records: Show Hide

Password: -Unassigned-

Password Features:

Forgotten Password...

Turn Off & Lock Device...

Figure 3-9:
Keep your
secrets
secret with
the Security
application.

Setting your password

Although you can keep confidential information on either a desktop computer or a Visor, very few people misplace their desktop computers in airports or restaurants the way they can misplace their handheld computers. That makes password-protecting your Visor data all the more important. Follow these steps to set a password:

1. **With the Security Preferences screen visible, tap Unassigned in the Password box.**

   The Password dialog box opens.

   If the word *Assigned* appears, you already have a password. If you want to delete your password, see the section "Deleting a forgotten password," later in this chapter.

2. **Enter the password that you want to set by using Graffiti (see Chapter 2 for more information about entering text).**

   The password that you enter appears in the Password dialog box, as shown in Figure 3-10. And don't forget to remember your password.

3. **Tap OK.**

   The Password dialog box opens again, asking you to verify your password.

4. **Re-enter the password that you entered in Step 4.**

   The password that you enter appears again in the Password dialog box.

5. **Tap OK.**

   The Password dialog box closes, and the word *Assigned* appears in the Password box.

Security

Private Records: Show Hide

Password

Enter a password:

BigSecret

If you assign a password, you must enter it to show private records.

(OK) (Cancel)

Figure 3-10:
Enter your
password
in the
Password
dialog box.

Deleting a forgotten password

So, what do you do if the worst thing happens? You've been asked to supply 1,001 passwords for various systems, your Visor is the 1,002nd, and you forgot your password. Of course, the easiest way to avoid this problem is to create a password that you're more likely to remember or re-use one of the passwords you use more frequently elsewhere. But if you can't remember it, you can delete the old password, as long as you can turn on the power and get to the Security application.

1. **With the Security screen visible, tap the Forgotten Password button.**

   The Delete Password dialog box opens, bearing a stern warning that all the items you've marked Private are removed until the next HotSync (see Figure 3-11). For more about marking items private, see Chapter 7.

If you've locked down your Visor by tapping Turn Off & Lock Device in the Security application and then forgotten your password, you're cooked. You can only get back into your Visor by performing a Hard Reset, which wipes out all the data on your Visor (see Chapter 1 for more information on resetting your Visor). You can recover all the items that you entered before your last HotSync by doing another HotSync. However, whatever you entered after the last HotSync but before you reset is gone for good. So, guess what you better do. . . .

2. **If you wish to proceed, tap Yes.**

   After a short pause, the word *Unassigned* appears in the Password box. You can then reassign a new password — just try not to forget it this time, okay?

Figure 3-11:
Try not to
forget your
password;
the Security
program
won't be
amused.

Hiding private items

It may not be *Saving Private Ryan,* but *Hiding Private Items* can be heroic stuff, too. The main reason to mark items private is so that you can hide them from the prying eyes of supervisors, paparazzi, and secret agents (or if you want to hide all the phone numbers of your Bond girls from Ms. Moneypenny — but I digress).

Follow these steps to hide private items:

1. **With the Security screen visible, tap the Hide button next to Private Records.**

   The Hide Records dialog box opens, telling you what happens when you hide records (see Figure 3-12).

Figure 3-12:
Hide your
private
items from
prying eyes.

2. Tap Hide.

The Hide Records dialog box closes, and the Security screen reappears. Visor highlights the word *Hide*, and your private items are hidden, as they should be!

TIP

After you've hidden your private items, you may want to make them appear again later. Just follow the preceding steps, but tap Show rather than Hide. If you've assigned a password, Visor makes you enter your password before revealing your private items. You can mark any item private by tapping the Details button and then tapping the Private check box.

Setting Up ShortCuts

One very cute feature in the Visor world is the ShortCut. A ShortCut is really an automatic abbreviation. For example, if you write the words *New York* frequently, you can make a ShortCut named NY. Then, when you want to write New York, just enter the ShortCut symbol in Graffiti, which looks like a cursive, lowercase *L,* and enter the letters NY. The words *New York* appear automatically. For more about entering Graffiti ShortCuts, see Chapter 2.

ShortCuts can save you lots of tapping and scratching when you want to enter information. Personally, I like to use the Time and Date stamp ShortCuts to measure how long I've worked on projects, especially when I'm billing those projects by the hour. You can create or edit your own collection of ShortCuts in a jiffy.

To access the ShortCuts screen, follow these steps:

1. Tap the Applications soft button.

The list of applications appears, showing icons for all the programs installed on your Visor.

2. Tap the Prefs icon.

The Preferences screen appears.

3. Tap the word displayed in the upper-right corner of the screen.

A pull-down list of preferences appears.

4. Choose ShortCuts.

The ShortCuts screen appears, listing all your current ShortCuts.

Read the following sections to figure out how to add, change, or delete your ShortCuts.

Adding a new ShortCut

A collection of ShortCuts is already set up for your use when you first buy your Visor. But to really get your money's worth out of ShortCuts, create some ShortCuts of your own. Adding a new ShortCut is this simple:

1. **With the ShortCuts screen visible, tap New.**

   The ShortCut Entry dialog box opens, as shown in Figure 3-13.

Figure 3-13:
Creating
a new
ShortCut
to save
time and
keystrokes.

```
Preferences          ▼ ShortCuts
         ShortCut Entry      ⓘ
ShortCut Name:
nwj..........................................

ShortCut Text:
No way, Jose!................................
.............................................
.............................................
.............................................
.............................................
( OK )  ( Cancel )
```

2. **Use Graffiti to enter the ShortCut name (abbreviation) that you want (see Chapter 2 for more information about entering text).**

   The text that you enter appears on the ShortCut Name line.

Don't use a period as the first character of your ShortCut name. For some reason, ShortCuts whose names start with a period (*Dot ShortCuts* to Visor programmers) do nothing useful for you and me, but they can do nasty things, such as erase all your data or drain your batteries. Try to stick to names made up of letters and numbers when creating your ShortCuts. Also, ShortCut names can't contain spaces.

You can also use the on-screen keyboard to enter your ShortCut name, but be sure that you can enter the characters that you want in Graffiti because you can't use ShortCuts from the on-screen keyboard, only from Graffiti.

3. **Tap the first line of the ShortCut Text section.**

   An insertion point appears at the point that you tap.

4. **Enter the text you want Visor to insert in place of the name; use either the on-screen keyboard or Graffiti.**

   The text that you enter appears in the ShortCut Text section.

5. **Tap OK.**

   Your new ShortCut appears in the list of ShortCuts.

Editing a ShortCut

At some point, you may want to change either the name or the contents of a ShortCut.

Follow these steps to edit a ShortCut:

1. **With the ShortCuts screen visible, tap the name of the ShortCut that you want to edit.**

   Visor highlights the ShortCut you've selected, as shown in Figure 3-14.

Figure 3-14: Choose a ShortCut to edit or delete.

2. **Tap Edit.**

   The ShortCut Entry dialog box opens.

3. **Select the part of the ShortCut that you want to replace.**

   Visor highlights the text.

4. **Enter the new text by using either the on-screen keyboard or Graffiti (see Chapter 2 for more about entering text).**

   Your new text replaces the old.

5. **Tap OK.**

   The ShortCut Entry dialog box closes.

Now your revised ShortCut is ready to use at the drop of a stylus.

Deleting a ShortCut

If you know how to enter or edit a ShortCut, you know how to delete one. Just follow the same steps in the preceding sections, but select Delete rather than Edit or New on the ShortCuts screen. Zap! Your ShortCut is long gone.

Hacking Up Your Visor

No, this isn't the latest sequel to *Halloween*. In the PalmPilot and Visor universe, *hacks* are applications that you can install on your Visor to add features or to make your Visor behave differently than it does when you first buy it. I'm not getting into hacks in any great degree here, but I do want you to know that they exist. Handheld computers are catching on in the corporate world in a big way, and some big outfits customize their Palm computers and Visors to suit the work they expect people to do. That means that you may have a company-issue Visor with pre-installed hacks that make it behave in a totally different way than the way I describe in this book.

You can install hacks that change the functions of your buttons, change the way your screen looks, change the things you can do with cut and paste, and lots more. Programmers are coming up with new hacks all the time. Most hacks are useful, such as AppHack, a program that enables you to assign up to six different programs to each of the four hard buttons. Other hacks are less useful, such as BackHack, which reverses the spelling of all text on your Visor, so the word *Record* comes out *droceR*. I can't begin to explain why someone would want a program to do that, but rest assured, one does.

One of the most important hacks is called HackMaster, the hack that manages other hacks (Geesh, can this get any more complicated?) Many hacks require you to install HackMaster before installing other hacks. If you're adventurous, check out the Palm-related Web sites listed in the appendix, and download some hacks to install to your Visor. When I say adventurous, I mean that you should be ready to deal with some problems, because some hacks are very experimental. But, fortunately, they're easy to uninstall. Personally, I stay away from hacks because when I have a hack installed I always spend more time resetting and fussing with my handheld computer than I really like. But if you really want to try something new and different, you'll find plenty of hacks to accommodate you.

Chapter 4

Springing Along with Visor Timesavers

*U*sing your Visor is pretty easy to begin with, and if you know the ropes, you can save steps here and there and really whiz through your work by using the following tips. You may even become a member of the elite ranks of Visor power users. Don't worry — you don't have to buy a uniform or learn a secret handshake, but just be ready for plenty of esprit de corps.

I'm going to focus on a handful of features that can make you a speedier Visor user without making you learn anything difficult. I also try to stick to tricks that are part of the Visor operating system and don't require any add-on programs. I deal with accessories and add-on software in Chapters 17 and 18. I've organized all these timesavers into categories so that you can easily find what you need. Enjoy!

General Timesavers

General timesavers are those that you can do at any time or in any application.

Using ShortCuts

The very best timesavers are cleverly named *ShortCuts*. You can expand short abbreviations into words and phrases of up to 45 letters (including spaces) by entering the Graffiti ShortCut symbol, which looks like a cursive lowercase letter *L,* and then the abbreviation. For more on the Graffiti ShortCut symbol, see Chapter 2.

When you first buy your Visor, several ShortCuts are already installed. To find out how to create your own ShortCuts, see Chapter 3.

Beaming a business card quickly

If you've set up your business card for beaming, just hold down the Address Book button for about two seconds. The Beam dialog box opens and your Visor searches for a nearby Visor ready to receive your card. For more on beaming, see Chapter 9.

Using your finger instead of the stylus

In a pinch, anything you can do with a stylus you can also do with your finger. The Visor screen is touch-sensitive, so your finger can serve as a perfectly good stylus at times, although touching the screen tends to smudge it up a bit. Beyond neatness, the main reason for using a stylus is that many Visor programs contain buttons that are too small to tap with your finger (unless you have very small fingers). A gentle tap with a fingernail can sometimes do just as well as a stylus tap. Be gentle, though; you don't want to scratch the screen.

Checking the time

If you tap the Date tab at the top of the Date Book display, the current time pops up for a few seconds. Also, the current time is always displayed at the top of the applications list when you tap the Applications soft button. See Chapter 8 for more about the Date Book.

If you want to enter the current time into a memo, you can call on the Time Stamp ShortCut. Just enter the Graffiti ShortCut symbol, which looks like a cursive, lowercase *L,* and then enter TS. I like to use the Time Stamp as a primitive way to "punch in" (my virtual time clock) when I'm trying to measure time spent on a job. I create a memo, enter a Time Stamp when I begin, and then enter another Time Stamp into the memo when I'm finished.

Reassigning a hard button to your favorite program

If you use another program more often than one of the standard Visor applications, you can reassign one of the four application hard buttons to start that program. Many people don't use the Memo Pad or To Do List nearly as much as the Date Book or Address Book, so they reassign the Memo Pad button to make it run another program. Because the Visor includes an alternate date book program, cleverly named DateBook+, which handles both appointments and To Do items, you might want to use the To Do hard button to start some other program. You can also get a "hack" program called AppHack that enables you to launch up to 24 different programs from the hard buttons by pressing two buttons at once (for more on "hack" programs, see Chapter 3). I still just go to the Applications screen to start my programs, but you can take your pick.

Application Timesavers

These timesavers apply directly to the four main applications that come with your Visor. They can save you loads of time.

Pressing hard buttons to change categories

When you first press the Memo hard button, you see all your memos. If you press the Memo button a second time, the memos in the Business category appear. Each time you press the Memo button again, you see a different category until you've cycled back around to the All category. All four standard application hard buttons behave the same way; push the button several times to run through several different categories. The Date Book hard button works a bit differently than the other three. The Date Book doesn't use categories, so when you press the Date Book button several times, you see your Date Book each time — day, then week, then month. Of course, if you don't have any items filed in a particular category, your Visor conveniently skips that category.

Viewing different dates by pressing buttons

When you want to check your schedule in a jiffy, remember that you can get to any date by pressing buttons, so you don't need to dig for your stylus. Just press the Date Book button once to see the daily view, twice for the weekly view, or three times for the monthly view. When you see the view you want, press the up or down scroll buttons to move to the next day, week, or month. By cleverly combining button clicks, you can see your schedule for any day on the calendar. Granted, you may find it easier sometimes to whip out the stylus and pick the date you want, but when your hands are full, the stylus can be one too many things to hold.

Uncluttering your Date Book

The Date Book shows a blank for every hour of your workday. That can make your schedule look cluttered and hard to read. If you set up your Date Book preferences to have your day start and end at the same times each day, the display shows only entries for the times at which you've scheduled appointments; the rest of the screen will be blank (see Figure 4-1). See Chapter 3 for more about setting preferences.

Figure 4-1:
Making your
schedule
easier to
read.

Drag and drop to change appointment times

If you press the Date Book hard button twice, you see the weekly view of your Address Book. The weekly view shows you a collection of bars representing your appointments for the week. If you want to change the scheduled time of an appointment, just drag the bar representing that appointment to the time you prefer (see Figure 4-2). Sad to say, you can't drag an appointment from one week to another.

Using cut, copy, and paste

Windows and Macintosh users have been cutting, copying, and pasting text for years. You can do the same trick with your Visor. Just select some text by drawing an imaginary line through the text with your stylus, and then tap the

Menu soft button and choose Edit⇨Cut or EditMemo Pad or To Do List⇨ Copy. Cutting makes the text you select disappear, but don't worry — it's not gone forever. The text goes to a place in memory called the *clipboard*. The same thing happens when you choose Copy, only the original text stays put, and a copy of that text goes to the clipboard. To make the text reappear in another place, just tap where you want to place the text and choose Edit⇨ Paste. Even if you turn off your Visor, the last text you put on the clipboard stays on the clipboard, so you may find that you can paste text that you copied weeks or months ago. Be aware, however, that every time you cut or copy text, that text replaces whatever text was previously on the clipboard.

Adding multiple items to a category

If you want to add a series of new items to a single category, simply display that category and start creating items. Whatever category you display before creating new items becomes the category assigned to the new items. For example, if I want to make a list of things I need to do at PC Expo, I press the To Do List hard button several times until my PC Expo category appears (provided that I created a PC Expo category), and then I just start adding items. Every new item I create while in a certain category turns up in that category, so I can see everything in the category as I add items.

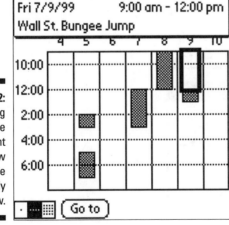

Figure 4-2: Dragging the appointment to a new time in the weekly view.

Graffiti Timesavers

If you've really taken to Graffiti, then you may appreciate these quick timesavers.

Creating new items by writing

If you want to add a new item to any standard Visor application except for the Address Book, press the hard button for that application and start entering text in the Graffiti area. This is one trick that works only if you use Graffiti. When the Visor senses that you're entering Graffiti, it naturally does the right thing — it opens a new item in which to store the new text.

Opening Graffiti Help with a single stroke

You can open Graffiti Help by drawing a line with your stylus from the Graffiti writing area to the top of the display. If you've already earned your black belt in Graffiti, you can assign that stroke to perform one of four other tasks: turn on the backlight, display the on-screen keyboard, beam the current item to another Visor, or turn off and lock your Visor. To reassign the upstroke command follow these steps:

1. **Tap the Applications soft button**
2. **Tap Prefs.**
3. **Choose Buttons from the pull-down menu in the upper-right corner.**
4. **Tap Pen, and the Pen dialog box appears (see Figure 4-3).**

   For more about customizing the functions of your Visor, see Chapter 3.

Figure 4-3: Customize what happens when you use the Graffiti upstroke.

Part II
Getting Down to Business

The 5th Wave   By Rich Tennant

Mitch would never be sure it was laughter he heard that day at the airport but he never again traveled with his Pez handheld computing device.

In this part . . .

The programs that come with your Palm device can do a great deal if you know all the options. You can create and manage appointments, addresses, tasks, and memos by following the steps in this part. You also find out how to beam data to other Palm devices with just the touch of a button.

Chapter 5

Names and Addresses in a ZIP

I find it incredibly handy to have all the names and addresses I need in electronic form rather than on paper. I love being able to find names in a flash, change details, and keep track of bits and pieces of information about everyone in my social and professional life.

You'd get pretty uncomfortable if you had to walk around with a desktop computer stuffed into your pocket or purse — and you'd look pretty funny, too. Just because I want you to be comfortable (and because I *know* you're good-looking), I'm going to show you how to do all your addresskeeping on the Visor, because your Visor can always be with you.

Accessing Your Address Book

To call up the Address Book on your Visor, just press the Address Book hard button (the second button from the left at the bottom of your Visor, as shown in Figure 5-1). My sample Address List is shown in Figure 5-2.

Address Book
hard button

Figure 5-1:
Starting the
Address
Book.

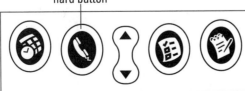

```
┌─────────────────────────────────────┐
│ ▐Address List▌              ▼ All    │
├─────────────────────────────────────┤
│ Alifont, "Bull"          555-9897 W  │
│ DeDark, Fredda           555-6457 W  │
│ Early, Otto B.           555-6472 W  │
│ ▐Snivel, Heather          555-3197 W▌│
│                                      │
│                                      │
│                                      │
│                                      │
│ Look Up:│             ( New )        │
└─────────────────────────────────────┘
```

Figure 5-2:
Viewing the
names
you've
entered.

Putting Names into Your Visor

I know more than a few people who enter and make changes to their Address Lists on a desktop computer, and then transfer the whole shebang to the Visor just to look up names while they're traveling, which works just fine. (Actually, many of those folks have employees who enter the information for them, which is the easiest method of all. But, most of us don't have that luxury.) But you don't have to wait to update your addresses; you can enter all the information you need right on the Visor, no matter where you are. See Chapter 12 for more about keeping up your Address List in the Palm desktop program.

Adding a new name

Many people have relied on a Little Black Book since even before Casanova. The paper kind served well until the computer came along. Computers enable you to find one name out of a list of thousands faster than you can say, "What's-his-name." Speed isn't the only advantage of electronic address lists; the Visor looks up a name from your list and plugs that name into an item in your To Do List, Memo Pad, or Date Book to save you the trouble of retyping. But before you can look up a name, you need to add the name to your Address Book.

Use these steps to store a name in your Address Book:

1. **With the Address List visible, tap the New button at the bottom of the Address List.**

   The Address Edit screen appears.

2. **Tap anywhere on the Last Name line and enter the last name, as shown in Figure 5-3.**

Figure 5-3: Visor highlights the line as you tap and enter information.

```
┌─────────────────────────────────────┐
│ Address Edit          ▼ Unfiled      │
│ Last name: Alifont                   │
│ First name: ........................ │
│      Title: ........................ │
│   Company: ......................... │
│    ▼ Work: ......................... │
│    ▼ Home: ......................... │
│     ▼ Fax: ......................... │
│   ▼ Other: ......................... │
│  ▼ E-mail: ......................... │
│    Address: ........................ │
│                                      │
│ ( Done ) ( Details... ) ( Note )  ▲  │
│                                   ▼  │
└─────────────────────────────────────┘
```

3. **Tap and enter information to fill in the First Name, Title, Company, and the Work and Home phone lines.**

4. **If you want to enter a type of phone number that isn't shown, tap Other.**

   A list appears, showing the different types of phone numbers that you can enter, including pager and mobile numbers (see Figure 5-4).

   Notice the pull-down list triangle next to each phone number line. As with the other applications in Visor, this arrow means that a pull-down list is hiding behind that button; here you can choose other options simply by tapping the triangle, and then tapping your choice. Although every address record contains three phone number lines and an e-mail line, you can use any of the phone number lines to store any of seven different types of phone number or an e-mail address. For example, if you want to save one person's work number and pager number, but not his home number, then tap the triangle next to Home and pick Pager from the list. Now the number you enter will be shown as a Pager number.

5. **Tap the name of the phone number type that you want to enter.**

   The type you choose, Fax for example, replaces Other.

Figure 5-4:
Add other
phone
numbers as
needed.

6. **Enter the phone number in the Graffiti number area.**

7. **If you want to enter your contact's mailing address, press the scroll-down hard button at the bottom center of the Visor.**

   The lower half of the contact form appears, enabling you to enter mailing address information, as shown in Figure 5-5.

Figure 5-5:
Wait! Scroll
to find more
at the
bottom of
the form.

8. **Enter mailing address information on the appropriate lines just as you did in the preceding steps.**

9. **When you finish entering the information, click Done.**

   The Address Edit screen disappears, and the Address List reappears.

Now you're ready to find anyone in your personal Who's Who almost faster than you can say, "Who?"

If you have a list of names and addresses in another contact program on a desktop or laptop computer, you can enter them in the desktop program as a list and then HotSync the whole bunch to your Visor.

As you can see, entering names and addresses in the Visor is easy, but when you have a large collection of names, you can save time by letting your computers take care of the job. For more about installing and operating the desktop programs for either Windows or Macintosh, see Chapters 11 and 12.

Editing an address record

It seems that some people change their addresses more often than they change their socks. You can't very well tell them to stop moving, but you can keep up with their latest addresses by editing their address records in your Visor. You may want to say something to them about their socks, though.

These steps help you to change an entry in your Address Book:

1. **With the Address List visible, enter in the Graffiti box the first few letters of the last name that you want to edit.**

   The letters that you enter appear on the Look Up line at the bottom of the display. Of course, if the name you're looking for is visible to start with, you don't have to look it up.

2. **Tap the appropriate name to edit the record.**

   The Address View screen, shown in Figure 5-6, appears, showing details about that contact.

Figure 5-6:
Viewing the
current
information
in Address
View.

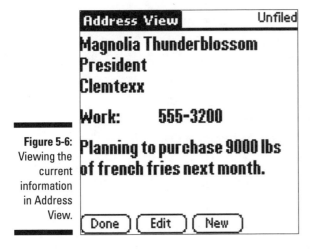

3. **Tap Edit at the bottom of the display.**

   The Address Edit screen appears.

4. **Enter new information by the tap-and-enter method.**

   For more on entering text, see Chapter 2.

   New information appears on the appropriate lines of the screen.

5. **To replace existing information, highlight the text that you want to replace by drawing a horizontal line through it.**

6. **Enter new text in the Graffiti box at the bottom of the display.**

   As in your favorite word processor, the text that you enter replaces the text that you selected. For more on entering text, see Chapter 2.

7. **When you've made all the changes that you want to make, tap Done.**

   The Address Edit screen disappears and the Address List screen reappears.

Visor saves all your changes as soon as you tap the Done button. If you want to change the person's address or other details back, you have to go through the whole edit process again. In other words, you don't have an Undo feature to put things back the way they were.

Attaching a note to an address record

You want to know lots of things about a person — where she likes to go; what he said to you the last time you spoke to him; how much she owes you; whatever. You can attach all sorts of information to a person's address record in the form of a note.

To attach a note to an address, follow these steps:

1. **With the Address List visible, tap the person's name to open that record.**

   The Address View screen appears, showing details about the contact that you chose.

2. **Tap the Menu soft button at the bottom of the display.**

   The menu bar appears at the top of the display.

3. **Choose Record⇨Attach Note, as shown in Figure 5-7.**

Record
Options
Delete Address... ✓D
Attach Note ✓A
Delete Note... ✓O
Beam Address ✓B
Select Business Card...
Beam Business Card
Done
Edit
New

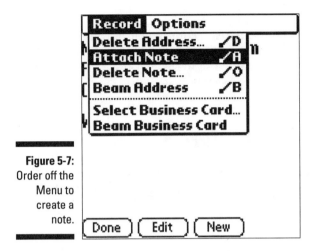

Figure 5-7: Order off the Menu to create a note.

A blank note screen appears.

4. **Enter the note text in the Graffiti box at the bottom of the display, or use the on-screen keyboard as shown in Figure 5-8.**

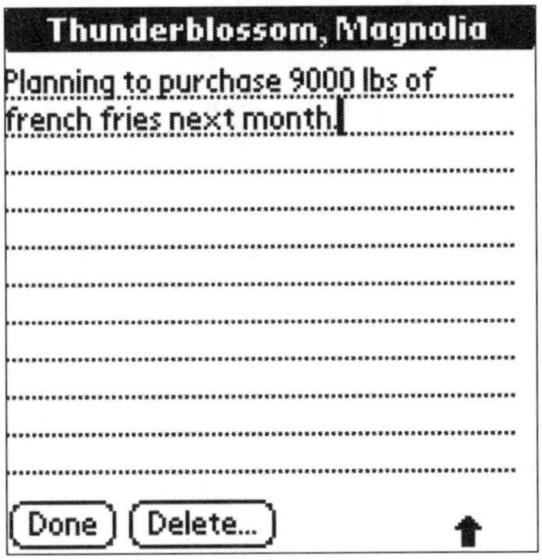

Thunderblossom, Magnolia
Planning to purchase 9000 lbs of
french fries next month.
Done
Delete...

Figure 5-8: Enter plain old text in the Note screen.

5. **Tap Done at the bottom of the Note screen.**

   The Note screen closes to return to the Address View screen.

6. **Tap Done again.**

   The Address View screen disappears, and the Address List reappears.

If you enter information in a note and want to find it again, you can use the Find tool to search all the data on your Visor. For example, if you added a note to someone's record that says `drives a Studebaker`, you can tap the Find soft button at the bottom-right corner of the screen and then enter `Studebaker` to find the person who drives one.

Managing Your Information

If you're one of those lucky folks who has an assistant to enter your Visor data so that all you do is use what's been entered, the rest of this chapter is for you. After you know how to find the stuff you've collected, you're in business!

Marking your business card

Now that everybody who's anybody has a Visor or PalmPilot (after all, you have one, and I have one, and that's all that matters to me), we can all take advantage of the Visor infrared port to exchange business cards. Before you beam your business card to anyone, you need to enter an address record containing your own name and contact information, as I describe in the section on adding a new name in this chapter.

An *infrared (IR) port* is standard equipment on your Visor. Infrared lets you *beam* information from one Visor to another Visor or PalmPilot. *Beaming* is when you point two Visors at each other and send data across the air using an invisible beam of light. See Chapter 9 for more on beaming. Someday, you'll be able to change the channels on your TV with Visor infrared, but for now, you can beam your business card (as well as other addresses, To Do items, memos, and appointments) to other Visor users.

When you send your business card to someone via Visor, what you're really doing is beaming a name from your Visor Address Book to the Address Book on the other Visor. The name you send just happens to be your own. Here's how to set up your Visor to send your business card:

1. **With the Address List visible, enter the first few letters of your last name in the Graffiti box.**

   The letters that you enter appear on the Look Up line at the bottom of the display.

2. **Tap your name in the Address List.**

   The Address View screen appears, showing details about your contact record.

3. **Tap the Menu soft button at the bottom of the display.**

   The menu bar appears at the top of the display.

4. **Choose Record⇨Select Business Card.**

   The Select Business Card dialog box opens, as shown in Figure 5-9.

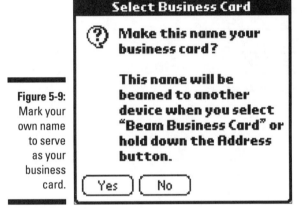

Figure 5-9:
Mark your
own name
to serve
as your
business
card.

5. **Tap Yes at the bottom of the Select Business Card dialog box to close it.**

   A small icon that looks like a file card appears at the top of the Address View screen.

6. **Tap Done at the bottom of the display.**

   The Address View screen disappears, and the Address List reappears.

You don't absolutely have to mark a business card if you don't plan to use this feature. If you use the beaming feature a lot, you can save time if you mark your business card because you won't have to spend time looking up your own name when you want to send a card. For the first several months after I bought my original PalmPilot, I never beamed a business card to anyone, but I marked my name anyway. If deep space aliens showed up like they did in the movie *Independence Day*, I'd have been ready to beam them my friendly greetings (for all the good it would've done — aliens all use Macs). Since then I've had plenty of occasions to beam my card to other friendly Palm and Visor owners, and I'm always glad when someone beams me his card; that way I don't have to retype his address.

Finding Mr. Right (or whoever)

If you took the time to enter a bunch of names into your Visor, I'd guess that you want to find the names again. Call me crazy, but you might get more good out of your Visor than you do that dating service you joined.

Here's the quickest way to find a name in your Address Book:

1. **With the Address List visible, enter in the Graffiti box the first few letters of the last name that you want to find.**

   The letters that you enter appear on the Look Up line at the bottom of the display, as shown in Figure 5-10.

Figure 5-10:
Your Visor figures out who you're looking for when you enter the first few letters of the last name.

Address List	▼ All
Alifont, "Bull"	555-9897 W
DeDark, Fredda	555-6457 W
Early, Otto B.	555-6472 W
Snivel, Heather	555-3197 W

Look Up: dedark   (New)

If you don't like messing with Graffiti, you can press the hard scroll-down button on the Visor to scroll through your address list. The Address Book can hold thousands of names, so if your list is long, scrolling can be laborious.

2. **Tap the name of the person whose record you want to view.**

   The Address View screen appears, showing details about the contact.

3. **When you're finished, tap Done at the bottom of the display.**

   The Address List reappears.

The Quicklist category is preset in the Address Book to make room for addresses you use frequently and need to find in a hurry. You can use it for the most important people in your life.

Deleting a name

The main reason to add a name to your Address Book is to help you remember important things about a person. However, sometimes you'd rather forget some people in your list. I won't mention any names. . . .

Assigning categories to contacts

If you want to make finding addresses easier, you can assign categories to names on your Address List. Then when you press the Address Book button several times, you cycle through the different address categories until you see the category that you want to use. For example, you can assign the category Business to some names and the category Personal to other names. When you press the Address Book button the first time, you see all the names in your collection. The second time that you press it, you see the names assigned to the Business category; the third time, you see the names assigned to the Personal category, and so on. You may be completely happy keeping all your names uncategorized, which is just fine, too.

To assign a category to any name in your list, open the record for editing, as I describe in editing an address record in this chapter, and then pick the category you want to assign to your contact in the upper-right corner of the form. You can manage Address Book categories in exactly the same way you manage categories of To Do items. See Chapter 6 for more about managing To Do item categories.

To delete an unwanted name from your Address Book, follow these steps:

1. **With the Address List visible, enter in the Graffiti box the first few letters of the last name that you want to delete.**

   The letters you enter appear on the Look Up line at the bottom of the display.

2. **Tap the name of the person whose record you want to delete.**

   The Address View screen appears.

3. **Tap the Menu soft button at the bottom of the display.**

   The menu bar appears at the top of the display.

4. **Choose Record⇨Delete Address.**

   The Delete Address dialog box opens, as shown in Figure 5-11. The dialog box asks if you want to archive the item. For more about archived items, see Chapter 12.

5. **Tap OK.**

   The Address List reappears, minus one name.

Figure 5-11:
Deleting the
names of
those who
no longer
interest you
is easy.

Delete Address

? **Delete selected
Address entry?**

☑ **Save archive copy on PC**

[OK] [Cancel]

TIP

If you delete a name in a fit of pique and then wish you could bring it back, all is not entirely lost. If you haven't used HotSync between the time you deleted the name and the time you want it back, you can find the name in the program on your desktop computer (provided the name isn't brand new and has never been HotSynced at all). To re-enter that address into Visor, make a slight change in the address information and then resynchronize to make the offending name a part of your list again. Then you can kiss and make up. I discuss synchronization in Chapter 11 and archiving in Chapter 12. Fractured friendships are another issue altogether.

Deleting a note from an address record

Sometimes the note you've attached to someone's address becomes out of date. You can change the contents of the note by using the same steps that you used to create the note, or you can just delete the entire note.

Here's how to delete a note attached to an address:

1. **With the Address List visible, tap the name with the obsolete note.**

   The Address View screen appears with the record details.

2. **Tap the Menu soft button at the bottom of the display.**

   The menu bar appears at the top of the display.

3. **Choose Record⇨Delete Note, as shown in Figure 5-12.**

   The Delete Note dialog box opens.

4. **Tap Yes at the bottom of the Delete Note dialog box.**

   The Delete Note dialog box closes, and the Address View screen reappears.

5. **Tap Done at the bottom of the Address View screen.**

   The Address View screen disappears, and the Address List reappears.

Zap! Your note is gone for good. You can also delete a note from within the note itself. Just open the note and tap Delete.

Figure 5-12:
You can delete only a note from a record but keep the record.

Setting Address Book preferences

If you don't like the way the Address Book looks when it first opens, you can change its appearance . . . a little. I think the Address Book is just fine as it is, but if you simply must rearrange your list, these steps show you how:

1. **With the Address List visible, tap the Menu soft button at the bottom of the display.**

   The Menu bar appears at the top of the display.

2. **Choose Options⇨Preferences.**

   The Address Book Preferences dialog box opens, as shown in Figure 5-13.

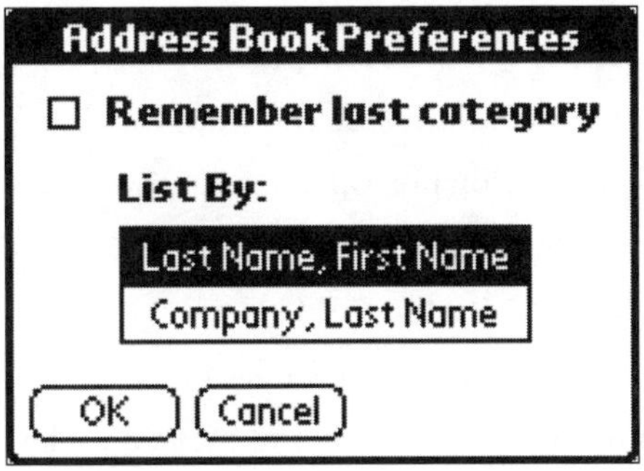

Figure 5-13:
Express your preferences through the Address Book Preferences dialog box.

3. **From the List By box, choose either of these options:**
   - Last Name, First Name
   - Company, Last Name

4. **Tap the Remember Last Category box if you usually want your Address Book to open to the most recent category you used.**

   If you don't check the Remember Last Category box, your Address Book always opens to the All category, showing you all names.

   I think it's better to leave the box unchecked, but that's a matter of personal preference. If you have a category that you use constantly, you might want the Visor to return to that category regularly.

The main reason to change the List By options is when you organize your contacts by company rather than by name. When you choose "Company, Last Name" you'll see a list of companies in your Address Book rather than a list of names.

Setting up custom fields

Sometimes you need to keep track of something about the people you know, and Visor doesn't already have a line (or field) for it in the Address List. For example, if your job involves selling merchandise to retail stores, your Address Book probably contains the names of all the store buyers to whom you sell. The Address Book includes four lines at the end of the Address Edit screen that you can rename to fit your needs. These four lines are called *custom fields*. You may want to set up one custom field to keep track of which type of merchandise each buyer buys, such as housewares, appliances, shoes, and so on. You can rename one of the custom fields Specialty to show each buyer's area of interest.

To set up your custom fields, follow these steps:

1. **With the Address List visible, tap the Menu soft button at the bottom of the display.**

   The menu bar appears at the top of the display.

2. **Choose Options⇨Rename Custom Fields.**

   The Rename Custom Fields dialog box opens, as shown in Figure 5-14.

3. **Select the field that you want to rename.**

4. **Enter the name that you want for the field.**

   The text that you enter appears as the new field name.

5. **Rename the other custom fields by following Steps 3 and 4.**

6. **When you've renamed all the fields that you want to rename, click OK.**

   The Rename Custom Fields dialog box closes, and the Address List reappears.

Rename Custom Fields

**Create your own field names
by editing the text on the
lines below:**

Specialty

Custom 2

Custom 3

Custom 4

(OK) (Cancel)

Figure 5-14:
Just replace
Custom 1
with your
own field
name.

You don't absolutely have to rename custom fields to use them. You can just enter information in the fields and remember that the field named Custom 1 contains a certain type of entry. Renaming the custom fields just makes them a little more useful and easier to understand. When you rename a custom field, the field name is changed in all address records.

Chapter 6

To Do's That YOU Do!

. . . .

In This Chapter

▶ Creating a list of tasks

▶ Entering To Do details

▶ Attaching and deleting notes

▶ Organizing items by category

▶ Beaming To Do's

▶ Changing and deleting To Do items

▶ Marking the To Do's you've done

▶ Setting To Do preferences

. . . .

*W*ho doesn't have a zillion things to do these days? Just keeping track of the tasks you need to take care of is a full-time job. The only thing worse than keeping track of your tasks is actually doing all those things. And even if you use a computer for many of your daily tasks, you probably can't stay chained to the desk all day. You need to move around, while keeping track of all the things you did in all the places you went.

The To Do List on your Visor can help you keep a handle on all those little errands and projects that take up all your time. You can add a task when you think of it, rather than waiting to get back to your computer. By the time I get back to my desk, I usually forget that terribly important detail that I need to take care of.

I assume in this chapter that you're using your Visor exactly the way it comes out of the box. Because your Visor includes a copy of a program called DateBook+ that also takes care of To Do items, you might prefer to handle your daily tasks through that program and ignore the regular To Do program. When you enter To Do items through DateBook+, the items appear in both the To Do List and in DateBook+, so you don't need to worry about losing anything. For more information about DateBook+, see Chapter 8.

If DateBook+ doesn't make the grade for you as a task manager either, a couple of other chapters in this book tell you how to find still more programs to replace the To Do List and how to install them. If you've replaced your To Do List with some other program, many of the instructions in this chapter won't work for you. I don't want to discourage you from trying other programs — lots of good ones exist — but, unfortunately, I can't cover all the third-party software out there for the PalmPilot and Visor.

Just push the To Do List hard button (second one from the right) to call up your To Do List (see Figure 6-1). Then do whatever you want to do with your To Do's!

To Do List
hard button

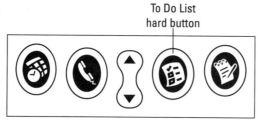

Figure 6-1:
Press the
To Do List
button to
bring up
your list of
To Do's.

Adding New To Do's

Adding items to your To Do List is as easy as you want to make it. If you want to keep track of short lists of simple projects, you can go a long way with the tools that come with the Visor. If your planning process involves long lists of elaborate plans and projects and goes beyond the ability of the Visor To Do List, you may need some extra help in the form of extra software or a daily download from your desktop computer. You can always rely on a desktop program such as ACT! or Goldmine to do all the heavy lifting, and you can just HotSync your Visor to your desktop every day to keep a handy portable copy of your information. For more about using your Visor with third-party software, see Part III.

Creating a To Do item

You can take advantage of the powers of your To Do List only if you've entered the To Do's that you have to do. No voodoo is involved with To Do — just press a button, tap with a stylus, and you're in business.

Follow these steps to add a new item to your To Do List:

1. **If the To Do List isn't already open, push the second hard button from the right and tap New at the bottom of the To Do List.**

   A new blank line appears in the To Do List.

2. **Enter the name of your task with either the on-screen keyboard or Graffiti (see Chapter 2 for more about entering text).**

   The name of the task you enter appears on the new line (see Figure 6-2).

Figure 6-2:
Just tap a line and enter the name of your task.

3. **Tap any blank area of the screen or press the Scroll Down button to finish.**

   Ta-da! Now you have a new task to call your very own.

Of course, you can use an even simpler way to enter a new To Do: Press the To Do List button and enter the name of your task with Graffiti. Your Visor automatically creates a new To Do with the name you enter.

Entering details for a To Do item

You may not be satisfied with a To Do List that only keeps track of the names of your tasks. Knowing what a productive, demanding person you are (or could be if you really wanted to be), your To Do List enables you to assign priorities, categories, and due dates to each task.

To add details to your tasks, follow these steps:

1. **With your To Do List open, tap the name to select the task.**

2. **Tap Details at the bottom of the display.**

   The To Do Item Details dialog box opens.

3. **To set the priority of your item, tap one of the numbers (1 through 5) next to the word Priority.**

   If the only detail you wanted to change about your task is the priority, you can simply tap the priority number in the To Do List and pick the priority number from the drop-down list.

4. **To assign a category to your task, tap the triangle next to the word Category.**

   A list of available categories appears. The option of assigning categories helps you organize your To Do List, but you don't have to assign a category to a task. I explain how to use categories in "Viewing Items by Category" later in this chapter.

5. **Tap the name of the category you want to assign to your task.**

   The list disappears, and the name of the category you chose appears.

6. **To assign a deadline to your task, tap the triangle next to Due Date.**

   A list appears, giving you these choices: Today, Tomorrow, One Week Later, No Date, and Choose Date (see Figure 6-3).

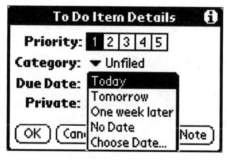

Figure 6-3:
Pick the due
date for
your task.

7. **Tap the option for the due date you want.**

   If you choose a pre-set time period, the list disappears, and the date you chose appears.

   If you tap Choose Date, the Due Date screen, which looks like a calendar, opens instead (see Figure 6-4). Tap the new deadline on the calendar, and the Due Date screen disappears. The date you chose appears in the To Do Item Details dialog box.

Due Date

◀ **2001** ▶

Jan	Feb	Mar	Apr	May	Jun
Jul	Aug	Sep	Oct	Nov	Dec

S	M	T	W	T	F	S
				1	2	3
4	5	6	7	8	9	10
11	12	13	14	15	16	17
18	19	20	21	22	23	24
25	26	27	28	29	30	31

(Cancel) (Today)

Figure 6-4:
Choose a
more
specific
date from
the
calendar.

8. **If you want to safeguard your entry, tap the check box next to the word Private to toggle this feature on or off.**

Private entries typically appear with your other entries, but you can also hide your private entries. Just tap the Applications soft button to call up your applications list, choose Security, and select Hide. For more about privacy and passwords, see Chapter 3.

9. **Tap OK.**

The To Do Item Details dialog box closes, and your To Do List reappears with the changes you made visible on the screen.

You may notice when you create a new task that the on-screen Details button is available the whole time. If you want to add all sorts of details while you're adding a new task, nothing can stop you. However, if you're in a hurry and just want to enter the task quickly, you can enter just the name of the task and then add details later.

Attaching notes to items

The popular book by Robert Fulghum tells us that we learn everything we need to know in kindergarten. That's okay, I guess, but if you didn't get past kindergarten, don't mention it in your next job interview.

In the same way, many tasks need a bit more explanation than a quick subject line can describe. So, you may need to add a note to your task if you need to keep track of a detailed explanation along with a task.

These steps show how to add a note to a To Do item:

1. **With your To Do List open, tap the task to checkmark it.**

2. **Tap Details at the bottom of the To Do List.**

   The To Do Item Details dialog box opens.

3. **Tap Note at the bottom of the To Do Item Details dialog box.**

   A blank Note screen appears.

4. **Enter text with either the on-screen keyboard or Graffiti.**

   Your note appears, as shown in Figure 6-5.

Figure 6-5:
If you have
more
detailed
instructions
about your
task, add
a note.

Spin straw into gold

Find out the name of that little troll
before tomorrow

(Done) (Delete...)

5. **Tap Done at the bottom of the Note screen.**

   The Note screen disappears and your To Do List reappears. As a reminder, a small square icon appears to the right of the items with notes. If you want to view a note attached to a To Do item, just click the square.

The Note screen also includes a Delete button that lets you delete a note as you read the note. I discuss another way to delete notes attached to To Do items in the section "Deleting a note" later in this chapter, but deleting a note from the Note screen is as good a method as any.

TIP

If you've created a note in the Visor Memo List, or if you've attached a note to an entry in your Address Book, you'll find the general idea of creating notes stays the same throughout your Visor. Unfortunately, notes attached to different types of Visor items don't have anything to do with each other. For example, you can't move a note from the Memo List to the To Do List, or from the To Do List to the Address Book — not now, at least, but maybe in the future.

Viewing Items by Category

To Do items always belong to a category of one type or another. If you don't assign a category yourself, your Visor automatically assigns the category Unfiled. You can see the name of the category you're viewing in the upper-right corner of the screen. When you first press the To Do List button, the word in the corner is All, which means that you're viewing all your tasks, regardless of category. You can change your view to a different category in two ways — the short way and the even shorter way. (They make these things so easy to use!) I start with the short way:

1. **With your To Do List open, tap the category name in the upper-right corner of the screen.**

   The list of available categories appears. The first time that you use your Visor, the list has four categories: All, Business, Personal, and Unfiled. After you have used your Visor the first time, a fifth option, Edit Categories, is available (see Figure 6-6). I talk about that option in the editing section.

Figure 6-6:
To switch categories, just pick from the list.

To Do List — All, Business, Personal, Unfiled, Edit Categories...

☐ 1 Spin straw into
☐ 1 Call Prince abo
☐ 1 Open a savings
☐ 1 Get new fillings

(New) (Details...) (Show...)

2. **Tap the category that you want to view.**

   The To Do List changes to display only the items assigned to the selected category, and the name of the category that you're viewing appears in the upper-right corner of the screen.

The shorter way to change the category you're viewing is — you guessed it — even shorter. Just press the To Do List button more than once. Each time you press the To Do List button, you see the next category for which you've created entries. The categories appear in alphabetical order, including any categories that you may have added yourself (see the section, "Adding categories," later in this chapter). Neat, huh?

Adding categories

If you're usually juggling too many tasks to fit on one little Visor screen, you'll find assigning categories to your tasks useful in tracking the scads of things you have to do. You can look through all categories, one at a time, with a few clicks of the To Do List button. Sooner or later, though, you may want to create categories of your own.

Follow these steps to create a new category:

1. **With your To Do List open, tap the category name currently in the upper-right corner of the screen.**

   The list of available categories appears.

2. **Tap Edit Categories.**

   The Edit Categories screen appears.

3. **Tap New.**

   The Edit Categories dialog box opens.

4. **Enter the name of the new category.**

5. **Tap OK.**

   The name that you entered appears in the Edit Categories dialog box, and the dialog box closes.

6. **Tap OK again.**

   The new category is ready for your tasks.

Remember that you're better off if you stick to a few well-used categories rather than dozens of categories that you never look at. A to-do list should focus on the things you really plan to do; otherwise you could just call it a "Round Tuit" list — things you'll do if you ever get around to it.

Deleting categories

If you've gone hog-wild and created categories that you never use, delete some of them. You can also create a category for a special event and then delete the category when the event ends. I do that for trade shows sometimes; I create a category for things I have to do during the show, and then delete the category when the show is over.

Follow these steps to delete a category:

1. **With your To Do List open, tap the category name in the upper-right corner of the screen.**

   The list of available categories appears.

2. **Tap Edit Categories.**

   The Edit Categories screen appears.

3. **Tap the name of the category that you want to delete.**

4. **Tap Delete.**

   If the category still contains items, the Remove Category dialog box opens, warning you that all the items in that category will be reassigned to the Unfiled category. If no items are assigned to the category you picked, the Remove Category dialog box doesn't open.

5. **Tap Yes.**

   The Remove Category dialog box closes, and your category is deleted.

6. **Tap OK.**

The All and Unfiled categories don't show up in the Edit Categories screen, because they're not really categories. You can't get rid of the view that shows all your tasks (a mistake you probably wouldn't want to make) because finding things that you categorized by mistake would be harder.

Renaming categories

What's in a name? Shakespeare's Romeo thought it didn't matter, but look what happened to him. Sometimes you want your categories to reflect what you're really doing, so you change the names to fit your style. Maybe you want to keep a list of "to get" items the next time you're at the store, so you make a Shopping category. Or, maybe your boss or the IRS forbids you to use your tax-deductible Visor for personal use, so why bother with a Personal category. Of course, if you just *happen* to put something personal in a Misc category, then what's in the name is up to you.

To rename a category, follow these steps:

1. **With your To Do List open, tap the current category in the upper-right corner of the screen.**

   The list of available categories appears.

2. **Tap Edit Categories.**

   The Edit Categories screen appears.

3. **Tap the name of the category.**

4. **Tap Rename.**

   The Edit Categories dialog box opens.

5. **Type or enter the new name.**

6. **Tap OK.**

   The name that you entered replaces the previous name of the category in the Edit Categories dialog box, and the dialog box closes.

7. **Tap OK again.**

Because your categories can be sorted and displayed in alphabetical order, you may want to pick category names that fall in line a certain way. Business tasks come before Personal tasks in more ways than alphabetical order. On the other hand, you can cycle through all your categories with a few clicks of the To Do List button, so you can see all your tasks without much fuss.

What to Do with the To Do's You Do

Even if you don't enter To Do items yourself, you may wind up with a collection of tasks in your list that got sent to you by another person or by a program on your desktop computer. (See Chapters 9 and 12 for more on beaming your To Do's and connecting your Visor to a desktop computer.) After you have To Do's, you need to know what to do. (Anybody else feel a little dizzy?)

Beaming To Do's

You don't have to keep your To Do's to yourself. You can beam tasks to other people if they have a Visor or PalmPilot too. Although beaming To Do's is reasonably safe and totally sanitary, beaming too many tasks at people can make them sick — that is, sick of all the tasks you're sending. You can read more about beaming in Chapter 9.

To beam a To Do item to another PalmPilot or Visor, follow these steps:

1. **With your To Do List open, tap the name of the task that you want to beam.**

   Visor highlights the check box to the left.

2. **Tap the Menu soft button at the bottom of the display.**

   The menu bar appears at the top of the display.

3. **Choose Record⇨Beam Item, as shown in Figure 6-7.**

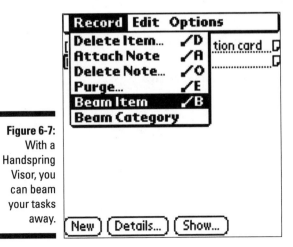

| Record | Edit | Options |

Delete Item... ✓D
Attach Note ✓A
Delete Note... ✓O
Purge... ✓E
Beam Item ✓B
Beam Category

[New] [Details...] [Show...]

Figure 6-7:
With a
Handspring
Visor, you
can beam
your tasks
away.

The Beam dialog box opens.

4. Tap OK.

The Beam dialog box closes, and your To Do List reappears.

Remember that the beaming feature of your Visor works just like the remote control for your TV. The two Visors have to be side by side and reasonably close together, within three feet. If you want to beam a task to someone in the office building across the street, or to the driver of an oncoming car, you're out of luck.

Changing To Do's

The French have a saying, *"Plus ça change, plus c'est le meme chose,"* which means "The more things change, the more they're the same." Even if you don't speak French, you know that makes no sense, but it sounds terribly charming in French.

The charming thing about changing To Do items is that you do pretty much the same things to change an item that you did to enter it in the first place. This section shows you how to alter the priorities, names, and details, of existing To Do items.

Switching priorities

To change the priority of a To Do item, follow these steps:

1. **With your To Do List open, tap the name of the task to checkmark it.**

2. **To change the priority of your task, tap the number next to the name of the task.**

   A list of numbers 1 through 5 appears (see Figure 6-8).

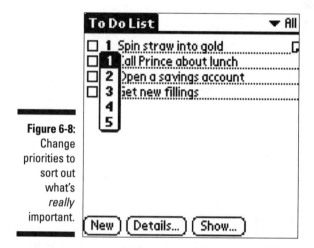

Figure 6-8:
Change
priorities to
sort out
what's
really
important.

3. **Tap the number for the new priority that you want to give your task.**

   The highest priority is 1; the lowest is 5. When you tap a number, the list disappears, and the new priority number appears next to your task.

Changing names

If you want to change the name of a To Do item, follow these steps:

1. **With your To Do List open, tap the name of the task to checkmark it.**

2. **Select the text you that want to change by drawing a horizontal line through it with your stylus.**

3. **Type or enter the new text.**

   The new task name replaces the selected text.

Updating details

If you want to make further changes to a To Do item, follow these steps:

1. **With your To Do List open, tap the name of the task to checkmark it.**

2. **Tap Details at the bottom of the To Do List.**

   The To Do Item Details dialog box opens.

3. **Make whatever changes you want in the To Do Item Details dialog box.**

   You can use the same methods for changing the details of your task that you did to enter the details in the first place (see "Entering details for a To Do item" in this chapter).

4. **Tap OK.**

   The To Do Item Details dialog box closes, and the To Do List reappears.

The one trick about changing To Do items is that the To Do List almost never displays all the things that you can change about a task. That means that you may change something that's not displayed, so at first you may think that your changes didn't take. See "Setting preferences for your To Do List" later in this chapter to find out how to show everything you want to see.

Undoing a mistake

If you make a mistake when changing the text in a To Do item, you can fix it in a jiffy by doing this:

1. **With your To Do List open, tap the Menu soft button.**

   The menu bar appears at the top of the display.

2. **Choose Edit⇨Undo.**

   Your text returns to the way it was before you changed it.

Undo works only when you change or replace text. You can't use the Undo command to recover a To Do item that you accidentally delete. If you have archived deleted items, you can go to the archive on the Palm Desktop to recover the item. See Chapter 12 for details on recovering items from the archive.

Marking the To Do's that you've done

As you finish the tasks that you've assigned to yourself, mark them as completed. Checking off To Do items does more than give you a feeling of satisfaction; it can also shorten that depressing list of things left to do. I say "can," because you can either set up your Visor to display all tasks, completed or not, or you can choose to hide completed tasks. See "Setting preferences for your To Do List" later in this chapter for information on hiding tasks.

To mark a task as completed, tap the check box next to the name of the task that you want to mark. A check mark appears in the check box to show that you've completed the item (see Figure 6-9). If you set the To Do Preferences to hide completed items, the item disappears from the To Do List.

```
To Do List                    ▼ All
☑ 1  Spin straw into gold          ▯
☐ 1  Call Prince about lunch
☑ 1  Open a savings account
☐ 1  Get new fillings




( New )  ( Details... )  ( Show... )
```

Figure 6-9:
When you
finish a task,
check it off.

Deleting a To Do

Perhaps you added a task to your To Do List and then lost your nerve and
decided to erase any trace of it. If you've made it your task to tell what's-his-
name that he's a dirty, rotten so-and-so, you may be wiser to delete the thing.
Some tasks are better deleted than done.

To delete a To Do List item, follow these steps:

1. **With your To Do List open, tap the task to checkmark it.**

2. **Tap the Menu soft button.**

   The menu bar appears at the top of the display.

3. **Choose Record⇨Delete Item.**

   The Delete To Do dialog box opens (see Figure 6-10).

   The Delete To Do dialog box offers a Save an Archive Copy on PC option
   for each item you delete. By checking this option, you can still dig up old
   deleted items through the Palm Desktop on your PC if you need them in
   the future. If you leave the box checked, each item is archived automatically. For more about archived items, see Chapter 12.

   If you click the archive check box to uncheck it, it stays unchecked for
   every item you delete until you check it again.

4. **Tap OK.**

   The Delete To Do dialog box closes, and your To Do List reappears.

Delete To Do ⓘ

? **Delete selected To Do item?**

☑ **Save archive copy on PC**

(OK) (Cancel)

Figure 6-10:
If you don't
want to
complete it,
delete it.

Some people like to delete tasks rather than marking them as completed because it keeps their list of tasks short. The reason not to delete completed tasks is so that you can brag about all the things you've accomplished. That's a particularly useful approach if you have a job that gives performance reviews. It's up to you: complete or delete.

Deleting a note

After you've done a task a few times, you may not need a note telling you how to do that task anymore. You can delete a note attached to a To Do item without deleting the item.

To delete a note, follow these steps:

1. **With your To Do List open, tap the task to checkmark it.**

2. **Tap the Menu soft button.**

   The menu bar appears at the top of the display.

3. **Choose Record⇨Delete Note.**

   The Delete Note dialog box opens, asking if you're sure that you want to do this.

   When you delete a note, it's gone for good; notes are not archived separately, and the Undo command doesn't bring them back. So, be sure that you *really* want the note that you pick to be deleted.

4. **Tap Yes.**

   The note is deleted, but the task remains.

Setting preferences for your To Do List

If you never change a thing about your To Do List, you can still get plenty of mileage out of your Visor. But everybody works a little differently, so you may want to slice and dice the items in your To Do List in a way that works better for you.

To change your To Do List preferences, follow these steps:

1. **With your To Do List open, tap Show.**

   The To Do Preferences screen appears.

2. **Tap the Sort By triangle to set up your sort order.**

   Your choices, shown in Figure 6-11, are

   - Priority, Due Date
   - Due Date, Priority
   - Category, Priority
   - Category, Due Date

Figure 6-11:
You can
sort your
tasks four
different
ways.

3. **Tap the check boxes that correspond to the elements that you want displayed in the To Do List.**

   The To Do Preferences screen has a half-dozen check boxes that set your display to show Completed Items, Due Dates, Priorities, Categories, and other items. If you display everything, your screen can get a bit crowded, but that's your choice.

If you check any of the following boxes, you get these results:

- **Show Completed Items:** Tasks that you complete stay on the list until you delete them so you can keep a running record.

- **Show Only Due Items:** Taskswith Due Dates set in the future don't show; only tasks with no Due Date or with a Due Date set for today or earlier appear. If you're one of those people who like to wait until the last minute, click this one.

- **Record Completion Date:** The Due Date of a task changes to the date when you mark the task as completed. For example, if you set the Due Date of a task for Friday but mark the task complete on Wednesday, the Due Date automatically changes to Wednesday.

- **Show Due Dates:** This option makes a Due Date appear on the screen along with the name of each task. Use this to put first things first.

- **Show Priorities:** This option makes the Priority number appear next to each task.

- **Show Categories:** Use this option to make the category of each task appear next to the name of the task.

4. **Click OK.**

   The To Do Preferences screen disappears, and your To Do List reappears.

 If you choose to sort by category or priority, displaying the category or priority is also a good idea. Otherwise, your screen looks confusing.

Looking up an address and phone number

Creating To Do items that involve other people is fairly common, even if the task is something as simple as calling someone on the phone. You can get your Visor to look up a name from your Address List and plug that person's name and phone number into the To Do item. Phone Number Lookup can save you the trouble of looking up the person's number when it's time to make the call.

Follow these steps to look up a name and phone number from your Address Book:

1. **With the To Do List open, tap the name of an existing task or create a new one.**

   If you're not sure how to create a new item, see "Creating a To Do item" in this chapter.

2. **Tap the Menu soft button.**

   The menu bar appears.

3. Choose Options⇨Phone Lookup.

The Phone Number Lookup screen appears. If this screen looks like your address book, don't be surprised — that's where the phone numbers come from (see Figure 6-12).

Address List	▼ All
Alifont, "Bull"	555-9897 W
DeDark, Fredda	555-6457 W
Early, Otto B.	555-6472 W
Rumpelstiltskin	555-6666 W
Snivel, Heather	555-3197 W

Look Up: [New]

Figure 6-12: Use the Phone Number Lookup feature to find important numbers.

4. Tap the name of the person

5. Tap Add.

The name and phone number appear as part of your To Do item.

Bear in mind that only the first phone number of the address record you pick appears in the To Do item, no matter how many phone numbers the address record contains.

Unfortunately, you can't get from the To Do List to the person's Address List entry to see other details about the person, such as the street address or other details. You have to press the Address List button and find the name.

Purging finished To Do's

The reason for keeping a To Do List is to help you get things done. After you've done the things on your list, you have no reason to leave them hanging around. The Purge function automatically deletes items that you've marked as completed. You could delete all your completed items one by one, but the purge function deletes them en masse.

To purge completed To Do items, follow these steps:

1. **With your To Do List open, tap the Menu soft button.**

   The menu bar appears at the top of the display.

2. **Choose Record⇨Purge.**

   The Purge dialog box appears. Make sure that a check mark appears in the box that says Save Archive Copy on PC. Otherwise, you won't have a record of all the things you've done.

3. **Tap OK.**

   The Purge dialog box closes, and the items you have marked as completed disappear from the screen, but Visor archives them at your next HotSync.

If you need to dig up a list of the things you've done to show your boss at review time or as dramatic courtroom testimony ("Just where were you the night of . . . ?"), you can go back to the archives of your To Do items, provided that you checked the archive box in the Purge dialog box. For more on retrieving To Do items from the archive, see Chapter 12.

Chapter 7

Memo Mania

● ●

In This Chapter
▶ Creating memos
▶ Viewing memos
▶ Changing and categorizing items
▶ Making a memo private
▶ Deleting memos
▶ Setting preferences
▶ Beaming memos

● ●

The Memo Pad isn't the flashiest feature of the Visor, but I must confess that it's my favorite. Like many writers, my best ideas always hit me when I'm farthest from my desk and least able to record them. Now I keep my Visor nearby 24 hours a day, 7 days a week, so that every brilliant flash of insight gets recorded to my Memo Pad, along with every foolish whim. At this point, the foolish whims outnumber the brilliant flashes by a long shot, but because I can change and delete a memo anytime, I can make myself look foolish less often. As you've probably noticed, I haven't yet figured out how to look brilliant.

When you synchronize your Visor with a desktop computer, you can copy and paste the text from your memos to regular word-processing programs. This method is the best way to format, print, or e-mail the precious prose you've collected in your Visor Memo Pad.

To access your Memo List, just press the Memo Pad button (the far right hard button), as shown in Figure 7-1 and continue with adding, deleting, or whatever you want to do with your memos.

Memo Pad
hard button

Figure 7-1:
Press the
Memo Pad
button to jot
down your
notes.

Taking Notes

If you plan to use the Memo Pad to write down large amounts of information while you're away from your desk, it really pays to learn Graffiti. You can get by in all the other Visor programs by using the little on-screen keyboard to tap out short pieces of text, but that gets tiresome quickly. (I discuss the keyboard and Graffiti in Chapter 2.) Even Graffiti can get a little tiring if you're used to the speed of a standard computer keyboard, but tapping the keyboard for this task can be less efficient.

Adding items

Making notes with the Visor Memo Pad is very straightforward. Even if you typically just read your memos downloaded from the desktop, you still might need to add memos about your notes.

To create a new memo, follow these steps:

1. **Use the far right hard button to open your Memo List and tap New.**

   A blank note screen appears.

2. **Enter the text by using either the on-screen keyboard or Graffiti.**

   The text you enter appears on the Memo screen (see Figure 7-2).

3. **Tap Done.**

   The Memo screen disappears, and your Memo List reappears.

Notice that the first line of text from the memo is what appears on the Memo List screen. You don't name memos unless you type the name of the memo as the first few words of the text. For this book, I call this line of text the name.

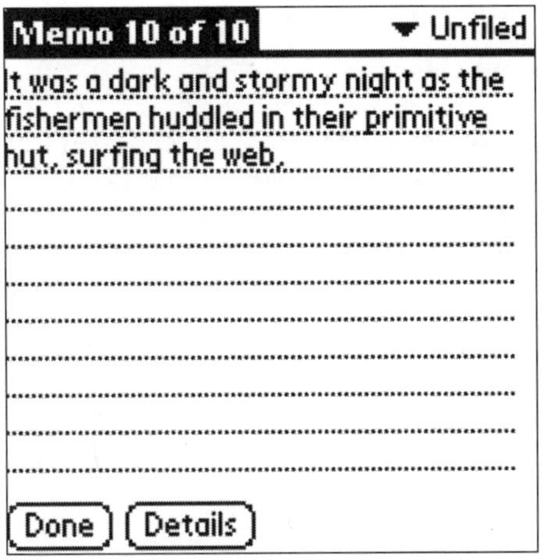

Memo 10 of 10   ▼ Unfiled

It was a dark and stormy night as the fishermen huddled in their primitive hut, surfing the web.

Done | Details

Figure 7-2:
Create memos using the Memo Pad.

These steps are the prescribed way of entering a memo. An even easier way is to press the Memo Pad button and just start writing stuff in the Graffiti box. The Memo Pad just assumes that you want to create a new memo and opens a new memo screen. You still have to tap Done to close the new memo.

Reading memos

The word *memo* looks like someone started to write the word *memory,* but forgot to finish. You don't have to worry about forgetting how to read your memos, though. These steps show that it's just a matter of press and tap:

1. **With your Memo List open, tap the name of the memo that you want to read, and it opens, as shown in Figure 7-3.**

Memo List   ▼ All

1. Handheld Basics
2. 3 Ways to Enter Text
3. A Night in Newark
4. Download Free Applications
5. It was a dark and stormy night
6. Nietzche was Pietzche
7. Power Tips
8. Sibling rivalry is for kids
9. Silicon Valley of the Dolls
10. The Zen of Visor

New

Figure 7-3:
Pick the memo you want to read from the list.

2. **Read your memo to your heart's content.**

3. **Tap Done, and your memo closes.**

The other sneaky thing I like about memos is that you can read them in the dark. The Visor has a backlight that goes on if you hold down the power button for two seconds. That way you can read (or write) memos after the lights go out, which feels just like being back in the days when you used to read comic books under the covers with a flashlight. Don't get caught, though.

Bear in mind that the backlight can drain your batteries rather quickly, so use the backlight sparingly.

Changing items

What's the difference between a foolish whim and a brilliant insight? Editing! (My editors certainly agree with me about that.) Editing your memos is just as easy as reading and creating them.

The simplest change you can make to a memo is adding new text. I have certain memos to which I add one or two lines every day. Adding more text to a memo only takes a second.

To add new text to a memo that you've already created, follow these steps:

1. **With your Memo List open, tap the memo that you want to change.**

2. **Tap the spot in the memo where you want to add new text.**

   A blinking line, called the *insertion point,* appears at the spot where you tapped.

3. **Enter the text by using either the on-screen keyboard or Graffiti.**

   The text you enter appears in the spot you tapped.

4. **Tap Done.**

   Your memo closes.

Another common way to edit a memo is to change the text that's already there. When you select any text you've entered in your Visor and then enter new text, the text you select is automatically replaced by the text you enter. Most Windows and Macintosh programs work pretty much the same way, so you should be ready to edit Visor memos in a flash.

To replace existing text in a memo, follow these steps:

1. **With your Memo List open, tap the memo that you want to change.**

   The memo opens on your screen.

2. **Select any text that you want to replace, and it appears in highlight as shown in Figure 7-4.**

   For more about selecting text, see Chapter 2.

Memo 5 of 10	▼ Unfiled

It was a dark and stormy night as the fishermen huddled in their primitive hut, ██████ the web.

(Done) (Details)

Figure 7-4:
Get rid
of pesky
typos by
highlighting
text to
change it.

3. **Enter your replacement text using either the on-screen keyboard or Graffiti.**

   The text you enter replaces the selected text.

4. **Tap Done.**

   Your memo closes.

If you want to select the whole memo and replace everything in it, you can open the memo, tap the Menu icon, and choose Edit⇨Select All. If you're going to go that far, though, you may as well just delete the memo and start over.

Because Visor uses the first line of the memo to display it on your Memo List, if you let your Visor sort alphabetically, the first word of the first line determines the order. You can make sure that a certain memo always ends up at the top of your memo list by making the first character in the memo zero.

Categorizing items

After you've created a large enough collection of memos, you may want to start organizing them so that you can find the information you want quickly. You can assign a category to each memo so that it shows up along with other memos with similar content. The following steps show you how to categorize:

1. **Open the Memo List (last hard button on the right) and tap the name of the memo.**

2. **Tap the category name in the upper-right corner of the display.**

   If your memo is uncategorized, Unfiled appears in the upper-right corner of the screen. When you tap the pull-down list arrow you see a list of categories, as shown in Figure 7-5. Categories work pretty much the same way in the Memo Pad as they do in the To Do List, so see Chapter 6 for more about dealing with categories.

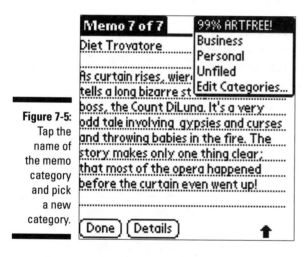

Figure 7-5:
Tap the name of the memo category and pick a new category.

3. **Tap the name of the category to assign your memo.**

   The list disappears, and the category you chose appears in the upper-right corner.

4. **Tap Done.**

   Your memo closes, and the Memo List reappears.

Making a memo private

If you want to be wise about recording your Foolish Whims, you can mark them all private so that only you know what you've entered. Keeping things private is a good way to keep from looking foolish if anybody else gets hold of your Visor. I've thought about marking my sillier memos private, but I suspect everybody already knows I'm foolish, so it's probably too late.

Follow these steps to keep private memos to yourself:

1. **With your Memo List open, tap the name to open the memo that you want to make private.**

2. **Tap Details.**

   The Memo Details dialog box opens (see Figure 7-6).

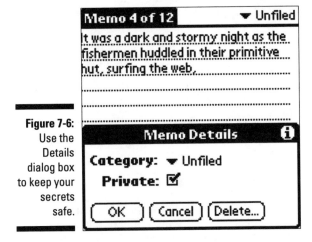

Figure 7-6: Use the Details dialog box to keep your secrets safe.

3. **Tap the check box marked Private.**

   A check mark appears in the check box.

4. **Tap OK.**

   The Private Records dialog box appears if you haven't elected to hide private records. The Private Records dialog box warns you that marking this item Private won't matter until you choose to hide private records. I discuss hiding and showing private records in Chapter 4. If you have elected to hide private records, the Memo Details dialog box simply closes at this point.

5. **Tap OK in the Private Records dialog box.**

   The Private Records dialog box closes.

6. **Tap Done.**

   Your memo closes, and the Memo List reappears. If you have chosen to hide private records, the memo that you marked Private is no longer listed.

You can choose whether to show or hide all private items on your Visor by going to the Security application and picking either Show or Hide. If you pick Show, all your items appear on-screen, private or not. If you pick Hide, the items marked Private seem to disappear. If you mark an item Private while hiding items marked Private, the item seems to vanish, only to reappear when you go back to the Security application and pick Show Private Items again. For more on hiding private items, see Chapter 4.

You can also set up a password to protect your private items. That's one more way of keeping your private items private. Check out Chapter 4 for more about passwords.

The tricky thing about items marked Private is that nothing appears on the screen to tell you whether you're seeing the private items. One way to remind yourself is to create a memo with a first line that starts with a zero and says O PRIVATE ITEMS SHOWING. Use this as a reminder to check for items that you previously marked as Private.

Managing Memos

Even if you don't enter memos directly into your Visor, you still want to read the memos you've collected and organize your memo collection in a useful way. The Visor Memo Pad offers you a collection of organizing tools that are simple but useful. You can sort your memos in different ways, view different categories, and change the font that the Visor displays to make your memos easier to read.

Deleting items

An old axiom says, "When in doubt, throw it out." Deleting a memo takes a few more steps than I wish it did, but not much mystery is involved.

To delete a memo, follow these steps:

1. **If your Memo List is closed, press the Memo List hard button and tap the memo to open it.**

2. **Tap the Menu icon.**

3. **From the menu, choose Record⇨Delete Memo, as shown in Figure 7-7.**

Figure 7-7:
Delete a
memo when
you don't
want it
anymore.

The Delete Memo dialog box opens and asks whether you want to delete the current memo.

4. **Tap OK.**

The Delete Memo dialog box closes, and your memo is deleted. If you've changed your mind about deleting this memo, you can tap the Cancel button in the Delete Memo dialog box to call off the deletion.

Be sure that a check mark appears in the box marked Save Archive Copy on PC. That's the only way that your deleted memos can be recovered at a future date. For more about archiving, see Chapter 12.

Viewing memos by category

My, how memos multiply! In no time at all, you may gather up dozens and dozens of memos, full of stuff that you're sure you want to keep handy at all times. Of course, the catch is this: The more memos you try to keep handy on your Visor, the less handy they get because you have so doggone many of 'em.

Earlier in this chapter, I show you how to assign categories to your memos (see "Categorizing items" for more information), but to really use categories, you need to be able to see which memos are in each category.

To view your memos by category, follow these steps:

1. **With your Memo List open, tap the name of the category in the upper-right corner of the screen.**

   The list of available categories appears. When you first use your Visor, the list has four categories: All, Business, Personal, and Unfiled.

2. **Tap the name of the category that you want to display.**

   The Memo List changes to display only the items assigned to the category you chose. The name of the category you're viewing appears in the upper-right corner of the screen.

If you really want to impress your friends with your Visor prowess, you can whip through your memo categories even faster by clicking the Memo Pad button more than once. Each time you press the Memo Pad button, you see a different category.

Changing fonts

Changing the font on your Visor means to change the size and style of lettering that you see in the display. The itty-bitty letters that the Visor usually displays allow you to show a lot of information on that tiny little screen, but if your eyes aren't so sharp or if the light isn't just right, your Visor can be tough to read.

To change the font in both the Memo List and in the text of your memos:

1. **Tap the Menu icon.**

   The menu bar appears.

2. **Choose Options⇨Font.**

   The Select Font dialog box appears.

3. **Pick the font that you want to display and tap OK.**

   You can choose from among three fonts. You have to choose the font for your memo text and your Memo List separately.

If you change the font for the Memo List, you haven't changed the font you see for the text of your memos. You need to open a memo to change the font for the body of memos. When you change the font for the body of one memo, all memos appear in that font until you pick another font.

Setting preferences to organize your memos

When it comes to organizing memos, you have two choices: alphabetical or manual. You can either let your Visor organize your memos by the first letter of the first word contained in each memo, or you can set up the Visor to let you drag the titles of memos around the Memo List and drop them off in the order you like. I prefer the alphabetical arrangement because I usually carry a few hundred memos around, so the alphabetical arrangement is the one I always remember.

If you choose to sort your memos alphabetically, you get the result you'd expect; all your memos line up in alphabetical order according to the first word in the memo. If you choose manual sorting, memos appear in the order in which you created them so that the last memo that you created appears at the bottom of the list. But when you sort your memos in manual order, you can also drag them to the point in your memo list where you want them to appear. Follow these steps to let Visor know your preferences:

1. **With your Memo List open, tap the Menu icon.**

   The menu bar appears.

2. **Choose Options⇨Preferences.**

   The Memo Preferences dialog box opens, as shown in Figure 7-8.

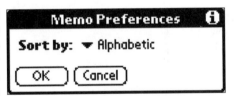

Figure 7-8:
Sort memos by your preference.

3. **Tap the pull-down triangle next to Sort By.**

   A list appears offering you two choices: Alphabetic and Manual.

4. **Tap the choice that you prefer to close the pull-down list.**

5. **Tap OK to close the Memo Preferences dialog box.**

   Your Memo List appears in the sort order of your choice.

It doesn't matter what category you're looking at when you set the preferences; the setting you choose applies to all categories.

If you've sorted your memos manually and then switch to alphabetical sorting, your manually sorted arrangement is lost for good. The memos are still there, but you have to re-sort everything.

Beaming your memos

Yes, Virginia, there is a Santa Claus, and if he has a Visor or Palm organizer next Christmas, you can write your gift list on your Visor Memo Pad and beam it to Santa. Of course, that way you don't get to sit on his lap.

You can beam nearly anything on one Visor to another Visor or Palm computer, not just memos. For more about beaming, see Chapter 9.

To beam a memo, follow these steps:

1. With your Memo List open, tap the name of the memo to open it.

2. Tap the Menu icon.

The menu bar appears.

3. Choose Record⇨Beam Memo, as shown in Figure 7-9.

> **Record** Edit Options
> **New Memo** ✓N
> **Delete Memo...** ✓D
> **Beam Memo** ✓B uttons
> turns on your Palm III and shows a
> specific screen. The Date Book
> button, for example, displays
> today's schedule.
>
> ▪ Select a record and tap the Details
> button to access more options. Some
> settings can be edited directly by
>
> (Done) (Details)

Figure 7-9:
Beaming makes passing notes a lot more fun.

The Beam dialog box opens.

4. Tap OK.

Your memo is magically sent to the other unit.

Of course, you have to set the Visors within about three feet of each other for the beaming process to work, which means that you can't beam solo. The Visors must also be within line of sight of each other, so you can't beam through walls; that's definitely a job for Superman — or a HotSynced e-mail.

Chapter 8

The Date Game

• •

In This Chapter

▶ Adding and deleting appointments

▶ Setting regular appointments

▶ Using alarms

▶ Marking items private

▶ Setting preferences

▶ Purging your Date Book

▶ Switching to DateBook+

• •

A recent study says that 92 percent of Visor and PalmPilot users consider the calendar the most important feature on their handheld computer. The Date Book certainly has a good chance of becoming your favorite Visor feature, too. You may already know how powerful a computer can be at keeping track of your schedule — you may use one at work to keep track of your appointments. The Visor lets you carry that power around in your pocket and keep your schedule up-to-date while you're carrying it out. Then, when you return to your office or your home, you can simply HotSync to your desktop computer to keep your Date Book current. For more on performing a HotSync, see Chapter 11.

The Visor actually comes with two calendars: the Date Book and DateBook+. One has a few more features than the other (guess which one). I tell you how to use the standard Date Book in the first part of this chapter, and in the second part I clue you in to the advantages of using the spiffed up DateBook+.

To access your Date Book, just press the Date Book hard button (the first one on the left), as shown in Figure 8-1 and then arrange your appointments, as you like.

Date Book
hard button

Figure 8-1:
Opening the
Date Book
with the
hard button.

Selecting a Date Book View

I think that you may find the Date Book pretty easy to use after you've tried it a bit. The only tricky part about understanding the Visor Date Book comes from the size of the screen. You can't really show a whole calendar on that little bitty display and still be able to show what's going on each day. So, the Visor breaks the calendar up into different views that show one day, a week, or a month at a time.

Each view of your calendar includes three icons at the bottom of the screen representing the three calendar views: Day, Week, and Month. The icon for the view you're seeing appears highlighted; if you want to switch to another view, tap a different icon. For example, when you look at the Day view, the far left icon highlights. When you tap the middle icon, the Week view appears.

Another way to switch between Date Book views is to press the Date Book button more than once. Each time you press the Date Book button, you cycle through the different views one at time. If you don't like the view you see, keep pressing the Date Book button until the view you want appears.

The Day view

The first time that you press the Date Book button, you see a daily schedule, as shown in Figure 8-2. It shows a line for each hour of the workday, and any appointments on your schedule are listed in order of starting time.

Your Visor usually shows today's appointments first. If you want to see appointments for a date earlier or later in the week, tap the letter for the day of the week at the top of the screen. You can also move from day to day by pressing the scroll buttons on the Visor case.

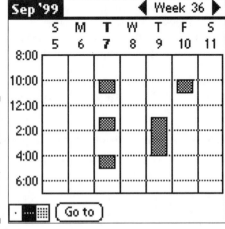

Figure 8-2: Checking daily appointments.

The Week view

The Week view, shown in Figure 8-3, just displays a diagram of your schedule for the week. It shows a grid of days and times, and shaded bars represent blocks of time when you have appointments scheduled. However, the bars don't tell you specifically what's scheduled. If you want to find out what you've scheduled at a certain time, tap the bar representing that scheduled item, and the information regarding the appointment appears at the top of the screen.

Figure 8-3: Viewing your appointments over the course of a week.

You can look at your weekly schedule for the future or the past by pressing the scroll buttons on the Visor case, just like you can in the Day view. You can also change the week you're looking at by tapping one of the triangles at the top of the screen.

The Week view has one important feature that the other two views don't have: You can change an appointment to a different time in the week by dragging the bar representing the appointment time and dropping it off at another time in the week. Figure 8-4 shows an appointment (represented by the box with the heavy border) being dropped in at 2 p.m. on September 10.

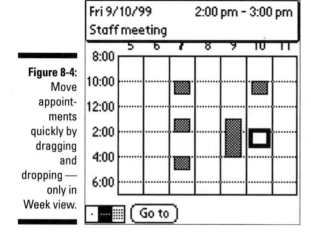

Figure 8-4:
Move appointments quickly by dragging and dropping — only in Week view.

As you're dragging and dropping, the name and time of your appointment appear at the top of the display to let you know exactly when you've set the new appointment time. You need to be pretty steady with the stylus if you drag and drop this way, but it's the fastest way to change an appointment time.

If you've never done the drag and drop (no, it's not a dance step from the 1960s; that was the Watusi), don't fret. These steps show you how simple the drag-and-drop method is:

1. **Put the tip of your stylus on the bar representing an appointment.**

2. **Slide the stylus tip along the screen to where you want the appointment set.**

   As you slide the stylus tip along the screen, a little box representing the appointment slides right along with your stylus, as if you are dragging the box along the screen. As you drag, the appointment listed in the banner at the top of the screen changes to show you what the new appointment time will be if you drop the appointment at the current position by lifting your stylus.

3. Lift up the stylus when the appointment is where you want it.

Now you're a drag-and-drop champ!

The Month view

The Month view, shown in Figure 8-5, is the most familiar-looking view in your Date Book because it resembles a regular wall calendar. Unfortunately, the Month view offers very little information about your schedule; only dots represent your appointments. The main advantage of the Month view is the ability to navigate through your schedule easily. If you tap any date in the Month view, you see the Day view for that date.

Figure 8-5:
View the whole month to see which days have appointments.

September 1999						◀ ▶
S	**M**	**T**	**W**	**T**	**F**	**S**
			1	2	3	4
5	6	**7** ▪	8	9 ▪	10 ▪	11
12	13 ▪	14	15	16 ▪	17	18
19 ▪	20	21	22 ▪	23	24	25 ▪
26	27	28 ▪	29	30		

▪ ⋯▦ (Go to)

As with the other views, the scroll buttons change the Month view from one month to the next. If you need to take a quick look at a date in the distant future (a year or more from now), tap Go to at the bottom of the Date Book screen and pick the date that you want to see.

The Go to icon shows you a calendar that enables you to tap the date you want to see. If you want to view a date later this month, tap Go to and tap the date you want to see. If you want to see a date in a different month of this year, tap the month you want from the list of months at the top of the screen, and then tap the day you want. If you want to look at a day in a different year, tap Go to, tap one of the triangles next to the year at the top of the screen (depending whether you want to time warp into the past or the future), and tap the month you want to see.

Making Dates

You can keep track of a surprising amount of detailed information in your Date Book. Thousands of appointments fit comfortably in your Date Book along with reminders, notes, and other details. You don't have to enter your appointments directly into your Visor if you don't want to. You can do most of the keyboard work on your desktop computer and then HotSync everything to your Visor. But in some situations, you may be better off entering appointments right in your Visor.

Adding appointments the simple way

Some folks are into dates; some aren't. You don't have to go crazy entering lots of details when you add an appointment to your Date Book. You can enter just the time and a phrase, and you can enter many types of appointments with very little effort.

Follow these steps to add a new appointment the simple way:

1. **Open the Date Book by pressing the first hard button on the left and tap the line next to the hour when your appointment begins.**

   A blinking line, called the *insertion point,* appears on the line.

2. **Enter the name of your appointment by using either the on-screen keyboard or Graffiti.**

   The name of your appointment appears on the line that you tapped. (See Figure 8-6.)

Figure 8-6:
Just write the name of your appointment in the appropriate time slot.

Sep 7, 99 ◀ S M T W T F S ▶

8:00	
9:00	
10:00	Interview
11:00	
12:00	
1:00	Lunch
2:00	
3:00	
4:00	
6:00	Reception
7:00	

(New) (Details) (Go to)

3. **To keep the setting, tap the blank spot on the bottom of the screen to the right of Go to.**

   The insertion point disappears, and your appointment is set. (If you don't complete this step, nothing terrible happens; your Visor just waits for you to do something else.)

Adding appointments the complete way

If all your appointments start right on the hour and last exactly an hour, the simple way to enter appointments, shown in the previous section, may suit you just fine. When you have appointments that start at odd times or don't last exactly an hour, you need to resort to the more complete method for entering appointments. Follow these steps to enter detailed information about an appointment:

1. **With the Date Book visible, tap Go to.**

   The Go to Date dialog box opens.

2. **Tap the date for your appointment.**

   The Date Book appears in Day view, showing you the appointments that you've scheduled for that date.

3. **Tap the hour closest to the starting time of your appointment.**

   The Set Time dialog box opens, as shown in Figure 8-7.

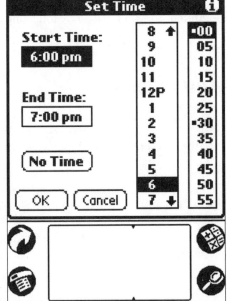

Figure 8-7:
Setting
more
accurate
appointment
times in the
Set Time
dialog box.

4. **Tap the hour and minute time for the starting time of your appointment.**

   The hour and minute time appear in the Start Time box.

5. **Tap the End Time box to highlight it.**

6. **Tap the hour and minute for the ending time of your appointment.**

   The new time appears in the End Time box.

7. **Tap OK.**

   The Set Time dialog box closes, and your Date Book screen reappears.

8. **Enter the name of your appointment, and it appears on the time line.**

   The name of your appointment appears on the line next to your starting time.

9. **Tap Details to open the Event Details dialog box.**

10. **If you need to make any changes to the details of your appointment, tap the appropriate box and enter that information.**

    Because you've already entered the date and time, you probably don't need to change those details. I explain more about setting alarms, setting private appointments, and repeating appointments in the related sections of this chapter.

11. **Tap OK.**

    The Event Details dialog box closes, and your Date Book screen reappears.

You've done it! Isn't that satisfying? Okay, maybe not, but you've done all that you can do, so take heart. If you didn't find this method helpful or efficient, you can enter your next appointment the simple way by following the steps in the preceding section.

Scheduling all-day events

Not everything on your schedule happens at a particular hour of the day. Birthdays and holidays, for example, just happen, all day long, even if it rains. If you want to enter an event without a time attached, just open the Date Book to the daily view, and then enter the name of the event in the Graffiti box. For more about using Graffiti, see Chapter 2. Your new event appears at the top of the screen. You can also use the complete method of entering an appointment in the preceding section and tap No Time in the Set Time screen in Step 6.

Setting alarms

I'm the first to admit that I need a lot of reminding. Fortunately, my Visor is always around to gently pester me into doing what needs to be done when it needs to be done. My Visor has become sort of a like an electronic mother-in-law. Even if your Visor is turned off, the alarm wakes up your Visor and makes a series of tiny beeps. You need to turn off the alarm by tapping OK on the Visor screen.

Follow these steps to set an alarm:

1. **With the Date Book visible, tap the name of the appointment for which you want to set an alarm.**

   The insertion point appears on the line with your appointment's name.

2. **Tap Details.**

   The Event Details dialog box opens.

3. **Tap the Alarm check box.**

   A check mark appears in the check box, and the alarm setting appears to the right of the check box, as shown in Figure 8-8. Typically, the alarm setting is 5 minutes, which means that the alarm will go off 5 minutes before the scheduled appointment time. However, you can change the alarm time.

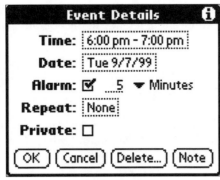

Figure 8-8: Checkmark the Alarm option so that your Visor can remind you of an important appointment.

4. **If you want to change the alarm time, tap Minutes.**

   A list appears with the choices of Minutes, Hours, or Days.

5. **Tap your choice of Minutes, Hours, or Days.**

   The list disappears, and the choice that you tapped appears.

6. **Enter the number of minutes, hours, or days before the appointment that you want the alarm to sound.**

   The number that you enter appears next to the Alarm check box.

7. **Tap OK.**

   The Event Details dialog box closes.

I usually check the Alarm check box while creating an appointment rather than after creating it.

Adding notes to appointments

Every Date Book item also can contain a note explaining details about the appointment. Date Book notes work exactly the same way as the notes you can attach to To Do items. Simply select the appointment and choose Record⇨Attach Note. Then, enter the note you want. See Chapter 6 for more about attaching notes.

Using the Address Book lookup feature

Another feature shared by the Date Book and the To Do List is the ability to look up a name in your Address Book and automatically copy that person's name and phone number into the appointment. To look up a name, tap the Menu soft button and choose Options⇨Phone Lookup. When the Address Book appears, tap the name you want to include in the appointment and then tap the Add button.

Repeating appointments

You certainly don't want to forget that important weekly meeting of Electronics Shoppers Anonymous. Rather than input each of those meetings individually, you can set up a repeating appointment.

To mark an appointment as a repeating appointment, follow these steps:

1. **With the Date Book visible, tap the name of the appointment that you want to set up as a repeating appointment.**

   The insertion point appears on the line with your appointment's name.

2. **Tap Details.**

   The Event Details dialog box opens.

3. Tap the Repeat box.

The Change Repeat dialog box opens, as shown in Figure 8-9.

Figure 8-9:
Come
again? Set
up your
recurring
appoint-
ments in the
Change
Repeat
dialog box.

4. Tap one of the interval pattern buttons to set the frequency that you want.

Your choices are None, Day, Week, Month, and Year. When you tap one, the screen changes to show intervals that are suitable to your choice. If you choose nothing, Visor assumes that you mean None.

5. Enter a number to indicate how often you want the appointment to repeat.

If you enter nothing, the Visor assumes that the number is 1, meaning the appointment occurs every day, week, month, or year, depending on which frequency you chose. If you change that number to the number 2, your appointment occurs every two days, two weeks, two months, or two years, and so on.

6. If your appointment repeats until a certain date, tap the End On box.

Some appointments repeat for a certain period of time. If you go to night school, for example, your class may occur once a week for ten weeks. When you tap the End On box, a menu appears giving you two choices: No End Date or Choose Date.

7. Tap Choose Date from the End On box.

The Ending On screen appears.

8. Tap your desired end date on the calendar.

The Ending On screen disappears, and the date that you chose appears in the End On box.

9. **Tap the appropriate detail to set other information about your repeating appointment.**

   You have one other choice to make if your appointment repeats on either a weekly or monthly basis. You can set weekly appointments to recur on several days of the week, such as Monday, Wednesday, and Friday, by simply tapping the various days. Notice that the days are set on a *toggle*, meaning that you must tap them again to deselect them. If you're setting up a monthly appointment, tap either Day (for example, the 3rd Monday of every month) or Date (for example, the 15th of every month).

   When you make any of these choices, text describing your recurrence pattern such as The 3rd Monday of every month appears in the box at the bottom of the Change Repeat dialog box. Keep an eye on this text to be sure that you've set up your appointment correctly.

10. **Tap OK.**

    The Change Repeat dialog box closes, and the Event Details dialog box opens.

11. **Tap OK.**

    The Event Details dialog box closes.

When you create a repeating appointment, each instance of the appointment looks like a separate item, but the occurrences are all connected in the mind of your Visor. So if you change or delete one occurrence of the appointment, your Visor wants to know if you're changing every occurrence or just that one. When your Visor asks, just tell it what you want.

Protecting private items

You can enjoy the thrill of a secret rendezvous with your Visor. I suppose that you can enjoy the rendezvous without your Visor, too, but your Visor helps you remember the rendezvous while keeping it a secret from anyone else who looks at your Visor.

Follow these steps to mark private appointments:

1. **With the Date Book visible, tap the name of the appointment that you want to make private.**

   The insertion point appears on the line with your appointment's name.

2. **Tap Details.**

   The Event Details dialog box opens.

3. **Tap the check box next to Private and toggle on the check mark.**

4. **Tap OK.**

   The Event Details dialog box closes. If you haven't set your security option to hide all private records, you see a dialog box telling you how to hide all private records. In case you forget, see Chapter 3 for more about hiding private items.

Of course, there is such a thing as too much secrecy. If you mark an appointment Private and then tell your Visor to hide all Private Records, the appointment doesn't show on your Visor. So, you can't even see your private records yourself, which could cause a serious problem. To prevent keeping your appointments secret from yourself, tap the Applications icon, choose the Security icon, and then pick Show Private Records.

Managing the Date Book

You may be the type of person who rarely enters anything directly into your Visor. If you enter everything via a HotSync from your desktop computer, you may still want to be able to delete existing appointments and set up your Visor's preferences to suit your fancy.

Deleting appointments

Sooner or later, all your appointments become history. Perhaps you want to save all your appointment records for posterity. Perhaps you think keeping dead appointments is baloney, and you want to get rid of the stuff once it's over. I go for the second choice.

Use these steps to delete an appointment:

1. **With the Date Book visible, tap the name of the appointment until the insertion point blinks.**

2. **Tap Menu.**

   The Menu bar appears at the top of the display, as shown in Figure 8-10.

3. **Choose Record➪Delete Event.**

   The Delete Event dialog box opens. If you check the Save Archive Copy on PC box, that wonderful archive thing happens: The next time you HotSync, the HotSync Manager saves a copy of the deleted item on your desktop computer. For more about archived items, see Chapter 12, and for more on HotSyncing, see Chapter 11.

```
┌─────────────────────────────────────┐
│ │Record│ Edit  Options               │
│ New Event         ╱N                 │
│ Delete Event...   ╱D ················ │
│ Attach Note       ╱A ················ │
│ Delete Note...    ╱O ·············· ⌐│
│ Purge...          ╱E                 │
│ 1:00 ································· │
│ 2:00 Staff meeting ················ ⌐│
│ 3:00 ································· │
│ 4:00 ································· │
│ 5:00 ································· │
│ 6:00 ································· │
│ ·⊡ ( New ) ( Details ) ( Go to )     │
└─────────────────────────────────────┘
```

Figure 8-10:
Want to
delete an
appoint-
ment?
Choose
Delete
Event from
this menu.

4. **Tap OK.**

   The Delete Event dialog box closes, and your appointment disappears —
   simple as that.

Another way to delete an appointment is to tap the appointment name, then
tap Details, and then tap Delete. You get the same result either way — no
more appointment.

Setting preferences

You can change your Date Book two ways: the number of hours it displays for
each day and the type of alarm.

To set Date Book preferences, follow these steps:

1. **With the Date Book visible, tap Menu.**

2. **Choose Options⇨Preferences.**

   The Preferences screen appears, as shown in Figure 8-11.

3. **To change the workday start time, tap one of the triangles next to the
   Start Time box.**

   Tap the upper triangle to make the start time later or the lower triangle
   to start earlier.

4. **To change the end time, tap one of the triangles next to the End Time
   box to end earlier or later.**

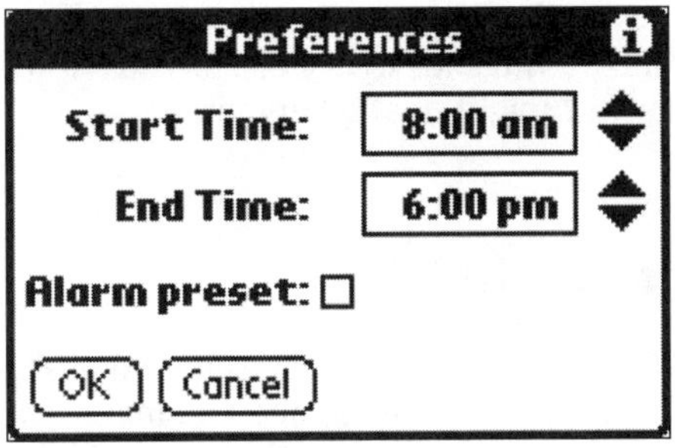

Figure 8-11:
Express
your
preferences
in the
Preferences
screen.

Preferences ℹ️

Start Time: `8:00 am` ↕

End Time: `6:00 pm` ↕

Alarm preset: ☐

(OK) (Cancel)

5. **To change the default alarm preset, tap the Alarm Preset check box.**

   A check mark appears in the check box, and the alarm setting appears to the right of the check box. The default alarm setting is 5 minutes.

6. **If you want to change the Alarm preset time, tap Minutes (or the unit of time on-screen).**

   A list appears with the choices Minutes, Hours, or Days.

7. **Tap your choice for the unit of time.**

   The list disappears, and the choice that you selected appears.

8. **Enter the number of minutes, hours, or days before the appointment you want the alarm to sound.**

   The number that you enter appears next to the words Alarm Preset.

9. **To change the sound you hear when the alarm goes off, tap the pull-down list triangle next to Alarm Sound.**

   A list of all the possible alarm sounds appears.

10. **Tap the type of the alarm sound that you want.**

    You have several squeaks and squawks to choose from. The sound that you tap plays a sample, and its name appears in the Alarm Sound box.

11. **Tap the Remind Me box.**

    A list appears with the number of times Visor can remind you before giving up. The choices range from Once to 10 Times.

12. **Tap the number of times, and your choice appears in the Remind Me box.**

13. **Tap the Play Every box to choose how often to replay the Alarm.**

    A list appears, offering various choices from 1 to 30 minutes.

14. **Tap your alarm interval choice.**

    The choice that you tap appears in the Play Every box.

15. **Tap OK.**

Maybe I'm boring, but I've never changed my Date Book preferences. You may have a reason to vary the settings for every alarm you set. If I could get the alarm to play "Tea for Two," I might change my mind.

Purging your Date Book

Your Visor can hold up to 10,000 appointments. That sounds like a lot, but sooner or later, you'll want to clear out some space and make room for more items. The fastest way to make room is to purge old Date Book items. Purging your Date Book is quick and easy, and it doesn't hurt a bit.

To purge your Date Book, follow these steps:

1. **With the Date Book visible, tap Menu.**

2. **Choose Record➪Purge.**

   The Purge dialog box opens, as shown in Figure 8-12. If you want to change the age of purged appointments, tap 1 Week (or the on-screen interval) and choose from the list that appears.

   By default, your Visor is set to purge appointments older than one week. This means, obviously, that your monthly calendar during the last week of the month won't show the appointments you had at the beginning of the month. Change the setting if you want to track earlier appointments for monthly reporting without having to consult your archive.

Figure 8-12: Is your schedule too full? Purge it to make room for more appoint- ments.

3. **Tap OK.**

   The Purge dialog box closes.

Now you're rid of all the great things that you've done, and you can move on to the great things you're going to do. Isn't that inspiring?

Using DateBook+

Your Visor includes two different date book programs to choose from. Visor offers the standard one that I describe in the first part of this chapter. The standard Date Book comes with any handheld computer that runs the Palm Operating System. The Visor people also include a second, enhanced date book program that you can use instead of the standard one if you want. This plus-sized version of the Date Book is conveniently named DateBook+. I recommend using it because you got it for free. The way you do things in Date Book doesn't change when you use DateBook+, but you can do lots more things with the Plus version. The most important extra features of DateBook+ include more views, better views, and the ability to deal with both appointments and To Do items in the same program.

Making DateBook+ your date book

I recommend that you make DateBook+ your main date book so that when you push the far left application button DateBook+ appears. To find out how to reassign your hard buttons to other applications, see Chapter 3. Why not use the best program you have for your all-important appointments and events? To make DateBook+ your main date book, follow these steps:

1. **With either Date Book or DateBook+ visible, tap the Menu soft button.**

2. **Choose Options⇨Default Date Book.**

    The Set Default dialog box appears (see Figure 8-13).

Figure 8-13: Take your pick; plus is better than no plus.

3. **Tap the box labeled DateBook+ to highlight it.**

4. **Tap OK.**

    DateBook+ is now installed as your main date book.

Don't worry if you've created appointments in both Date Book and DateBook+. All of your appointments still appear in both versions. The main difference is that you can't use the enhanced features of DateBook+ when you're in the standard Date Book screen.

Selecting DateBook+ views

DateBook+ gives you a few more ways to view your entries than standard Date Book and gives you more information in the views that both programs have in common. The DateBook+ views are

✔ **The Enhanced Week View**: This view shows your appointments somewhat like the Date Book Week view but also includes the names of your appointments, plus your events and current To Do items (see Figure 8-14).

Tap the 2 at the top of the screen shown in Figure 8-14, and you can also see two weeks of appointments.

If you want to make a change in an appointment from the Enhanced Week View, just tap the name of the item, and the one-day view that includes that appointment appears. You can edit the appointment from the one-day view.

✔ **The Year View**: This view displays a diagram of the current year (or any year you select) with X marking each day that contains an appointment (see Figure 8-16). If you're planning to go around the world in 80 days, you can see when you have 80 days free.

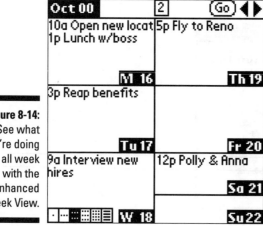

Figure 8-14:
See what you're doing all week with the Enhanced Week View.

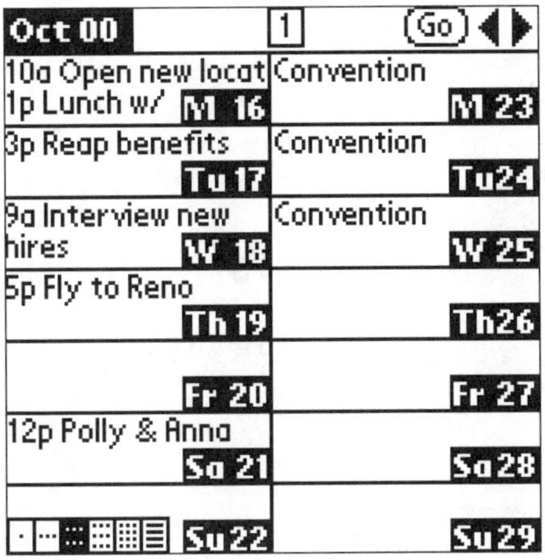
Oct 00
1
Go
10a Open new locat
1p Lunch w/
M 16
Convention
M 23
3p Reap benefits
Tu 17
Convention
Tu24
9a Interview new hires
W 18
Convention
W 25
5p Fly to Reno
Th 19
Th26
Fr 20
Fr 27
12p Polly & Anna
Sa 21
Sa 28
Su22
Su29

Figure 8-15: Toggle between the 1 and 2 for twice the excitement.

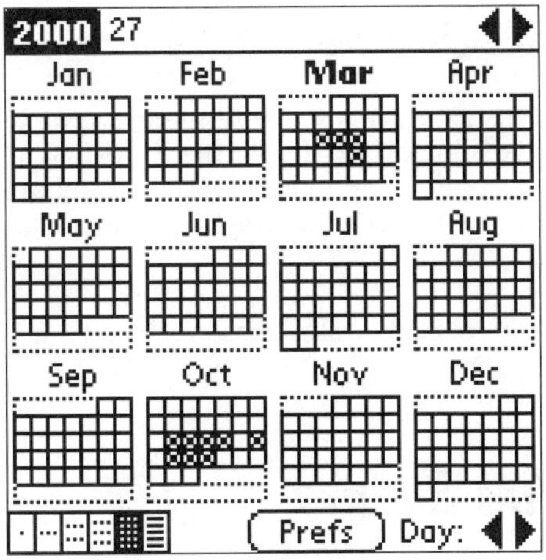
2000
27
Jan
Feb
Mar
Apr
May
Jun
Jul
Aug
Sep
Oct
Nov
Dec
Prefs
Day:

Figure 8-16: Use the Year View when you're planning a *really* long vacation.

- **The List View**: This option does just what it says; it makes a list of your appointments, events, and tasks and doesn't pretend to be a calendar at all (see Figure 8-17).

  TIP

  You can also set the List View to display only items that contain a certain text string. For example, if you want to see only a list of upcoming appointments that include the word `review`, tap the Menu button at the bottom of the display, choose Options⇨List View Preferences, and tap the Find check box. Enter the word `review` in the Find text box and tap OK. The List View reappears, showing only the appointments that include the word `review`. If none of your appointments contain that word, no appointments appear.

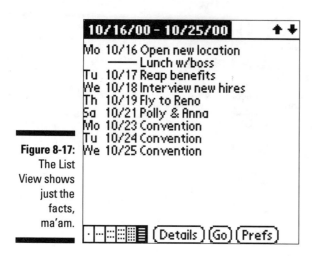

Figure 8-17:
The List
View shows
just the
facts,
ma'am.

Adding new DateBook+ items

The standard Date Book works nicely if you live in a very predictable world where everything happens like clockwork. If your life is normal, though, you end up with lots of odd things on your schedule that don't behave so neatly. DateBook+ has ways of dealing with lives that might be a little messier (and more like the rest of us).

DateBook+ includes other types of schedule items, such as Floating Events, To Do's, and a journal.

Creating Floating Events

Do you have a "round tuit" list, that is things you figure to do if you ever get a round tuit? Floating events are the kinds of things you definitely want to take care of as soon as you get the time. Floating events appear on your schedule next to a little circle (the "round tuit" you've been talking about all these years). Until you complete the event, your floating event appears at the top of your daily list every single day. When you finish the event, tap the circle to mark the item complete and leave you to rest — until the next round tuit shows up. You know how they are.

To enter a new floating event, follow these steps:

1. **With DateBook+ Day view visible, tap Menu.**

2. **Choose Record⇨New Floating Event.**

A new text insertion line appears at the top of your calendar to show you where the name of your floating event goes. The new line displays an unfilled circle to indicate that you're creating a Floating Event.

3. **Enter the name of your floating event.**

   The name of your floating event appears in the display.

4. **Tap any other part of the display to set your Floating Event.**

That little empty circle next to the name of your floating event shows you that you haven't gotten around to this event yet (see Figure 8-18). When you do finish the event, tap the circle to make a check mark appear in the circle. Ah! The satisfaction of being finished!

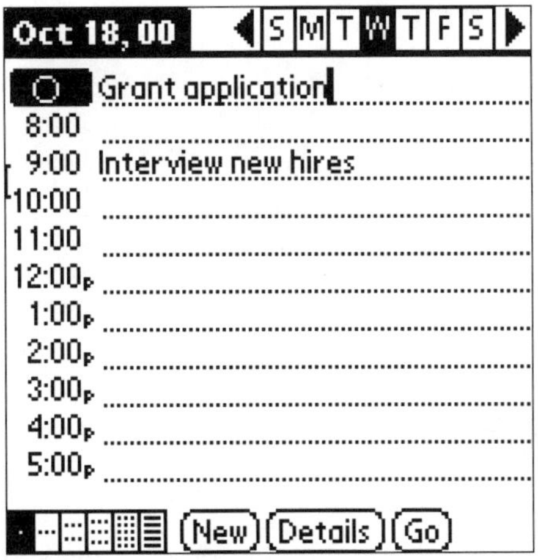

Figure 8-18: That round icon is that "round tuit" you've been meaning to do.

Using the DateBook+ To Do's

You may be wondering why I'm talking about To Do's again when I just spent a whole chapter on 'em in Chapter 6. I'm not testing your memory, I'm just mentioning the subject twice because the souped-up DateBook+ lets you enter and view both appointments and To Do items. The To Do items that you enter in either DateBook+ or the To Do List appear in both places. Some people prefer to use one program for dealing with the things they have to do and the times they're supposed to do them. If you manage your To Do's in DateBook+, you may not want to use the regular To Do program at all. It's your call. These steps show you how to enter a To Do item in DateBook+:

1. **With the DateBook+ Day View visible, tap Menu.**

2. **Choose Record⇨New To Do.**

A blank insertion line appears at the top of the daily calendar view. The blank line starts with an unfilled check box to indicate that this is a To Do item.

3. **Enter the name of your To Do.**

The text you enter appears on the new line.

4. **Tap any other part of the screen to set the To Do (see Figure 8-19).**

The check box tells you that this is a To Do and that today's the day to do it.

Figure 8-19:
Add a To Do
to the day's
events.

```
┌─────────────────────────────────┐
│ Oct 18, 00  ◀ S M T W T F S ▶   │
│ ☐ 1 Tax report.................. │
│  ○   Grant application.......... │
│ 8:00 ........................... │
│ 9:00  Interview new hires....... │
│ 10:00 .......................... │
│ 11:00 .......................... │
│ 12:00ₚ......................... │
│  1:00ₚ......................... │
│  2:00ₚ......................... │
│  3:00ₚ......................... │
│  4:00ₚ......................... │
│ ▪ ⋯ ▦ ▦ ▤  (New)(Details)(Go)   │
└─────────────────────────────────┘
```

If you tap the Details button at the bottom of the screen while you're creating your To Do, you can set a priority, due date, or category for the item. You can also mark the item private if you want do something but you don't want anyone to know you did it. It's pretty sneaky, but some people like that sort of thing.

Using the Daily Journal feature

On Monday, May 21, at 11:07 a.m. a suspicious red sedan pulled into the parking lot of the bank. At 11:18 a team of three little old ladies got out of the car carrying piggy banks. At 11:30 they entered the bank.

If you like keeping detective style notes like Joe Friday on Dragnet, the Daily Journal is for you. Every time you create a new Daily Journal item, the date and time are automatically entered, and all you have to do is enter a quick description of what you want to record at the moment (see Figure 8-20). Just tap the Menu icon, choose Record⇨New Journal Entry, and enter your astute observation. Then when you confront your suspect at the dramatic climax of the show (right before the last commercial), you can whip out your badge and your Visor and say, "We know where you were at 11:07 on Monday, Granny!" Case closed.

Figure 8-20:
Keep very
detailed
records with
your journal.

Journal entries appear next to a diamond-shaped icon to distinguish themselves from To Do's, Floating Events, and regular appointments. You can only create a journal entry from the day view of DateBook+.

Setting appointments

If you know how to enter appointments in Date Book, you can do exactly the same things to enter appointments in DateBook+. You have a few more options in DateBook+, like Floating Events and added views, but otherwise the methods I describe in the first part of this chapter work just fine.

Saving time with templates

You know the routine: SSND (Same Stuff, New Day), or something like that. If you find yourself making the same old entries over and over and get a little tired of writing it all out again and again, you can save an entire DateBook+ entry as a template and just call it up each time you need to make that same old entry.

One reason you might use a template is to keep track of a meeting you attend over and over. If each meeting features a rotating chairperson (on his or her rotating chair), invocation, joke, report, speech, and so on, you can make a template of the roles and fill in the names each time. In fact, if you have the names of all the people who attend the meeting in your Address Book, you can just use the Address lookup feature to plug the names in, too. You may discover even more timesaving ways to use templates in DateBook+.

Creating a new template

You can't use something that hasn't been created yet, except next month's credit card balance . . . but that's a different story. You need to create a template first, like this:

1. **Create an appointment or event in the Day View of DateBook+.**

   You don't actually have to create one; you can also pick one you've already created.

2. **Tap the item you want to turn into a Template to select it.**

   You'll see a blinking bar in the item you tap to show that it's selected.

3. **Tap the Menu button and choose Record⇨Create Template.**

   A screen appears confirming that you've created a template.

4. **Tap OK.**

   Your template is created and ready to be used.

Using a template

When you tap the New button at the bottom of the DateBook+ screen, a little list pops up offering five choices: Floating Event, To Do, Daily Journal, Template, or Appointment. If you tap the word Template, the Appointment Templates screen appears, showing you the list of templates you've created (see Figure 8-21). Just tap the name of the appointment you want to use and tap OK. The template appears in your calendar. If you haven't created any templates yet, choosing Template opens a screen asking you to create one.

Undeleting items

A very cool feature of DateBook+ is the ability to undelete items that you've zapped away (see Figure 8-22). Just go to the Day View of DateBook+ and tap the Menu button; then choose Record⇨Undelete from Archive and Poof! Your most recently deleted item reappears like Freddy Kruger in those horror movies. OK, they reappear like Casper the Friendly Ghost. However you like to put it, they come right back.

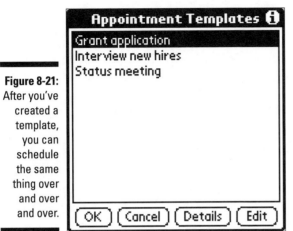

Figure 8-21:
After you've created a template, you can schedule the same thing over and over and over.

Figure 8-22:
Bring back lost appointments by Undeleting.

Chapter 9

Beaming Visor Data through the Air with Infrared

● ●

In This Chapter

▶ Sending and receiving items

▶ Sending and receiving categories

▶ Sending and receiving applications

● ●

*P*eople are often willing to pay more for something cool than they would pay for something useful. At the moment, the ability to *beam,* or send, information between two Visors is very cool and just beginning to be useful. In fact it's very, very cool, and fortunately, it doesn't cost you anything extra. However, you may not find yourself in many situations in which you can use it — at least not until more people are suitably equipped with a Visor, PalmPilot or other compatible device. In this chapter, I give you the skinny on beaming so that you can be ready when that first momentous beaming occasion presents itself. In the following sections, I explain how beaming works and show you how to beam individual items, categories, and even applications.

Beaming — What You Need to Know

Beaming is a feature of Palm-OS-based computers like the Visor that enables you to send information from one device to another. The beaming feature uses infrared (IR) light, which is what the remote control for your TV uses. You must directly point the two units' IR ports at each other to properly send and catch the beam. The IR port on your Visor is that little red place on the left side of the case. As long as the units are within about three feet of one another, the process is quick and simple. My very subjective tests show that two Visors lose sight of each other when they're four feet apart, and they also have some trouble communicating at less than three inches or so. At a typical meeting table, you should have no trouble beaming information to a person across from you.

Computer manufacturers have begun to include IR communications on laptops and printers. You also can find IR capability on certain advanced pagers and cellular telephones. But until more people own more devices that use IR, you won't get much mileage out of the technology.

Beaming is new enough to the Visor world that few applications other than the standard Visor applications have been built to use it. Even the Visor Mail and Expense programs can't beam items at this point. Being able to forward e-mail by beaming would be useful, but probably won't be available for a while.

Sending an Item

When you beam information between a pair of Visors, you're copying information from one Visor to the other. The data that you send remains on your unit and is duplicated on the second unit. The process resembles sending a fax: Before you send a fax, only you have a copy of the information; after you're done, you and the receiver both have a copy of the information — only without the annoyingly poor quality of faxing!

These steps show you how to send an item:

1. **Make sure that both Visors are turned on and sitting with IR ports facing.**

   Keep the two Visors within three feet of each other.

   The recipient must be set to receive beaming. To find out how to toggle beaming reception on and off, turn to Chapter 3.

2. **Select the item that you want to beam.**

   The item appears on your Visor screen. You can send a memo, an address, a To Do item, or an appointment.

3. **Tap Menu.**

   The menu bar appears.

4. **Choose Record⇨Beam Event.**

   The menu indicates Beam *Event* for a Date Book appointment (as shown in Figure 9-1), Beam *Address* for an Address Book entry, and so on.

   The Beam dialog box opens for a short time, first telling you that it's preparing to beam and then that it's searching for another Visor. After your Visor finishes beaming the item, the dialog box closes.

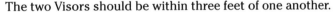

Record	Edit	Options

New Event   /N
Delete Event...   /D
Attach Note   /A
Delete Note...   /O
Purge...   /E
Beam Event   /B

2:00
3:00
4:00
5:00 Big Whoop!
6:00

(New) (Details) (Go to)

Figure 9-1:
Beaming
an event.

If all goes well, both Visors beep to let you know that the item reached its destination. Recipients actually know more about the transfer than you do because dialog boxes pop up on their Visors to say what's been received. If your transfer fails, your Visor displays a message saying that something's wrong and that you should try again.

If you enter your own address in your Visor Address Book and mark it as your business card, all you need to do when you want to beam your business card is hold down the Address Book button for about two seconds until the beaming process starts. Chapter 5 shows you how to mark your business card for beaming.

Receiving an Item

Just because you're receiving an item rather than sending one doesn't mean that you can just stand there and do nothing. You can stand there and do *almost* nothing. Just watch the screen and tap Yes when the time comes, like this:

1. **Make sure that both Visors are turned on with the IR ports facing.**

   The two Visors should be within three feet of one another.

   The recipient must be set to receive beaming. Use the General Preferences dialog box to turn beaming reception on. Chapter 3 has more information.

2. **When your buddy sends an item to you, wait for the Beam dialog box to open.**

   The Beam dialog box tells you what's being beamed to you and asks whether you want to accept the item.

3. **Tap Yes or No.**

   If you tap No, the Beam dialog box closes to end the process. If you tap Yes, the application to which the beamed item belongs opens, and shows you details of the item. For example, if the beamed item is someone's business card, your Address Book screen appears, showing the new address record that you're about to add to your Address List.

4. **Make any changes that you want to the beamed item.**

   You may want to change the category of the item, or just make a note about when or where the beamed item originated. For example, if someone beams you her business card at a trade show, you may want to make a note of the trade show at which you met.

5. **Tap Done.**

   The item closes, and you see the main screen of the application to which the beamed item belongs.

People can beam unsolicited items to you, but you can always refuse them by tapping No. My only gripe about how the routine works is that once you say Yes, your Visor buries the item in the list of items in the Unfiled category. If I want to go through the items that I receive in a day, I have to guess which item came in when. If you assign categories to everything promptly, you won't have trouble figuring out what's new. For more about using categories, see Chapter 6.

Sending a Category

You don't have to beam items one at a time. You can send an entire category at once. Of course, you're limited to sending bunches of items that can handle categories; for example, the Date Book has no categories, so you can beam only one appointment at a time. For more about using categories, see Chapter 6.

To beam an entire category, follow these steps:

1. **Make sure that both Visors are turned on with IR ports facing and within three feet of each other.**

2. **Display the category that you want to beam.**

   The category appears on your Visor screen.

3. **Tap Menu and choose Record⇨Beam Category, as shown in Figure 9-2.**

   The Beam dialog box opens for a moment and then closes.

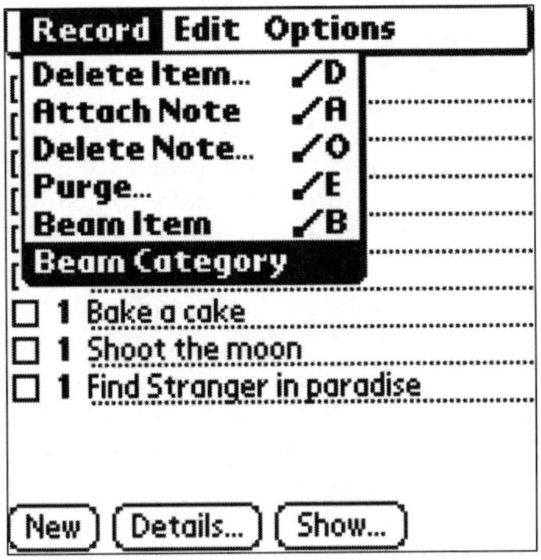

Record	Edit	Options
Delete Item...	✓D	
Attach Note	✓A	
Delete Note...	✓O	
Purge...	✓E	
Beam Item	✓B	
Beam Category		

☐ 1 Bake a cake
☐ 1 Shoot the moon
☐ 1 Find Stranger in paradise

(New) (Details...) (Show...)

Figure 9-2: Beam a whole category of tasks for someone else to do. That's how I spell relief.

Before the Beam dialog box closes, it tells you very briefly the name of the category that you're sending. A Cancel button in the dialog box enables you to cancel the transfer if you've sent the wrong thing, but the dialog box closes so quickly that you really can't stop the transfer. Therefore, be sure that you really want to send the items that you're beaming.

Receiving a Category

The process of receiving a whole category of items works just like receiving a single item (see the section on receiving an item).

Keep in mind that receiving a category of items sometimes creates a problem for two reasons:

1. When you tap Yes to accept incoming items, the Visor opens only one of the items that you received. If you want to edit or categorize the incoming items, you can do so only with the first item — all the others get mixed up with your unfiled items. As a result, you have to dig them out one by one. Because you have no way of knowing exactly which items the other person sent, you may have trouble figuring out which items were sent by whom.

2. Another problem is that the category markings are removed from incoming items; they're all marked Unfiled. Visor does have good reason for that, though because it can handle only 15 categories. If you were able to accept categorized items from lots of different people, you could end up with a messy collection of categories. However, if someone sends you a category, you logically expect to get that category. I figure that the Palm people will address this issue in a future upgrade.

Sending an Application

Believe it or not, you can beam an entire application from one Visor to another. Frankly, beaming programs between Visors is much easier than installing programs from your desktop computer. Of course, you have to install the program first on your Visor before you can share it with anyone else.

Some Visor applications refuse to be beamed. The standard Visor applications, for example, appear in the Beam list with a padlock icon next to them, which means that you can't beam those programs because they're locked. In the future, many other Visor programs will be locked the same way to prevent software piracy. At the moment, though, you can beam most Visor software between Visors by following these steps:

1. **Make sure that both Visors are turned on, with IR ports facing and within three feet of each other.**

2. **Tap the Applications soft button.**

   The Applications screen appears.

3. **Tap Menu and choose App⇨Beam.**

   The Beam screen appears, as shown in Figure 9-3, listing all your applications. The applications with little padlocks next to them are locked and can't be beamed.

Beam		ⓘ
Address	🔒	2K
AirCalc		45K
BrainForest		80K
Date Book	🔒	1K
DietLog		87K
DigiPet		21K
EEToolkit		30K
Flash!		61K
Mail	🔒	2K
Memo Pad	🔒	2K
(Done) (Beam)		

Figure 9-3: The locks show the programs that can't be beamed.

4. **Tap the name of the application that you want to beam.**

5. **Tap Beam.**

   The Beam dialog box opens, indicating which program you're sending. If you change your mind, tap Cancel.

Programs usually take longer to beam than individual items based on their size, so keep the Visors pointed at each other until the Beam dialog box closes, indicating that the process is complete. You can see how big a program is by checking the number next to the name of the program in the Beam screen. I've never seen it take more than a few minutes to beam a program between Visors.

Receiving an Application

The process of receiving a beamed application is just like receiving anything else (see the section on receiving an item for details). After you agree to receive the application by clicking Yes in the Beam dialog box, your display switches to the Applications screen, showing the new program.

Here's the big catch to beaming applications: Only the actual program is copied to the receiving Visor. Files created or used by the program don't come over with the program. For example, if you beam AportisDoc (the document-reading program from Aportis Technologies) from a Visor that has several text files in AportisDoc, those files aren't copied — only the program itself is. You can't beam AportisDoc files; you have to install the documents through the regular Palm Install Tool from a desktop.

Beaming into the Future

Naturally, plenty of people want to write Visor programs that take advantage of the ability to sling data through the air, but only a few programs are finished so far. A couple of products that I've heard of (but not tested myself) sound pretty interesting.

PalmPrint from Stevens Creek Software offers a program that enables you to print via infrared to any suitably equipped printer. At this point, HP, Canon, and other companies have printers with IR capability. With the PalmPrint IR program, you can point your Visor at a printer and print a memo, task, or appointment on the spot. For more information, check out Stevens Creek Software on the Web at www.stevenscreek.com.

Several software vendors also offer IR HotSync products that enable you to point your Visor at a desktop or laptop computer and perform a HotSync without placing your Visor in a cradle. IBM has a utility called IR Sync that's designed to synchronize a Visor or Palm computer with an IBM ThinkPad, but it works with other brands of laptop computers as well. See the details at IBM's Web site at www.ibm.com.

I've even tried products that enable you to use your Visor as a remote control for your TV or VCR. The IR capabilities of the Visor would be useful that way, but some folks say that the tiny IR transmitter in the Visor is too weak to get all the way from your couch to your TV. If you have to get off the couch to move within three feet of your TV, I guess that you may as well make the rest of the journey, right? But I like the idea anyway.

Chapter 10

Special Delivery: Using Palm Mail

E-mail is pretty convenient, but the business of sitting in front of a computer to read and write e-mail isn't so convenient. Your Visor includes Palm Mail, a rather basic e-mail program that enables you to carry a little bucket of messages wherever you go. You can read messages and compose replies whether you're sitting at the beach or riding on the subway. I have to admit that the program has its limits, but I often find it handy to deal with my e-mail on my Visor; plugging in my desktop computer on the cross-town bus can be a bit difficult.

Don't let the convenience of reading e-mail on your Visor lull you into carelessness. Reading your e-mail while driving is probably more dangerous than talking on a cell phone or doing something else distracting behind the wheel, so use your judgment. I don't want anyone arrested for DUIV (Driving Under the Influence of a Visor).

Making Sense of the Palm Postal System

The Palm Mail program doesn't exchange messages like a desktop e-mail package does. Like the Visor itself, the Mail program acts as an accessory to the programs on your desktop, in this case your e-mail program. When you perform a HotSync, the Palm Mail program copies the messages in your desktop e-mail program's Inbox and stores those copies on your Visor. You can read or reply to those messages or compose new messages on your Visor when you're away from your desktop computer. When you get back to your desktop computer, you need to perform another HotSync to move your outgoing messages to your desktop e-mail program, which does the work of actually delivering the messages.

The Palm Mail program can't send messages directly to their recipients without a desktop e-mail program acting as a middleman (or middleperson for all you politically correct readers out there). That's not what it's designed to do.

You can overcome this limitation by taking a few extra steps. If you want to send e-mail directly from your Visor, you need something that connects your Visor to the Internet: either the Visor Modem or one of those very cool wireless modems that I mention in Chapter 19. You also need to buy an independent e-mail program for your Visor, such as MultiMail, HandMail, or One Touch Mail, which I mention in Chapter 20.

In the following sections, I focus on showing you how to use what comes out of the box with your Visor.

Working with Your Messages

You can use the built-in Palm Mail program only if you have a desktop mail program with which to synchronize it. You can do many of the same tasks with Palm Mail that you can with your desktop e-mail program, such as read and write messages, reply to messages, and forward messages. However, some popular e-mail features aren't available in Palm Mail, especially the ability to attach files or read files that are attached to incoming messages. You may be willing to trade those features for the ability to read your e-mail on a bicycle built for two (preferably on the backseat), but the choice is up to you.

To access your Palm e-mail program, tap the Applications soft button and then choose the Mail application. The Mail program's Inbox opens.

Creating a message

Creating a new e-mail message is a lot like writing a regular paper letter. All that you need is an address and a message. Actually, all that you really need is an address, but actually adding a message is a sign of good manners.

Follow these steps to create a new message:

1. **Use the Applications soft button, choose Mail, and tap New.**

   The New Message screen appears. If you know your recipient's e-mail address by heart, then simply enter that address by using Graffiti or the on-screen keyboard. If you do this, skip ahead to Step 7.

   If you don't know your recipient's address, you can look it up in your Address Book. Continue with Step 2 if you're in this particular boat.

2. **Tap the word To.**

   The To screen appears.

3. **Tap Lookup.**

   The To Lookup screen appears (see Figure 10-1), showing the e-mail addresses of the people that you entered in your Address List. It doesn't show everyone in your Address Book, just those who have e-mail addresses. Convenient, eh?

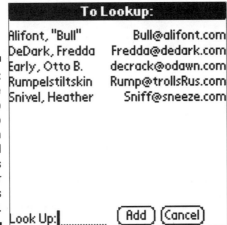

Figure 10-1:
Use the
Lookup
feature to
find an
e-mail
address
in your
Address
Book.

4. **Tap the name of the person to whom you're sending your message.**

   The name that you tap is highlighted to show that you selected it.

5. **Tap Add.**

   The e-mail address of the person that you selected appears in the To screen. You can repeat Steps 3 through 5 for each person to whom you want to send copies of the message.

6. **Tap Done.**

   The New Message screen reappears showing the names of the people that you've chosen to send your message to.

7. **If you want to send copies of your message to additional people, tap the line to the right of CC.**

TIP

CC is highlighted to show that you selected it. If you know your recipient's e-mail address, just write it in by using Graffiti or the on-screen keyboard. If you don't know the e-mail address and want to check your Address Book, repeat Step 2 (tapping CC instead of To) through Step 6 for each CC addressee that you want to add.

8. Tap the line to the right of Subj.

The insertion point appears in the highlighted subject line, as shown in Figure 10-2.

Figure 10-2: In the New Message screen, enter the subject of your message as you would any other text.

New Message

To: fredda.dedark@night.com
CC: obearly@snoozer.com
Subj:
Body:

(Send) (Cancel) (Details...) ↑

TIP

If you tap Subj itself, the Subject screen appears. Opening the Subject screen is an extra step that you don't really need to take because you can enter your subject in the New Message screen. But if you prefer to use the Subject screen, enter the text, tap Done when you finish, and continue to Step 10.

9. Enter the subject of your message.

The text that you enter appears on the Subject line.

10. Tap to the right of Body.

The insertion point appears, and Body is highlighted.

If you tap Body itself, the Body screen appears. Just like with the Subject line, this is an extra step that you don't really need to take. But if you prefer using this screen to enter your message, just tap Done when you finish, and continue to Step 12.

11. Enter the text of your message by using either the on-screen keyboard or Graffiti.

The text that you enter appears on the screen.

12. Tap Send.

Your message closes and moves to the Outbox.

Even though you tapped Send, your message isn't on its way to your recipient. Tapping Send simply moves your message to the Outbox. The next time that you HotSync your Visor, everything in the Outbox moves to your desktop e-mail program, which then sends your message off.

Reading a message

A true boon to humanity, the Visor now enables me to read my e-mail while waiting for the bus, so I can waste time two ways at once. While I'm at it, I can also do some deep knee bends to make myself look foolish in public. (I don't need a Visor to make me look foolish; I do that quite nicely on my own, thank you very much.)

To read your messages follow these steps:

1. **With the Mail program open, tap the pull-down list in the upper-right corner of the Mail screen to see the list of available folders.**

   The list includes Inbox, Outbox, Deleted, Filed, and Draft. You can expect to find new messages in the Inbox.

2. **Tap the name of the folder that you want to view.**

   The folder that you tap appears on the screen, showing a list of messages.

3. **Tap the message that you want to read.**

   The text of the message appears.

4. **After you finish reading the message, tap Done.**

   Your message closes, and the list of messages reappears. A check mark appears next to the message that you just read.

If you want to cycle through your messages but don't want to return to the message list, just use the left or right triangles at the bottom of each message screen. Tapping one of those triangles enables you to see the next message or the previous message. That feature is useful, but for some reason I think of the next message as being *below* the current message, rather than to the right. Anyway, that's what those triangles do, in case you were wondering.

While you're reading a message, you may also notice a pair of icons in the upper-right corner of the message screen. One looks like a tiny message containing a lot of text, and the other looks like a tiny message with only a little bit of text. If you tap the icon that looks like it holds a lot of text, you can view the message headers. *Headers* hold the information that comes before the body of the message, including who the message is to and from, the subject of the message, and the date the message was sent. The other icon conceals everything except the name of the person who sent the message and the subject of the message. You can tap either icon any time to see as much or little header information as you want. I prefer to see less header information.

Replying to a message

The simplest way to address a message to somebody is to reply to a message that they've sent you. These steps show you what to do:

1. **With the Mail program open, tap the message that you want to reply to.**

   The text of the message appears.

2. **Tap Reply.**

   The Reply Options dialog box opens, as shown in Figure 10-3.

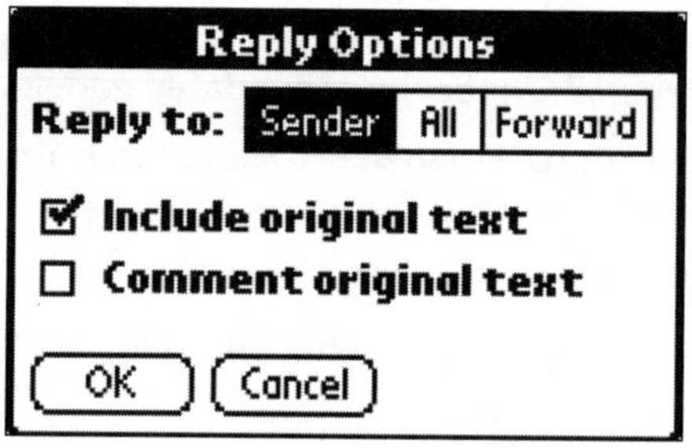

Figure 10-3:
You can
reply just to
the person
who sent
you the
message or
to everyone
that it was
addressed
to.

Reply Options

Reply to: Sender | All | Forward

☑ **Include original text**
☐ **Comment original text**

(OK) (Cancel)

3. **Tap either Sender or All.**

   If you choose Sender, your reply goes only to the person(s) listed on the From line of the original message. If you choose All, your reply goes to the person(s) on the CC line as well. To see what happens when you tap Forward, see the next section of this chapter.

   You probably notice two additional options: Include Original Text and Comment Original Text. If you check the first option, the text of the message that you're replying to is included with the message that you're sending. Checking the second box puts a caret symbol (>) in front of every line of the original text so that the person getting your reply can quickly distinguish the original from the text you're adding. You can check the first box, neither box, or both boxes, but if you just check the second box, nothing happens. You can't add comment marks to the original text unless you include the original text. Typically, I leave both boxes checked.

4. **Tap OK.**

   The New Message screen appears. Your recipient's e-mail address appears on the To line, and the Subject line shows Re: followed by the subject of the original message. If you chose in Step 3 to include the original message text in your reply, that text appears in the body of your new message.

   You can change any of this text by deleting and adding text as you usually would.

5. **If you want to add new addresses to either the To or CC line of the message, enter the new addresses on those lines.**

   You can add an address to a message that you're replying to the same way that you do when you create a message. See "Creating a message," earlier in this chapter for details.

6. **If you want to add text to your message, tap to the right of Body.**

   If you chose to include the original message's text, your Visor conveniently leaves you a blank line to start writing your reply text.

   If you tap the word Body, the Body screen appears with the subject of your message at the top. If you enter your text in the Body screen rather than the New Message screen, just tap Done when you finish entering your text, and continue to Step 8.

7. **Enter the text at the insertion point.**

   The text that you enter appears with the original message's text.

8. **Tap Send.**

   Your message closes and moves to the Outbox to await delivery.

Forwarding a message

Forwarding a message is just like replying to a message (see the previous section), except that instead of sending a message back to the person who sent you the original message, you send the original message on to a third person.

To forward a message follow these steps:

1. **With the Mail program open, tap the message that you want to forward.**

2. **Tap Reply.**

   The Reply Options dialog box opens.

3. **Tap Forward.**

   When you forward a message, the text of a message that you received from one person is sent to another person.

4. **Tap OK.**

   The New Message screen appears, containing the text of the message that you're forwarding. In the Subject line, you see `Fwd:`, followed by the subject of the original message.

5. **On the To line, enter the e-mail address of the person to whom you're forwarding the message.**

   Address a message that you're forwarding either by typing or looking up the address. See "Creating a message," earlier in this chapter for the lowdown.

6. **If you want to add text to your message, tap to the right of Body.**

   If you tap Body, a new screen appears for the body text, with the subject of the message at the top. You can enter text in either this screen or the New Message screen, according to your choice. If you choose to enter text in the Body screen, just tap Done when you're finished, and continue to Step 8.

7. **Enter the text at the insertion point.**

   The text that you enter appears with the message text.

8. **Tap Send.**

   Your message closes and moves to the Outbox to await delivery.

People seem to enjoy forwarding jokes by e-mail. I guess forwarding a joke to 25 people is faster than standing around the water cooler, waiting for them to show up so you can repeat the joke to each of them, one by one. Also, using your Visor to forward jokes by e-mail makes you look like you're working (except to those who know better).

Deleting a message

Your Visor seems to have plenty of space until you start loading it with e-mail. It may take a while to collect enough e-mail to fill 8MB of memory, but if you get a lot of e-mail, filling up your memory is pretty easy to do. Fortunately, deleting a message is just as easy, following these steps:

1. **With the Mail program open, tap the message that you want to delete.**

   The text of the message that you tap appears.

2. **Tap Delete.**

   Your message disappears. If you have Confirm Deleted Message checked in the Preferences dialog box, the Delete Message dialog box opens, as shown in Figure 10-4. Just tap Yes to get rid of that pesky message. To set the Delete preference, tap the Menu soft button and then choose Options⇨Preferences.

Figure 10-4:
Tap Yes to
delete.

Presto! Your message has magically disappeared — sort of. Actually, when you choose to delete messages, they move to the Deleted folder and wait for you to purge them.

If you change your mind after deleting a message, you can undelete a message from the Deleted Items folder. Open the Deleted Items folder by tapping the list of folder names in the upper-right corner of the Mail screen, and then choose Deleted. Tap the message that you want to undelete to open it, and then tap the Undelete button at the bottom of the message screen. When you tap Undelete, your message returns to the Inbox.

When you HotSync, your Visor Inbox is forced to match the Inbox on your desktop e-mail program. Therefore, if you delete a message from your desktop e-mail program, the next HotSync removes that message from your Visor Inbox as well. You may find it easier to delete messages from your desktop and then HotSync. Most desktop e-mail programs enable you to delete batches of messages all at once, which is faster and easier than deleting messages one by one on your Visor.

If you want to take a message out of the Inbox but leave it on your Visor, you can move the message to the Filed folder. Just tap the Menu soft button and then tap Message⇨File. Now, when all the messages in your Inbox are replaced by a new set during the next HotSync, the ones that you sent to the Filed folder stay put. To see the contents of your Filed folder, tap the folder list in the upper-right corner of the Inbox screen and then tap Filed.

Purging deleted messages

Deleting a message doesn't totally eliminate that message from your collection. A deleted message moves to the Deleted folder until you purge your deleted items like this:

1. **With the Mail program open, tap Menu.**

2. **Choose Purge⇨Deleted.**

   The Purge Deleted Message dialog box opens, as shown in Figure 10-5.

Figure 10-5:
The Purge
Deleted
Message
dialog box
warns you
about
wiping out
your deleted
messages.

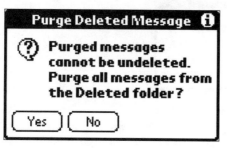

3. **Tap Yes.**

The Purge Deleted Message dialog box closes, and your messages are gone forever.

The Deleted folder exists to save you if you accidentally delete an item and then change your mind and want to undelete it. But the best way to save space on your Visor is to purge deleted messages frequently.

One big difference between deleting e-mail messages and deleting other items on your Visor is that no archive for deleted messages exists on the Palm Desktop. Your desktop e-mail program serves as the archive. So make sure that you really want those messages to disappear forever before you delete them.

Saving drafts

If you tap Cancel while composing a new message, the Save Draft dialog box asks you if you want to save a draft of the message. If you tap Yes, your incomplete message moves to the Drafts folder where you can return to it later. Isn't that thoughtful?

Tapping No deletes your incomplete message forever, and Cancel simply returns you to the message itself.

Sending a blind copy

Sending blind copies of your messages is a sneaky way to inform someone about your communications with a third person without that third person knowing. For example, if you need more cooperation from someone in another department of your company, you can send that person an e-mail asking for the help that you need, and at the same time, send a blind copy to the person who supervises both of you. The person that you're addressing the message to doesn't know that you've clued in the boss.

Blind copies, or BCCs, are so sneaky that the line for them is hidden unless you know how to find and use it. Here, I let you in on the secret:

1. **With the Mail program open, tap New.**

   The New Message screen appears.

2. **Tap Details.**

   The Message Details dialog box opens.

3. **Tap the check box labeled BCC.**

   A check appears in the box, as shown in Figure 10-6.

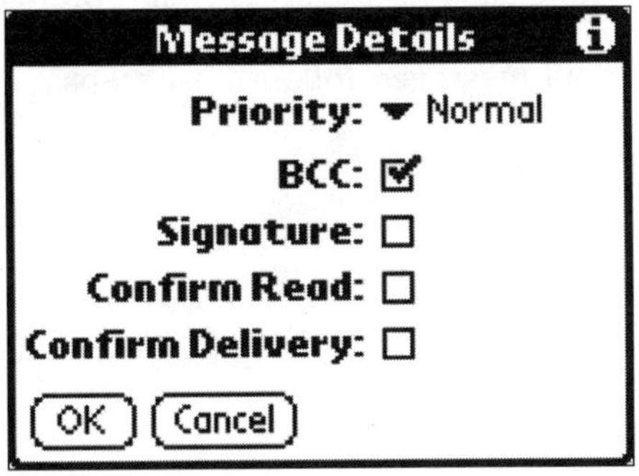

Figure 10-6:
To send a secret blind copy of a message, find the check box in the Message Details dialog box.

4. **Tap OK.**

   The Message Details dialog box closes, and the BCC line appears in the New Message screen.

5. **Tap BCC in the New Message screen.**

   The BCC screen appears. If you know the e-mail address of your BCC addressee by heart, enter the address by using Graffiti or the on-screen keyboard, tap Done, and continue creating your message. If you need to look up the address of the BCC addressee, continue to Step 6.

6. **Tap Lookup.**

   The BCC Lookup screen appears, showing all the names and e-mail addresses in your Address Book. Not everyone in your Address Book shows up on this list, only the ones with e-mail addresses.

7. **Tap the name of the person to whom you want to send a blind copy.**

8. **Tap Add.**

   The name that you chose appears in the BCC screen.

9. **Tap Done.**

   The name that you chose appears on the BCC line of your message.

10. **Continue creating your message.**

Well, now the secret is out. Don't forget; you saw it here first.

Sorting messages

Usually I like to read messages in the order in which I receive them, but sometimes I like to see all the messages from a certain person lined up in a row. Other times I want to read all the messages about a certain subject all at once. You can sort your messages three different ways, depending on what you need.

To change the sort order of your messages, follow these steps:

1. **With the Mail program open, tap Show.**

   The Show Options dialog box opens.

2. **Tap the triangle next to Sort By.**

   A list of ways to sort your messages appears with these options: Date, Sender, and Subject (see Figure 10-7).

3. **Tap your choice.**

   The sort type appears next to Sort By.

4. **If you want to display the date that you received each message, tap the check box next to Show Date.**

5. **Tap OK.**

   Your messages appear sorted the way that you chose.

This sort order remains in effect until you choose a different sort order.

Figure 10-7:
In the Show
Options
dialog box,
you can
sort your
messages
by date,
sender, or
subject.

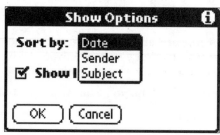

Customizing Your Palm E-Mail

After you develop a serious Visor e-mail habit, you may need to know some techniques for managing the messages that you get, customizing the messages that you send, and speeding up the process of synchronizing your messages with your desktop. You may never use these tricks, but I want you to know they're available.

Setting HotSync options

After you gather a healthy-sized collection of items on your Visor, the HotSync process may slow down quite a bit. At first a HotSync should take only a few seconds, but after a couple of months, a HotSync may take several minutes, which is a big deal for people as busy as you and me. You may want to shorten your HotSync time by telling your Visor to limit e-mail activity to just sending or just receiving messages that you haven't read yet. You can ignore the HotSync options if you want, with no ill effect.

To set HotSync e-mail options, follow these steps:

1. **With the Mail program open, tap Menu.**

   The menu bar appears.

2. **Choose Options⇨HotSync Options.**

   The HotSync Options screen appears, as shown in Figure 10-8.

Figure 10-8: In the HotSync Options screen, you can take your pick of HotSync e-mail options.

3. Tap the triangle next to Settings For.

A list appears that enables you to choose either Local HotSync or Remote HotSync.

You may want to make different things happen when you perform a modem HotSync than when you do a local HotSync. Modem HotSyncs are slower than local HotSyncs, so if you download only unread messages, for example, you save time and money when you do a long-distance modem HotSync. Otherwise, you may want to get all your messages when you do a local HotSync, so you need to be able to create different settings for the two types of HotSyncs. If you never attach your Visor to a modem, you don't need to think about modem HotSync options.

4. Tap either Local HotSync or Remote HotSync.

Your choice appears next to Settings For. You're not limited to setting only Local or only Remote HotSync options, but you do have to set the options for each type of HotSync one at a time.

5. Tap one of the boxes below Settings For.

Visor offers four options. The following list gives you the skinny on each setting:

- **All** means that all messages in your desktop Inbox are copied to your Visor and all outgoing messages are transferred to your desktop when you HotSync.

- **Send only** means that only outgoing messages are transferred to your Visor when you HotSync. Incoming messages stay on your desktop computer.

- **Filter** means that you can tell your Visor to accept certain kinds of messages and reject others. For example, you can set up a filter to accept only messages marked high priority. I discuss message filtering in greater detail in the "Filtering messages" section later in this chapter.

- **Unread** means that your Visor accepts only those messages that you haven't read yet. The ones that you've read stay on your desktop.

6. Tap OK.

The HotSync Options screen disappears, and your message list reappears.

If you frequently perform remote HotSyncs via a modem, you can set remote HotSync options separately from your local HotSync options. Your Visor automatically picks the options that you want depending on which type of HotSync you're doing. For example, you may want to exchange all messages when you're doing a local HotSync, but only send messages when you do a remote HotSync.

Filtering messages

Filtering is a fairly sophisticated HotSync option. Filtering enables you to set up rules to limit the messages that the system copies to your Visor, based on the priority of the message, the name of the person whose address appears in the To or From line, or the text in the Subject line.

I know people who get hundreds of e-mail messages every day. If performing a HotSync copied all their messages to their Visors, eventually there'd be no room on their Visors for anything but e-mail. Filtering is a good idea for those who get more e-mail than they want on their Visors, but still want to take some messages with them. These steps show you how to filter your messages:

1. **With the Mail program open, tap Menu.**

2. **Choose Options⇨HotSync Options.**

   The HotSync Options screen appears.

3. **Choose either Local or Modem HotSync.**

4. **Tap Filter.**

   Options for filtering messages appear, as shown in Figure 10-9.

Figure 10-9:
You filter the junk out of your water, so why not filter the junk out of your e-mail messages, too!

```
┌──────────────────────────────────┐
│  HotSync Options            ⓘ    │
│ ┌──────────────────────────────┐ │
│ │Settings for: ▾ Local HotSync │ │
│ │                              │ │
│ │ ┌───┬──────────┬──────┬──────┐│ │
│ │ │All│Send only │Filter│Unread││ │
│ │ └───┴──────────┴──────┴──────┘│ │
│ │                              │ │
│ │ ☑ Retrieve All High Priority │ │
│ │ ▾ Ignore Messages Containing │ │
│ │                              │ │
│ │   To:   ...................  │ │
│ │ From:   ...................  │ │
│ │ Subj:   ...................  │ │
│ │ ( OK ) ( Cancel ) (Truncate...)│ │
│ └──────────────────────────────┘ │
└──────────────────────────────────┘
```

5. **If you want to copy only high priority messages to your Visor, tap the check box next to Retrieve All High Priority.**

6. **If you want to create a rule for selecting a type of message to retrieve, tap the triangle at the left edge of the screen.**

   A list appears with two choices: Ignore Messages Containing and Retrieve Only Messages Containing.

7. **Choose the type of rule that you want to create.**

8. **If you want to ignore or receive messages according to the address of the person they're sent to, enter that e-mail address on the To line.**

   "Wait a minute," you say. "I'm the recipient of my own e-mail, so if I choose to ignore my own e-mail address, then I won't get any messages, right?" Well, technically, yes. It may seem silly to filter messages addressed to yourself, but you may discover reasons to exclude certain messages. First, you may get e-mail addressed to a mailing list. People on mailing lists often get dozens of messages every day, and you may not want to clutter up your Visor with that kind of stuff. Besides, you can still look at the excluded messages on your desktop computer. Another reason is that your desktop e-mail program may collect messages from two e-mail addresses. If you have one e-mail address for business and another for personal, you can filter out one or the other type of message by putting that e-mail address on the To line.

9. **To ignore or receive messages from a particular sender, enter that sender's address on the From line.**

   You can enter multiple addresses on this line; just separate them with a comma.

10. **To ignore or receive messages in which the subject line contains a certain word or phrase, enter that text on the Subj line.**

11. **Tap OK.**

    The HotSync Options screen disappears, and your message list reappears.

If you're used to the more elaborate rules and filters in your desktop e-mail program, you can have your desktop computer do all the filtering for you before you HotSync your Visor. Remember, only the items in the Inbox of your desktop program are copied to your Visor, so if you sort your desktop Inbox before running HotSync, only the messages that make the cut on the desktop find their way to your Visor. Most people I know are perfectly happy to not use any kind of e-mail rule or filter. So if you ignore filtering, you're probably just as well off.

Using signatures

Lots of people like to personalize their e-mail with a standard bunch of text at the end of each message. Most popular e-mail programs enable you to set up a signature, so why not use signatures on the messages that you create with your Visor? Why not, indeed, when the process is this simple:

1. **With the Mail program open, tap Menu.**

2. **Choose Options⇨Preferences.**

   The Preferences screen appears, as shown in Figure 10-10.

Figure 10-10:
Individualize
your e-mail
with a flashy
signature.

3. Enter your signature text.

The text that you enter appears on the Preferences screen.

4. Tap OK.

The Preferences screen disappears, and your message list reappears. Visor automatically adds your signature to all your outgoing messages from now on.

One little detail about signatures: You can't see them yourself when you create your messages. The Mail program adds the signature when you send a message, so don't worry if you don't see your signature.

Setting truncating options

One of the shortcomings of using a tiny device like a Visor for reading e-mail is the severe space limitation. You may not care much about megabytes or RAM until you run out of them. That's why the Palm Mail program automatically truncates, or chops off, messages at a certain length. You can determine the length, but you're still limited to 8,000 characters. Because the full text of your messages is stored on your desktop computer, you can always look in your desktop e-mail program to see what got lopped off of the messages on your Visor.

Set the length at which Visor truncates messages by following these steps:

1. With the Mail program open, tap Menu.

The menu bar appears.

2. Choose Options⇨HotSync Options.

The HotSync Options screen appears.

3. Tap Truncate.

The Truncate Options dialog box opens, as shown in Figure 10-11.

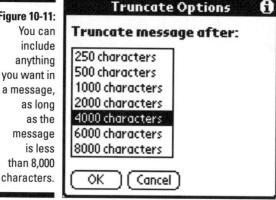

Figure 10-11:
You can
include
anything
you want in
a message,
as long
as the
message
is less
than 8,000
characters.

Truncate Options

Truncate message after:

250 characters
500 characters
1000 characters
2000 characters
4000 characters
6000 characters
8000 characters

OK   Cancel

4. Tap the maximum message length that you want.

5. Tap OK.

The Truncate Options dialog box closes, and the HotSync Options screen appears.

6. Tap OK.

The HotSync Options screen disappears, and your message list reappears.

The other thing that your Palm Mail program chops off is attachments. If someone sends you a file — such as a word processing document or a spreadsheet — that's attached to a message, you won't see the extra file on your Visor. You can still see the file on your desktop computer, but the Visor just doesn't have space for the extra file. Instead, it simply tells you that a file was attached. If you do need to receive attachments on your Visor, check out one of the third-party mail programs such as HandMail or MultiMail.

Part III
Visor and the Outside World

The 5th Wave   By Rich Tennant

"Let's see if I can get a menu any faster from their web site than I can from the waiter."

In this part . . .

Your Palm device isn't meant to be left all alone. You have to hook it up to a regular desktop or laptop computer to take full advantage of a Palm device's features. In this part, you find out how to help your Palm device and your regular computer carry out a meaningful relationship.

Chapter 11

Installing and HotSyncing to the Desktop Program for Windows

• •

In This Chapter

▶ Preparing hardware and Palm Desktop for Windows

▶ HotSyncing between your Palm device and your PC or Mac

• •

*I*n theory, you could use your Visor all by itself, with no other computer involved. But if you're only interested in doing things the easiest way possible (my favorite way), then the Palm Desktop programs may be the best way to put things in your Visor. You can carry it around to read your saved data and fiddle with it a little bit, as you see fit. I still prefer to enter most of my Visor data by using Graffiti, but most people that I know don't. Although you can put information into your Palm device in many clever ways, the desktop program is the simplest and most understandable method for anyone who has used a computer. In this chapter, I show you how to install the Palm Desktop, and I tell you all you need to know about HotSyncing your Visor to your desktop computer. In Chapter 12, I show you how to do all that cool Palm computing-type stuff on your desktop computer.

If you're a Mac user, see *Palm Computing For Dummies* by yours truly (IDG Books Worldwide, Inc.) for the full lowdown on connecting a Visor or other Palm organizer to a Mac. The Visor comes Mac-ready right out of the box, so Mac owners should have no problem.

Installing Palm Desktop for Windows

Hold up! Stop! Whoa, Nellie! (Did I get your attention?)

Before you install your desktop software, you need to hook up the Palm cradle to your desktop computer.

The cradle comes first

Typically, you can simply plug your Palm cradle into the only plug — or USB port — on the back of the PC in which it fits. If you can plug the cradle into the back of your PC easily, you've got it made. Just shout, "Hooray!" Pass Go, and collect $200 (or just jump ahead to the next section). If you can't plug the cradle right in, you may not have a USB port on your computer. If that's the case, you'll need to contact Handspring and buy a Serial Cradle to plug in. A Serial Cradle will synchronize your data just as well as the standard USB cradle. Some people think the USB cradle is faster, but you probably can't tell the difference.

Now, you get to install Palm Desktop

Palm Desktop for Windows enables your computer to talk to and work with your Visor through a process called HotSyncing. You have to install the desktop software only once, and then you're through. All you need to do after that is place your Palm device in the cradle and press the HotSync button on the cradle every day or so. The next section covers HotSyncing.

After you connect the cradle to your computer, you can install Palm Desktop by following these steps:

1. **Put the CD that came with your Palm device in your CD-ROM drive.**

   The Palm Desktop Installer Menu appears, as shown in Figure 11-1. If for some reason the screen doesn't appear automatically, use the Start⇨Run option to browse the CD for the SETUP.EXE file.

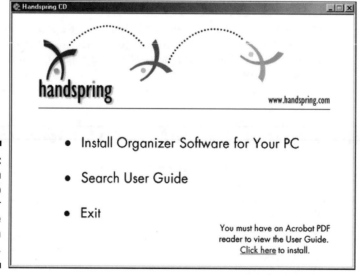

Figure 11-1:
The Palm Desktop Installer kicks off the installation process.

2. Click Install Organizer Software for Your PC.

The Welcome screen appears and tells you what's about to happen, as shown in Figure 11-2.

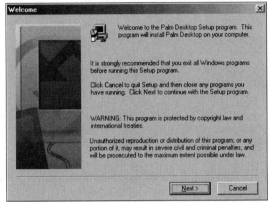

Figure 11-2:
The Welcome screen explains what you're getting into.

3. Click Next.

The Setup Type dialog box opens, as shown in Figure 11-3. You can choose between a typical installation and a custom installation. I recommend leaving Typical checked.

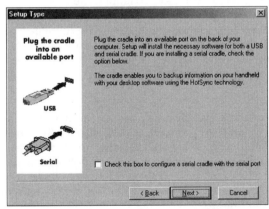

Figure 11-3:
The next screen gives you a choice between a typical or a custom installation. Keep it simple; pick Typical.

4. Click Next.

The Setup Type dialog box opens. The only reason for this dialog box is to remind you to put your Palm device in the cradle and plug the cradle into your computer so that the Install program can test the connections between your Palm device and your desktop computer.

5. **Place your Visor in the cradle and click Next.**

   The Install program copies files for a few moments, then the Perform Mail Setup dialog box appears. If you wish to set up your Visor to pick up e-mail from your desktop e-mail program, click Yes and follow the instructions.

6. **Press Enter.**

   The Setup Complete dialog box opens.

7. **Click Finish.**

   The Palm Desktop Installer closes.

Keeping Data in Sync

When you install the Visor, you end up with a good tool for tracking all your To Do's, addresses, memos, and appointments. That's fine if you're always at your desk. But if you divide your time between sitting at your desk and being on the go (and who doesn't, nowadays?), then keeping track of the data on two different machines can be a real pain. That's where HotSyncing comes in.

HotSyncing your Visor with your desktop computer is kindergarten simple. All you do is make sure that your desktop computer is running, put the Visor in the cradle, and push the HotSync button. That's it. The HotSync button is the only button on the cradle and has two arrows pointing at each other, so you can't go wrong. You don't even have to launch the desktop program. Pressing the HotSync button calls the HotSync Manager into action, which coordinates the whole process of swapping data. The HotSync Manager automatically turns on your Palm device, compares the data on it with the data on your desktop computer, and updates each machine with the most current info. After a few minutes, you end up with the same data on two different machines.

Most of the time, you don't need to know how the HotSync process works. However, every once in a while, you have to deal with HotSync problems, which happen most often when you synchronize your Visor with other personal information managers, such as Microsoft Outlook, Goldmine, or Act! Then you need to mess around with something called a *conduit,* which moves data between your Palm device and non-Palm-computing programs. I explain more about conduits in Chapter 20.

Chapter 12

Operating the Palm Desktop
Program for Windows

"**I**f the Visor is so great, why use a desktop computer at all?" you ask. Now take a breath. I know how enthusiastic people get about their handheld computers, but the little critters were never intended to send your desktop computer the way of the dinosaur. Not yet, anyway. The people who designed the Visor intended the two to work as a team, so you need a program for your desktop computer that talks to your Visor and makes it a little easier to enter and retrieve information from such a tiny device.

In this chapter, I'll tell you all about the Palm Desktop program for Windows that comes with your Visor. It's a perfectly good program for keeping track of appointments, addresses and the other stuff that most people keep on their Visors, but you may decide not to use the Palm Desktop for a couple of good reasons, such as these:

✔ **You use Microsoft Office 97 or 2000 for Windows.** You may already be keeping track of names and dates in Microsoft Outlook because it's included with Microsoft Office. Outlook is a very rich program; so rich that I've written an entirely separate book to cover it. Check out *Microsoft Outlook For Dummies* (IDG Books Worldwide, Inc.). Outlook thinks the same way your Visor does and ties in with Office so well that it only makes sense to use Outlook instead of the Palm Desktop. Also, the Visor installation program automatically links your Visor to Outlook if it finds Outlook on your computer. So, using Outlook is far and away the easiest way to go.

✔ **You use a Macintosh.** In that case, consider consulting my other book *Palm Computing For Dummies* (IDG Books Worldwide, Inc.). This book gives a comprehensive view of the ins and outs of using a Palm computer (such as the Visor) with a Mac.

✔ **You use ACT!, Goldmine, or one of those other high-falutin' contact managers.** A number of other programs for managing names and dates are available, and you may be deeply attached to one of them. Your current preference is probably okay because you can connect your Visor with most personal information managers.

If your program doesn't connect with a Visor or PalmPilot without help, you should check out a program called Intellisync from Puma. Check out Puma's site at www.pumatech.com for more information. Intellisync can connect your Visor to nearly anything but the kitchen sink (and they're probably working on the kitchen sink, too).

Palm Desktop Basics

A Visor does an amazing amount of work for a little gizmo with a tiny screen and barely a half-dozen buttons. But there's nothing like a big old computer with an old-fashioned keyboard and mouse for whipping off appointments, memos, To Do's, and addresses in a flash. Don't be prejudiced, though. You can use both the Palm Desktop and your Visor to enter your data — whatever suits your fancy. In this section, I give you an overview of the Palm Desktop interface and take you on a tour of the basic applications of the Palm Desktop.

Understanding the Palm Desktop interface

Interface is a techie term that computer geeks use to describe what you see on your computer screen after you launch a program. The interface of the Palm Desktop is made up of the same elements as the screens of most computer programs, combined with elements of the Palm device screens. You can see the name of the program in the upper-left corner of the screen, in the *title bar* area. Figure 12-1 shows a typical Palm Desktop screen. Below the title bar is the *menu bar,* which works just like the menu bar in other programs you use on your computer. Below the menu bar sits the *toolbar,* containing a row of icons you can click to perform the tasks you need to do most often.

On the left edge of the Palm Desktop screen is a column of buttons called the *launch bar.* The names of the buttons correspond to those of the standard Visor applications: Date, Address, To Do, and Memo. Clicking any of these buttons launches the corresponding application.

Below the four application buttons are two more icons labeled Expense and Install. The Expense icon starts the special Microsoft Excel spreadsheet that's filled with data from your Palm Expense application (if you use it). If you don't have Excel on your computer, the Palm Desktop Expense button does nothing, although you can still see it.

Launch bar

Palm Desktop toolbar

Figure 12-1:
Use the
Palm
Desktop
toolbar or
launch bar
to get
started.

Arranging appointments in your Date Book

The Date Book on the Palm Desktop has many of the same parts as the Date Book screens, but the Palm Desktop organizes things a bit differently because your computer screen has more room to display items than your Visor screen does. Also, your computer monitor probably has a color screen, which is something that your Visor might not have (yet). To bring up your Date Book in Palm Desktop, just click the Date button on the left side of the screen or choose View⇨Date Book.

Along the right edge of the Date Book, you can see three tabs labeled Day, Week, and Month. When you click any of those tabs, the view on the screen changes to that view. Here's the lowdown on what you see in each view:

✔ **Day:** The left side of the Palm device in Day view shows a list of appointments for a single day, as shown in Figure 12-2. The right side of the screen shows a miniature monthly calendar. When you click a date on that calendar, the list of appointments for that date appears. A list of the months of the year appears above the monthly calendar. Tap the month, and the calendar for that month appears. Above the list of months is a box showing the current year. If you want to see a date in a past or future year, click the triangle on either side of the year display. You may end up using Day view more than the other views (at least I do).

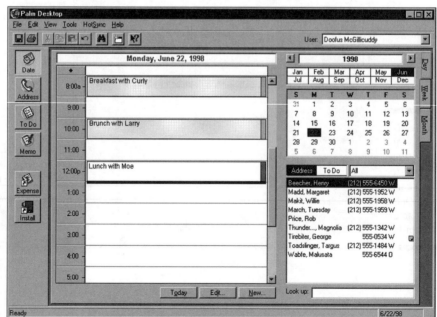

Figure 12-2:
Whaddya doin' today, knuckle-head? Check your Date Book! Nyah!

Below the calendar, Palm Desktop conveniently displays your To Do List or your Address Book so that you don't have to keep clicking the buttons on the left to switch between them. To toggle between your To Do List and Address Book, just click the name of whichever one you want to see.

✔ **Week:** Whenever you want to see how your week is shaping up, Week view shows a grid representing the whole workweek. Week view works just like it does on your Palm device. However, Palm Desktop shows you the names of your appointments, whereas your Palm device shows you only bars representing the appointments.

✔ **Month:** If you like to think ahead, Month view shows you what you're doing for the whole month. Palm Desktop gives you more detail, however, than Month view on your Palm device because your computer screen is larger.

For more info about using the Date Book on your Visor, refer to Chapter 8. The following sections give more details for using the desktop Date Book.

Adding appointments

Entering appointments in your Palm Desktop is undoubtedly faster than entering them on your Visor, as long as you're sitting at your big computer. If you're out in the field or at a meeting, it's a different story.

While you're sitting at the keyboard, follow these steps to add an appointment to the Palm Desktop:

1. **With the Date Book visible, click the Day tab on the right edge of the screen (or press Alt+D).**

   Day view of your Date Book appears.

2. **Click the date of your appointment on the calendar on the right side of the screen.**

   The Date Book shows the appointments scheduled for that date.

3. **Click the line next to the hour when you want your appointment to begin.**

   A box opens where you click the schedule, and an insertion point appears.

   The first line of Day view, next to the black diamond, has no time assigned to it; you can click there to enter events that last all day or that have no specific time assigned.

4. **Type a subject for your appointment.**

   The subject appears on the schedule.

5. **Click any other part of the screen (or press Tab).**

   Your appointment appears in yellow to show that you entered it.

I describe the method of adding appointments to Day view of your calendar on the Palm Desktop because it is similar to the way you add appointments on the Visor itself. You have more flexibility in how you enter appointments on the desktop, though. For example, Palm Desktop enables you to add appointments in Week view and in Month view — something you can't do on a Visor. Figure 12-3 shows you what Week view looks like. Just follow Steps 3 through 5 in the preceding example.

You may have noticed the New button at the bottom of the screen. (No, that doesn't make you a new person — you're fine the way you are.) The New button opens the Edit Event dialog box. You can always use the Edit Event dialog box for entering a new appointment, which is frankly the most complete and detailed way to enter information, but I think that it's a little cumbersome. You can read more about the Edit Event dialog box in the following sections.

Repeating appointments

Anything worth doing is worth doing at least once a week — that's my opinion — especially having days off. Try to make a habit of those, won't you? Note those repeating appointments in your Palm Desktop like this:

1. **With the Date Book visible, click the Day tab on the right edge of the screen (or press Alt+D).**

   Day view of your Date Book appears.

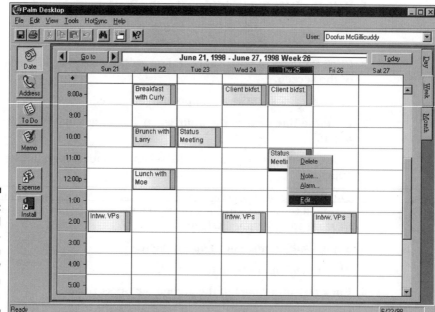

Figure 12-3:
You can add appointments in Week view of the Palm Desktop.

2. **Click the date of your appointment on the calendar on the right side of the screen.**

   The Date Book shows the appointments scheduled for that date.

3. **Click the appointment you want to set as a repeating appointment.**

   The appointment's yellow box appears shadowed to show that you selected it.

4. **Click Edit at the bottom of the screen (or choose Edit⇨Edit Event).**

   The Edit Event dialog box opens, as shown in Figure 12-4.

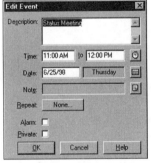

Figure 12-4: Change appointment details in the Edit Event dialog box.

5. **Click the button next to Repeat in the Edit Event dialog box.**

   The Change Repeat dialog box opens, as shown in Figure 12-5.

Figure 12-5: Do it again! Set up appointments that repeat as often as you want.

6. **Click the time period for the repeat pattern you want.**

   Based on your selection, the options for that pattern appear.

7. **Enter the choices you want for the repeat pattern you chose.**

   The choices you make appear in the Change Repeat dialog box. The text box at the bottom of the dialog box confirms your choices.

8. Click OK.

The Change Repeat dialog box closes.

9. Click OK again.

The Edit Event dialog box closes, and a little circle appears next to your appointment to show that it repeats.

One tricky thing about repeating appointments is that every time you change one, the Visor asks whether you're just changing this one appointment or the whole series. Don't be alarmed; just click the All button if you want to change all instances of the appointment, or click Current if you just want to change this instance of the appointment.

Making appointments private

Protecting private appointments works pretty much the same way as securing private memos does (see the section "Making a memo private," later in this chapter). The exception is that the check box in which you mark the appointment as private isn't on the main screen; it's hidden. To find the check box to mark an appointment as private, click the appointment to select it and click the Edit button at the bottom of the screen. That action opens the Edit Event dialog box, which contains the Private check box (refer to Figure 12-4).

Whenever you mark an appointment as private, a tiny key appears in the upper-left corner of the appointment box. You can hide all private records by choosing View➪Hide Private Records. When you hide private records, a key appears on the toolbar. You can show private records again by choosing View➪Show Private Records.

Deleting appointments

When you set up an appointment you're not entirely sure about, you may tell a person that you'll "pencil him in," which implies that you may erase him, too. All appointments on your Visor are somewhat penciled in because it's so easy to erase them.

Take these steps to delete an appointment from your Palm Desktop:

1. With the Date Book visible, click the Day tab on the right edge of the screen (or press Alt+D).

Day view of your Date Book appears. You can also choose the Week tab. If you prefer to view your whole week at a glance, jump ahead to Step 3.

2. Click the date of your appointment on the calendar on the right side of the screen.

The Date Book shows the appointments scheduled for that date.

3. Click the appointment you want to delete.

4. **Click Delete (or choose Edit⇨Delete).**

   The Delete Datebook Event dialog box opens, as shown in Figure 12-6.

Figure 12-6:
Simply
delete an
undesirable
appoint-
ment.

5. **Click OK if you want your appointment to disappear, or click Cancel if you have a change of heart.**

   If you leave the Archive box checked in the Delete Datebook Event dialog box, the appointment isn't lost forever; it automatically moves to an archive file, where you can look it up later.

Arranging entries in your Address Book

Keeping that little black book on a pocket computer is wonderfully efficient and amazingly quick. Using a little computer for all that crucial stuff has one big drawback: What if you lose the thing? Yikes! Losing a contact lens is nothing compared to losing your personal organizer — not to mention how it can put a crimp into your social life!

Fortunately, you can maintain the whole mess on your desktop computer, where it's all safe and sound and backed up. What are the chances of losing both your desktop computer and your Visor at the same time? Do you really want to find out? I didn't think so.

To bring up your Address Book, just click the Address button on the left side of the screen, or choose View⇨Address Book, and continue to the following sections. You won't have a problem making sense of the Address Book; when you open it, you see a list of names from which to select on the left side of the screen and full details of the person you select on the right side.

Adding a new Address Book entry

You can keep track of as little or as much information as you want about each person in the Address Book. Just fill out the form, please.

To add a new entry to your Address Book on the Palm Desktop follow these steps:

1. **With the Address Book visible, click New at the bottom of the screen (or choose Edit⇨New Address).**

   The Edit Address dialog box opens.

2. **Type the last name of the contact in the Last Name text box.**

   The text appears in the Last Name text box, as shown in Figure 12-7.

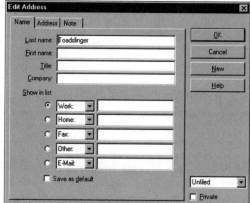

Figure 12-7:
To add a new address, fill in the form, please.

3. **Enter the contact's first name, title, and company in the appropriate boxes.**

4. **Enter the contact's telephone number in the appropriate phone number box.**

   Your choices for telephone number are work, home, fax, and other.

5. **Click the radio button to the left of the phone number you want shown on the Address List.**

6. **Click the Address tab at the top of the Edit Address dialog box.**

   The Address page of the Edit Address dialog box opens, as shown in Figure 12-8.

7. **Type the street address of your contact.**

8. **Enter the contact's city, state, ZIP code, and country in the appropriate boxes.**

9. **Click OK.**

   The Edit Address dialog box closes.

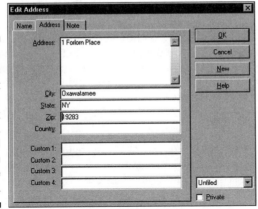

Edit Address

Name | Address | Note

Address: 1 Forlorn Place

City: Oxawatamee
State: NY
Zip: 19283
Country:

Custom 1:
Custom 2:
Custom 3:
Custom 4:

OK
Cancel
New
Help

Unfiled
☐ Private

Figure 12-8:
Put the
street
address in
the big box
and the city,
state, and
ZIP code in
the little
box.

Although you can enter plenty of information in an Address Book entry, you can get away with just filling in one blank. If you enter just a phone number and not the name of the person at that phone number, of course, you don't get much benefit other than a way to start a weird party game. It depends on what kind of parties you go to. I probably won't be there, thanks.

Editing an address record

I think that most people who carry Visors are upwardly mobile, and so are most of the people that they know. Don't you? Of course. We both carry Visors. What else would we think?

As you'd expect, all these upwardly mobile people are continually moving to better jobs and better addresses, so plan on making lots of changes to your Address List. And, please, don't forget the little people.

These steps show you how to edit an address in your Palm Desktop:

1. **With the Address Book visible, double-click the name of the person whose record you want to change.**

   The Edit Address dialog box opens.

2. **Add new information the same way you entered it originally.**

   For more information, see the preceding section, "Adding a new Address Book entry."

3. **Select any information you want to change and type the new information.**

   The text you enter replaces the information you selected.

4. **Click OK when you finish.**

   The Edit Address dialog box closes.

A big advantage to making your changes on the Palm Desktop rather than on the Visor is that you can save the old address in your archive. Just select the address record, and then press Ctrl+C to copy and then Ctrl+V to paste, and you have two identical records. If you delete one of the two and change the one that's left, you have the old address safely stored for posterity. To dig an old address from your archive, see the section "Archiving Your Palm Computing Stuff," later in this chapter.

Attaching a note to an address record

"Always tell the truth," a wise person said. "It's the easiest thing to remember." If you can't always recall what you say and to whom, you may benefit from keeping track of those important conversations. The perfect way to store these gems is in the form of notes in your Address Book. That way, you won't get caught.

Follow these steps to attach a note to an address record on your Palm Desktop:

1. **With the Address Book visible, double-click the record you want to annotate.**

   The Edit Address dialog box opens.

2. **Click the Note tab.**

   The Note page of the Edit Address dialog box appears, as shown in Figure 12-9.

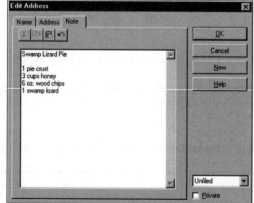

Figure 12-9:
Notes have their own page in the Edit Address dialog box.

3. **Enter the text of your note.**

   The text you type appears in the Note box.

4. Click OK when you finish.

The Edit Address dialog box closes. To view your note, just click the person's name on the Address List; the note appears with the other contact information in the box on the right side of the screen.

If you still can't remember what you said, keep your fingers crossed.

Finding the name you want

If you need to find a person's vital statistics quickly, you can just type the first few letters of the person's last name in the Look Up text box at the bottom of the Address List screen. When you type a letter or two in the Look Up text box, the Palm Desktop highlights the first name on the list that starts with those letters. If that's not the exact name you're looking for, the one you are looking for probably isn't far away. Keep typing letters until the name you want to find is highlighted. You can open that person's address record by double-clicking her name.

Deleting a name

Some names just don't make your list anymore. It's sad but true. To gently but firmly remove the name of someone who just isn't close to your inner microprocessor anymore, just click her name on your Address List and press Delete. A dialog box opens to make sure that you really want to do the deed; if you're sure, click OK.

If you change your mind, you can always restore any address record you saved in an archive. See the section "Archiving Your Palm Computing Stuff," later in this chapter, for details.

Setting up custom fields

If you keep track of lots of people who have a few important things in common, it's useful to set up special fields in your Address Book to help you keep track of what you need to know. If you're a teacher, for example, you may want to keep track of each student's age or grade level. If you're a Realtor, you may want to distinguish buyers from sellers and renters from landlords. Whatever your specialty, it's good to know that you can customize four of the Address Book fields for your own use.

These steps help you set up custom fields in the Palm Desktop:

1. With the Address Book visible, choose Tools⇨Custom Field Labels.

The Custom Field Labels dialog box opens, as shown in Figure 12-10.

Figure 12-10:
You can
customize
four fields
in your
Address
Book.

2. Type the name you want to assign to the first custom field.

The name you type appears in the Label 1 box.

3. Press Tab and enter the name you want to assign to each successive custom field.

4. Click OK.

The Custom Field Labels dialog box closes.

After you define the name of a custom field, all your address records have a field by that name. For example, if you rename a field as Grade Level, every record on your address list has a field by that name, even if the records aren't for students.

Doing stuff with your To Do's

Knowing what to do isn't enough if you don't remember to do it. The To Do List lets you add to your Visor the items you need to do so that the Visor can remind you to do them.

To bring up your To Do List, just click the To Do button on the left side of the Palm Desktop screen, or choose View⇨To Do List, and continue to the following sections. The left side of the To Do screen looks much like the Visor To Do screen. It's just a list of your tasks. The right side shows details of the To Do you select.

Creating a To Do item

Nothing could be easier than entering a task on your To Do List. If only doing the tasks were so easy! Use these steps to create a new To Do task.

1. With your To Do List visible, click New at the bottom of the screen (or choose Edit⇨New To Do).

A rectangle appears at the bottom of the To Do List, and the insertion point appears in the To Do text box on the right side of the screen, as shown in Figure 12-11.

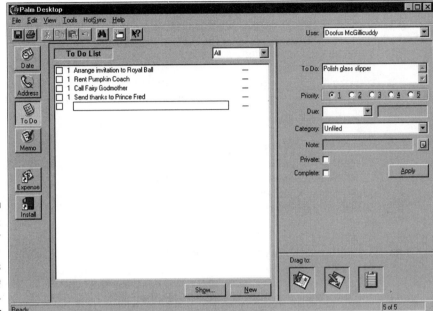

Figure 12-11:
Whatever
you type
appears
in the
rectangle.

2. Type your task in the To Do text box on the right.

3. Click the Apply button.

The name of your task appears on the To Do List on the left.

Setting the priority for a To Do item

With so many important things on your To Do List, how do you know what to do first? You need to set priorities. You have only the numbers 1 through 5 to assign as the priority for each task, but that's enough to make sure that you get to the important things first.

Here's how to set the priority of a To Do item:

1. With your To Do List visible, click the name of the To Do item for which you want to set a priority number.

2. Click one of the radio buttons next to Priority on the right side of the screen.

The radio button next to the number you click is blackened to show which number you selected.

3. Click the Apply button.

The priority you assign appears next to your To Do item.

Another trick you can try is simply clicking the priority number on the To Do List. Clicking a priority number makes a list of priority numbers appear, as shown in Figure 12-12. You can choose the number you want by picking it from the list with a single mouse click.

You can have more than one To Do with the same priority. You can make every task your top priority or your bottom priority. Whatever you pick, it's *your* priority.

Assigning a category to a To Do item

Another way to keep track of what task you need to do next is to assign categories. For example, some tasks must be done at home, and others can be done only at work. When you're at the office, you don't need to remind yourself to mow the lawn (although if it gets you out of the office early, it's worth a try).

To assign a category to a To Do item, follow these steps:

1. **With your To Do List visible, click the name of the To Do item to which you want to assign a category.**

2. **Click the Category box on the right side of the screen.**

   The drop-down list of available categories appears.

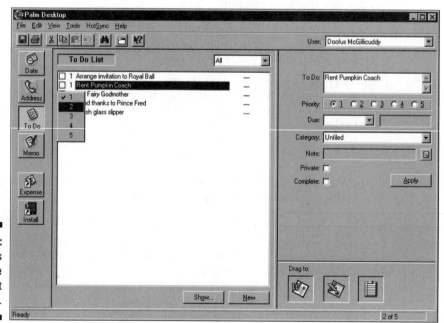

Figure 12-12: Some tasks are more important than others.

3. **Click the category you want to assign to your To Do item.**

   The category you click appears in the Category text box.

4. **Click the Apply button.**

   The priority you assign appears next to your To Do item.

Adding categories

You can maintain your collection of categories on either your Visor or the Palm Desktop. Every time you HotSync your data, the categories you set up on your Visor are mirrored on the Palm Desktop and vice versa.

Follow these steps to create a new category:

1. **With your To Do List visible, click the arrow next to Category on the right side of the screen.**

   The drop-down list of available categories appears.

2. **Click Edit Categories.**

   The Edit To Do Categories dialog box opens, as shown in Figure 12-13.

Figure 12-13:
Create new
categories
in the Edit
To Do
Categories
dialog box.

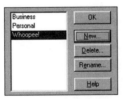

3. **Click New.**

   The New Category dialog box opens.

4. **Enter the name of the category you want to add.**

   The name you enter appears in the New Category dialog box.

5. **Tap OK.**

   The new category appears in the Edit To Do Categories dialog box.

6. **Tap OK again.**

   The Edit To Do Categories dialog box closes.

You can have no more than 15 categories on your Visor or on the Palm Desktop. If you try to exceed 15 categories, the program adamantly (but nicely) refuses to add new categories.

Deleting categories

If you went wild and added some categories you now regret, you can just zap your excess categories and get back to basics.

Follow these steps to delete a category:

1. **With your To Do List visible, click the downward-pointing arrow next to Category on the right side of the screen.**

   The drop-down list of available categories appears.

2. **Click Edit Categories.**

   The Edit To Do Categories dialog box opens.

3. **Select the name of the category you want to delete.**

4. **Click Delete.**

   The Delete Category dialog box opens, asking whether you want to move all items in the category to the Unfiled category or delete all items, as shown in Figure 12-14.

Figure 12-14:
Rename 'em
or remove
'em. Take
your pick.

5. **Choose either Move All Items to Unfiled or Delete All Items.**

   The circle next to the choice you click appears darkened to show that you selected it.

6. **Click OK.**

   The Delete Category dialog box closes, and your category disappears.

7. **Click OK.**

   The Edit To Do Categories dialog box closes.

At least when you delete a category on the Palm Desktop, you get a choice between deleting all the items in the category and sending all the items to the Unfiled category. On the Visor itself, you can only send everything to Unfiled.

Renaming categories

Did you know that Whoopi Goldberg changed her name from Caryn Johnson? Go figure. Changing the names of your categories is easier than changing your name for show business, but it won't make you a star.

To rename a category, follow these steps:

1. **With your To Do List visible, click the downward-pointing arrow next to Category on the right side of the screen.**

   The drop-down list of available categories appears.

2. **Click Edit Categories.**

   The Edit To Do Categories dialog box opens.

3. **Click the name of the category you want to rename.**

4. **Click Rename.**

   The Rename Category dialog box opens, as shown in Figure 12-15.

Figure 12-15:
You can rename your categories at any time.

Rename Category

Enter a new category name:

one of a kind

OK   Cancel

5. **Enter the new name of the category you want to change.**

   The name you type replaces the old name in the Rename Category dialog box.

6. **Tap OK.**

   The new category name replaces the old one in the Edit To Do Categories dialog box.

7. **Tap OK again.**

   The Edit To Do Categories dialog box closes.

In case you're interested, Hal Linden started off as Harold Lipshitz, and Peter Marshall's original name was Pierre LaCock. But that's a totally different category.

Assigning a due date to a To Do item

Your To Do List can do more than tell you what tasks to do; it also helps you remember when to do them.

Follow these steps to assign a due date to a To Do item:

1. **With your To Do List visible, click the name of the To Do item to which you want to assign a due date.**

2. **Click the drop-down list arrow to the right side of the Due text box on the right side of the screen.**

   A drop-down menu of available choices appears, offering five options: Today, Tomorrow, One Week Later, No Date, and Choose Date.

3. **Click the date you want to assign to your To Do item.**

   If you select anything other than Choose Date, the date you pick appears in the Due text box, so you can click the Apply button and you're done.

4. **Select Choose Date if you need to assign a specific date to your task.**

   The Select Date dialog box opens.

5. **Click the date you want to assign as your due date.**

   Figure 12-16 shows the date I selected for my To Do item.

Figure 12-16:
Give your
task its due
date in the
Select Date
dialog box.

6. **Click OK.**

   The Select Date dialog box closes, and the date you chose appears in the Due text box.

7. **Click Apply.**

Unfortunately, the To Do List doesn't have reminders for the list itself, so you have to remember to look at your list from time to time.

Marking a To Do item private

You may have things to do that other people shouldn't know about. Shhh! Keep them under your hat — or at least under a password.

These steps show you how to mark a To Do item private on the Palm Desktop:

1. **With your To Do List visible, click the name of the To Do item you want to mark as private.**

2. **Click the Private check box on the right side of the screen.**

3. **Click the Apply button.**

   A little key appears next to your item on the To Do List to show that it's now marked as private, as shown in Figure 12-17.

If you want your private items to remain private, you should choose, of course, View⇨Hide Private Records. This step makes your private items invisible until you choose View⇨Show Private Records. If you want to password-protect your private items, you have to set your password on your Visor. For more info about setting up passwords, refer to Chapter 3.

Attaching notes to To Do items

You know what you need to do and when you need to do it, of course, but do you always remember how or why? Perhaps you just need a more detailed explanation of some part of the task, such as driving directions or a secret formula. If you need some elaboration on your task, add a note.

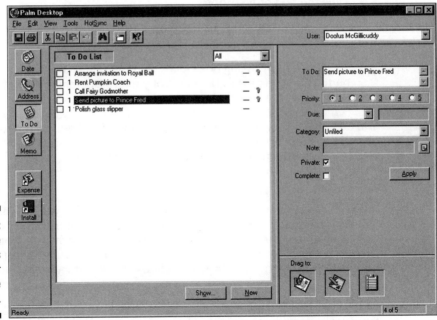

Figure 12-17:
Those little keys mark your private tasks.

To add a note to a To Do item in the Palm Desktop, follow these steps:

1. **With your To Do List visible, click the name of the To Do item to which you want to attach a note.**

2. **Click the Note icon button to the right of the Note text box on the right side of the screen (it looks like a piece of paper with the lower-right corner lifted up).**

   The Note Editor dialog box opens, as shown in Figure 12-18.

Figure 12-18:
Make a note
of what to
do in your
To Do.

3. **Type the text of your note.**

   The text you type appears in the Note Editor dialog box.

4. **Click OK.**

   The Note Editor dialog box closes, and the same icon that's on the Note button appears next to the name of your To Do item to show that the item has a note attached.

You don't have to type lots of text into the note if you don't want to. You can always copy text from another document on your desktop or from a Web page and paste the text into the Note Editor dialog box.

Viewing items by category

If you make the effort to assign categories to your tasks, you get some real mileage from that feature by viewing your tasks according to their categories. The name of the category you're viewing is always shown at the top of the To Do List. If you click the name of the category you're viewing, a drop-down list of the other categories appears. Just choose the category you want to see.

Deleting a To Do item

Some tasks become unnecessary before you even do them. If you planned to water the lawn and it rains, you're in luck.

Follow these steps to delete a To Do item on the Palm Desktop:

1. **With your To Do List visible, click the name of the To Do item you want to delete.**

2. **Press Delete.**

   The Delete To Do Items dialog box opens, as shown in Figure 12-19.

   The Archive Deleted To Do Item(s) at Next HotSync check box enables you to send deleted items to the archive for storage. I discuss how to deal with stored items in the "Archiving Your Palm Computing Stuff" section later in this chapter.

Figure 12-19:
Tasks
can be
completed
or deleted.
Take your
pick.

3. **Click OK.**

   Your To Do item is deleted.

If you actually did the task, then your best bet, of course, is to mark the task as complete. The little check box next to the name of the task is put there for that very reason. One click and you're the hero — mission accomplished!

Setting preferences for your To Do List

Setting preferences is, well, a matter of preference. You don't need to make any changes in your To Do List preferences if you don't want to. But if you like your To Do List just so, you can change several little things.

To set your To Do List preferences on the Palm Desktop, follow these steps:

1. **With your To Do List visible, click the Show button at the bottom of the screen (or press Alt+O).**

   The Show Options dialog box opens, as shown in Figure 12-20.

2. **Click the arrow to the right of the Sort By text box to see your list of choices.**

   The drop-down list of sorting options for your To Do List appears.

Figure 12-20:
When it
comes to
sorting
tasks, you
have
several
options.

3. **Choose the way you want to sort your To Do List.**

   The choice you click appears in the Sort By text box. The sort options on the Palm Desktop are identical to the choices on the Visor, as I discuss in Chapter 6.

4. **Click the check boxes next to the options you want for your To Do List.**

5. **Click OK.**

   The Show Options dialog box closes, and your To Do List reflects the preferences you set up. Figure 12-21 shows the new sort order.

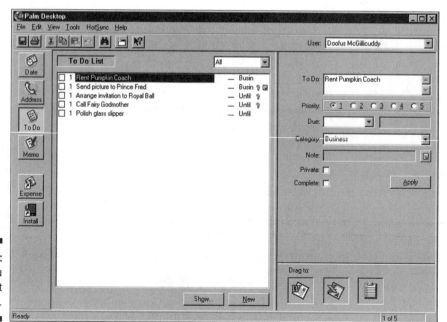

Figure 12-21:
What you
see is what
you set.

If you set up your preferences and then decide that you'd prefer something else, just change everything again.

Working with memos

The best reason to enter memos on the Palm Desktop rather than use Graffiti is that memos usually contain lots of text, and typing is much faster than scribbling with Graffiti or punching in individual letters on the Visor's on-screen keyboard. You can also copy and paste text to a memo from other desktop programs, such as your word processor.

To open the Memo Pad, just click the Memo button on the left side of the screen or choose View➪Memo Pad, and continue to the following sections.

Creating a memo

Sometimes, you need certain information that's not exactly an appointment and not exactly a To Do item, but you still need it on your Visor. The simplest way to keep miscellaneous information on hand is to create a memo. Nothing could be easier.

Use these steps to create a new memo on the Palm Desktop:

1. **With the Memo Pad visible, click New at the bottom of the screen (or choose Edit➪New Memo).**

   A new line appears on your list of memos, and the insertion point appears in the memo area on the right side of the screen.

2. **Type the text of your memo.**

   The text you type appears in the memo area on the right side of the screen, as shown in Figure 12-22.

3. **Click the Apply button below the memo area.**

   The title of your memo appears on the list of memos on the left side of the screen.

If you hate to type, you can also copy and paste text into your Memo Pad, too. Just select text from a word-processing document or even from the Web. Press Crtl+C to copy the text and start the Palm Desktop Memo Pad. Then press Ctrl+V to paste the text directly into the memo. You don't even need to create a new memo. The Palm Desktop figures out that you want a new memo and creates one automatically.

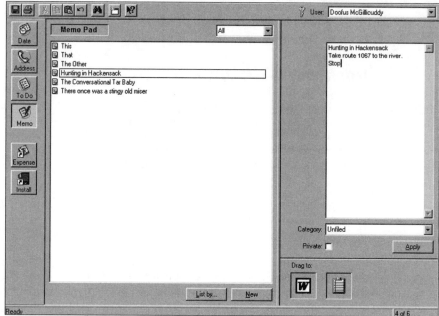

Figure 12-22:
Type or
copy
whatever
you like into
a memo.

Reading a memo

You may not want to hang around reading your memos on the Palm Desktop because you can send them all to your Visor and then go sit in the park to read them. Even so, you may need to check what you put in your memos now and again, and, fortunately, I can show you a way to do just that.

To read a memo, all you have to do is click the Memo Pad button on the left side of the screen (or choose View⇨Memo Pad) and then click the memo you want to see. Read away!

If you need to read through all the memos on your desktop quickly, you can whip through the whole list by pressing the down-arrow key. Each time you press the down-arrow key, the next memo on the list appears in the memo area on the right side of the screen.

Printing a memo

Another big thing you can do from the desktop is print things. Yes, some people out there have clever schemes for beaming their Palm computing data to specially equipped printers. But the whole scheme is still tricky, and most printers aren't up to the job. You probably have a printer hooked up to your desktop computer, so printing from the desktop is the quickest way to see your Palm computing data on paper.

To print a memo from the Palm Desktop, follow these steps:

1. **With the Memo Pad visible, click the title of the memo you want to print.**

   The text of the memo appears in the memo area on the right side of the screen.

2. **Choose File⇨Print (or press Ctrl+P).**

   The Print dialog box opens.

3. **Click OK.**

   Palm Desktop prints your memo.

The Palm Desktop doesn't let you do any fancy formatting of your memos; it's all plain vanilla. If you need to format and fiddle around with your text, you can drag the memo you want to work with to the Microsoft Word icon at the bottom of the Palm Desktop for Windows screen. Dragging a memo to the Microsoft Word icon opens Word and copies your text into a new Word document that you can beautify as you please. You also can drag text to Excel if you want. See the "Working with the Drag To icons," section later in this chapter. If you don't have Word installed on your desktop computer, you have to drag text to the clipboard icon, open any word processor or text editor, and paste the text into another document.

Editing a memo

If you use memos often, as I do, you certainly want to change a few of them now and then. The biggest advantage to keeping memos in an electronic form is that the text is so easy to change.

Follow these steps to edit a Memo on your Palm Desktop:

1. **With the Memo Pad visible, click the title of the memo you want to edit.**

   The text of the memo appears in the memo area on the right side of the screen.

2. **Click in the memo area on the right side of the screen at the point where you want to edit.**

   An insertion point appears where you click your mouse.

3. **Make any changes you want to the memo.**

4. **Click the Apply button below the memo area to save your changes as part of the memo.**

If you replace a large amount of the text in a memo, the text you replace is ordinarily gone for good. Typically, that's fine by me, but sometimes you may want to save a copy of the original memo. One thing you can do with memos on the Palm Desktop that you can't do on the Visor itself is copy whole memos and then just change one of them. To copy a whole memo, click the name of the memo to select it, press Ctrl+C to copy the memo, and then press Ctrl+V to paste it. You then have two identical memos. Just change one, and you have two different memos.

Categorizing a memo

Categories are particularly useful after you've collected more than a few dozen memos. Categorizing not only makes memos easier to find but also lets you see your memo collection more easily on your Visor because that little screen can show only 11 memos at one time.

Follow these steps to assign a category to a memo on the Palm Desktop:

1. **With the Memo Pad visible, click the title of the memo you want to categorize.**

   The memo text appears in the memo area on the right side of the screen.

2. **Click the Category drop-down list arrow and choose the category you want, as shown in Figure 12-23.**

   The category you assign appears below your memo text.

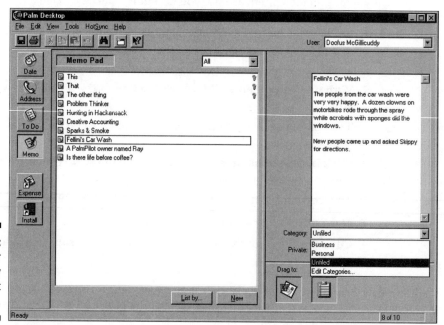

Figure 12-23: Change your category with just two clicks.

If you want to create several memos in the same category, switch to that category and then create the new memos. For example, if you switch to a view of your business memos and start creating new memos, all the new memos are automatically assigned to the Business category.

Making a memo private

I'm sure that you have some things you don't want just anybody to see, but you don't want to forget them yourself. You can mark certain memos as private to protect them from prying eyes.

To mark a memo private in the Palm Desktop, follow these steps:

1. **With the Memo Pad visible, click the title of the memo you want to mark as private.**

2. **Click the Private check box below the memo text on the right side of the screen.**

   A check mark appears in the Private check box to show that this memo is private, as shown in Figure 12-24. A key also appears next to the subject of any memo that's marked as private.

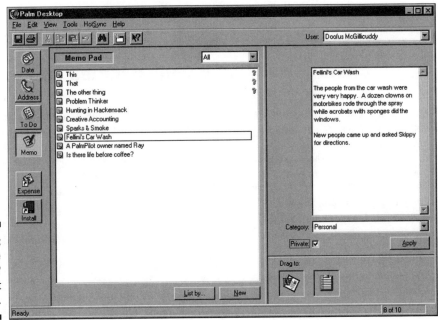

Figure 12-24:
Do you have a secret? Mark it private.

You can make all your private items disappear by choosing View⇨ Hide Private Records. If you want to make them reappear, choose View⇨ Show Private Records. Presto! If you want to be sneaky, you can set a password on your Visor to keep anyone from seeing your private records unless he knows your password. For more information about setting passwords, refer to Chapter 3.

Deleting a memo

You know how memos are — easy come, easy go . . . especially go. Follow these steps to make your memos go away:

1. **With the Memo Pad visible, click the title of the memo you want to delete.**

   The memo text appears in the memo area on the right side of the screen.

2. **Choose Edit⇨Delete (or press Delete).**

   The Delete Memo Pad Items dialog box opens, as shown in Figure 12-25. If you check the Archive Deleted Memo Pad Item(s) at Your Next HotSync check box, your memo is stored in an archive file.

3. **Click OK.**

   Poof! Your memo is gone.

What does that Expense button do?

Your Visor includes an Expense application to help you track how much money you spend as you spend it. When you perform a HotSync, the information you've gathered is pulled into a file on your desktop. Frankly, the program is limited and is best for people who need to track business spending in order to file expense reports. Even for those people, the program has major drawbacks. It requires you to choose a description of each expenditure from a noncustomizable list of 28 choices ranging from Airfare to Telephone. It's hard to make the Expense application useful if you can't enter the exact type of expenses you incur.

You can start the Expense application by tapping the Applications soft button and tapping the Expense icon on your Visor. Write in the amounts you spend and pick the description that you think fits best. The program automatically assigns the current date to each expenditure unless you tap the date and pick another one from the calendar.

The Expense button on the Palm Desktop for Windows automatically starts up a special Excel spreadsheet that captures data you've entered in the Expense application on your Visor. If you don't have Excel installed on your Windows PC, the button is still present, but it doesn't do anything. Plenty of Visor users have complained that the Expense program is too weak, so I hope that future versions will be more useful.

Figure 12-25:
The Delete
Memo Pad
Items dialog
box makes
sure that
you want to
delete that
memo.

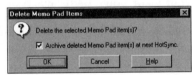

If you left the Archive box checked, you can go back and find the deleted memo later. See the section "Archiving Your Palm Computing Stuff," later in this chapter, for more information.

Working with the Drag To icons

If you use Microsoft Word and Microsoft Excel on your desktop computer, the Palm Desktop for Windows displays a set of icons labeled Drag To in the lower-right portion of the screen. Two of the icons look just like the icons for Word and Excel, and the third icon looks like a little clipboard. When you drag any item from the Palm Desktop to the Word icon, Word opens and creates a copy of the item, and converts it to a Word document. Dragging an item to the Excel icon creates a copy of the item, formatted as an Excel spreadsheet. The most useful thing you can do with this feature is to turn a memo into a Word document so that you can save, format, or print the text of the memo.

If you don't have Word or Excel installed on your computer, the Word and Excel icons don't appear. Even without Word or Excel, you can still drag items to the clipboard icon and then open a document in any word processor and choose Edit⇨Paste to insert the text that's on the clipboard.

Furnishing Your Visor

What is a home, after all, without some furnishings? You may have a lovely breakfast nook, but eventually you want a dinette, at least. You can furnish your Visor as lavishly (or sparingly) as you'd furnish your home — a few games, a spreadsheet — who knows what may strike your fancy?

Checking memory

Before you start adding things to your Visor, you'd better make sure that you have room for the stuff. The 8MB of memory installed on your Visor seems endless at first, but after a while you'll probably find a way to fill it up. Unlike my hall closet, which I seem to be able to cram anything into, your Visor protests if you try to put too much stuff on it.

You can see how much space is available on a Visor by following these three steps:

1. **Tap the Applications soft button.**

2. **Tap the Menu soft button.**

3. **Choose App⇨Info.**

   The Info screen appears. The line at the top of the Info screen says something like Free Memory: 849K of 960K, as shown in Figure 12-26.

Figure 12-26:
Before you install a new program, check your memory to see whether you have enough room.

Info	
Free Memory: 7974K of 8064K	
People Srch	8K
System	11K
To Do List	1K
Travelocity	16K
Weather	7K
wsj.com	2K
YellowPages	11K

(Done) Version Records Size

Most Palm computing applications are small, so as long as you have a few hundred kilobytes of memory (abbreviated *K* by computer geeks), you should be okay. Remember, though, that every time you add an item to one of the standard Palm computing applications, like the Address Book or the Date Book, you tie up a bit more memory. So leave yourself some breathing room. You can free up some memory either by deleting applications (see the section,"Deleting applications," later in this chapter), or by deleting bunches of items from the standard Palm computing applications. The easiest way to delete records en masse is to use the Palm Desktop, as I describe in the previous sections of this chapter.

Installing applications

Remember that the Palm Install Tool doesn't install applications; it *prepares* applications for installation. After picking an application with the Palm Install Tool, you have to perform a HotSync. Just place the Visor in its cradle and press the HotSync button (for more info about HotSyncing, refer to Chapter 11).

To install Palm computing programs using the Palm Desktop, follow these steps:

1. **Launch the Palm Desktop.**

2. **Click the Install button on the left side of the screen, or choose View⇨Install.**

   The Palm Install Tool dialog box opens.

3. **Click Add (or press Alt+A).**

   The Open dialog box appears.

4. **Click the name of the file you want to install as shown in Figure 12-27.**

Figure 12-27:
Add new programs with the Palm Install Tool.

If you downloaded the application from the Internet or are installing applications from the CD, browse until you find the application you want to install.

5. **Click Open.**

   The Open dialog box closes, and the filename appears in the Palm Install Tool dialog box list.

6. **Click Done.**

   Another dialog box opens, telling you that Palm Desktop will install the applications the next time you HotSync.

7. **Click OK.**

   The Palm Install Tool closes.

8. **Press the HotSync button on the cradle of your Visor.**

   The HotSync process begins, and the Desktop program installs the application on your Visor.

You have an even easier way to install Palm applications if you're comfortable dealing with files in Windows. Just find a Palm application file in Windows Explorer (Palm files end with .PRC, .PDB, or .PQA). Double-click the name of the file when you find it with Windows Explorer, and your Palm Install program opens, already showing the name of the file. Just click OK in the Palm Install Tool dialog box, and the install program will install the app on your next HotSync.

Deleting applications

Eventually, you may tire of your once-fashionable furnishings. I mean, orange shag carpet? Lava lamps? Please! Martha Stewart would send you straight to K-mart!

Discarding unwanted applications from your Visor is even easier than dumping those old Woodstock posters. You'll also be less embarrassed if someone catches you at it. You don't need to launch Palm Desktop to delete applications, either. Here's how to delete a program from your Visor:

1. **Tap the Applications soft button.**

   The applications screen appears.

2. **Tap the Menu button.**

   The menu bar appears.

3. **Choose App⇨Delete.**

   The Delete screen appears, as shown in Figure 12-28.

4. **Tap the name of the application you want to delete.**

5. **Tap Delete.**

   The Delete Application dialog box opens, as shown in Figure 12-29.

6. **Tap Yes if you're sure. If you change your mind, tap No.**

   If you tap Yes, Visor deletes the application, and the app's name disappears from the list on the Delete screen. If you tap No, the dialog box closes, and the application is still there.

7. **Tap Done.**

   The Delete screen closes.

Figure 12-28:
Clear out the clutter by deleting unwanted applications.

Figure 12-29:
Zap pesky programs from the Delete Application screen.

There you are! And there it isn't! Your unwanted application is gone like platform shoes. Oops, I guess platform shoes have made a comeback. Well, you can always reinstall the applications by using the same procedure shown in the section "Installing applications," earlier in this chapter.

Protecting Your Turf

Sometimes the worst does happen; your little Visor gets lost, stolen, or destroyed. You can always buy a new Visor — that's the easy part. But what about all your data? You're in luck — the Palm Desktop makes it easy to reinstall all your precious data, as long as you consistently back it up.

Restoring Palm computing data

In the best of times or in the worst of times, you may need to restore all your Palm computing data. The best of times may be when you upgrade to a new Palm organizer model; the worst of times may be when you replace a lost, stolen, or destroyed Visor. Either way, you can restore everything that was on your old Visor with a simple HotSync:

1. **Put your Visor in its cradle.**

   Nothing happens. Surprise!

2. **Press the HotSync button on the Palm cradle.**

   The HotSync Manager on your desktop PC launches, and the Users dialog box opens on your desktop PC screen.

3. **Click the name of the user whose data you want to install on the Visor — it's probably your name as shown in Figure 12-30.**

Figure 12-30: Pick the name of the user whose data should go on this Visor.

4. **Click OK (on the desktop).**

   The HotSync Progress dialog box opens. After a few minutes, the dialog box closes, your Visor plays some tinny little fanfare, and a button labeled Reset appears on the screen.

5. **Tap the Reset button on the screen.**

   The General Preferences screen appears on your Visor. You don't need to do anything in the General Preferences screen after a reset; you can either turn off the Visor or go right on and use any application.

If you use one desktop computer to synchronize more than one Visor or other Palm device, don't assign the same username to more than one Palm device. The HotSync program can get confused and send the wrong data to the wrong Palm device or, worse, make data disappear.

Backing up your data

If you use only the programs that come in the box with your Visor, you don't need to worry about backing up. If you HotSync regularly to keep your data current, you're covered. Your data from all the standard Palm computing applications gets saved and archived by the Palm Desktop every time you HotSync. It's a good idea, of course, to back up the data on the desktop machine regularly.

On the other hand, if you install programs that don't come preinstalled on your Visor, those programs may not automatically back themselves up like your standard Palm computing apps do, so you need a backup program to keep those files safe. One program, Backup Buddy, is available to help you back up your nonstandard programs automatically. To find out more, see the manufacturer's Web site:

www.backupbuddy.com

If all you've added to your Visor is a few games, I wouldn't worry about backing up. You need to be concerned with backups if you've added programs that add data themselves, like spreadsheets, databases, time and billing applications, or similar programs. If your Visor was issued to you at work, you should check with your system administrator about whether you need to do anything special with backups.

Archiving Your Palm Computing Stuff

Your Visor can hold only a fraction of the information your desktop computer can. To save space on the Visor, clearing things out regularly is a good idea. The Visor has a Purge function in the Date Book and To Do List that automatically gets rid of unneeded items and moves them to an archive file, if you checkmark the archive options. When you archive files to the desktop, you can later view or restore them. For more info about purging Palm organizer items, refer to Chapter 6.

Viewing archived items

The Palm Desktop is the only place where you can open and view archived items. Even if you use another personal information manager, such as Microsoft Outlook or Lotus Organizer, to put items into your Visor, you still need to look in the Palm Desktop to view your archived items.

These steps show you how to view your archived items on the Palm Desktop:

1. **Click the button on the launch menu (or from the <u>V</u>iew menu) for the type of archived item you want to view.**

   Calendar items are archived separately from items deleted from the Address Book, To Do List, or Memo Pad, so you need to open the part of the Palm Desktop that handles the type of item you want to see.

2. **Choose <u>F</u>ile⇨<u>O</u>pen Archive.**

   The Open Archive dialog box opens, as shown in Figure 12-31.

Figure 12-31:
Find those old deleted items by opening an archive file.

3. **Click the name of the archive file.**

   Usually, only one file appears on the archive list. If more than one archive file is listed and the archive you open doesn't contain the item you want, repeat Steps 2 and 3 until you find the archive containing the item you want.

4. **Click OK.**

The items in the archive you open appear as a new list of items on your Palm Desktop.

If you're looking at the archive of items assigned to categories, the archive files are organized by category — personal, business, or whatever you assign.

Returning an archived item to your Visor

Another benefit of keeping archive files is to help you get back items you accidentally delete. Don't be embarrassed — it happens to everybody.

To recover an item from an archive on the Palm Desktop, follow these steps:

1. **Click the button on the launch menu (or select from the <u>V</u>iew menu) the type of archived item you want to recover.**

   Choose Date Book, Address Book, To Do List, or Memo Pad.

2. **Choose <u>F</u>ile⇨<u>O</u>pen Archive.**

   The Open Archive dialog box opens.

3. **Click the name of the archive file you want to recover.**

4. **Click OK.**

   The items in the archive file you picked are listed on the Palm Desktop.

5. **Click the item you want to return to your Visor.**

6. **Choose <u>E</u>dit⇨<u>C</u>opy (or press Ctrl+C).**

   A copy of the item goes to the Clipboard. Nothing happens on the screen.

7. **Choose <u>F</u>ile⇨Open <u>C</u>urrent.**

   Your collection of current items appears.

8. **Choose <u>E</u>dit⇨<u>P</u>aste (or press Ctrl+V).**

   The item appears as part of your collection of current items.

9. **Place your Visor in its cradle, and press the HotSync button on the cradle.**

   The HotSync dialog box opens and shows the progress of your synchronization.

The whole reason for archiving items is to save space on your Visor, so don't load old items back up to your Visor unless you really need them.

If you're using your Visor with Microsoft Outlook, you have to do your archiving from Microsoft Outlook rather than from the Visor itself. Outlook doesn't keep track of items you've deleted from the Visor.

Accommodating Multiple Users

Most people use a Visor in conjunction with a desktop computer in order to simplify data entry and keep the data on their Visors safe. But you don't have to limit yourself to one Palm device per computer. The Palm Desktop enables you to synchronize Palm devices with different users.

The first time you HotSync your Visor, the HotSync Manager asks for your username. The Visor username you enter (or choose) is added to the list of usernames on the Palm Desktop. Each time you put a Palm device in the cradle attached to that desktop computer, the program recognizes which Palm device is in the cradle when you press the HotSync button. After you've set up a computer to HotSync a particular Palm device, the desktop computer always knows which Palm device it's dealing with and synchronizes to that particular person's information.

It's not a good idea to set up multiple users on the same computer if you don't use the Palm Desktop program. It's possible to make your Visor information synchronize to other programs, such as Microsoft Outlook or Act!, but you could encounter some confusion if you try to synchronize more than one Palm device to one of those programs. It's not impossible to use several Palm devices with those programs; it's just not certain that everything will work right if you do it all through the same computer. If you want to host several Palm devices on the same desktop PC, your best bet is to stick with the Palm Desktop.

The Visor Name Game

Although all Palm devices look pretty much alike in those little tiny boxes, each one has one important difference: the name of the user. You can find out which name is assigned to the Palm device you're using by tapping the Applications soft button and then tapping HotSync. The HotSync screen displays the name of the user assigned to it. Also, when you perform a HotSync, the name of the user whose data is being synchronized appears in the HotSync Progress dialog box. You determine the Palm device username the first time you perform a HotSync. If you try to HotSync your Visor to a computer that hasn't ever seen a Palm device with that username, the HotSync Manager asks whether you want to set up a new account for that user.

Chapter 13

Using the Visor Modem

*T*he amount of power that you can pack in a little bitty Visor is amazing. But that's not all — pop in a Handspring Modem and look out! The modem adds only a half inch or so to the length of your Visor, but it extends the little gizmo's reach far enough to explore the entire Internet. The modem also enables you to exchange messages with people all over the world from nearly anywhere or synchronize with your desktop over the phone. Granted, a modem sets you back by about $129, but that's a small price to pay to put that much power in your pocket.

Handspring Modem Basics

If you've just purchased a shiny new, store-bought Visor and Handspring Modem, making them work together is fairly simple. When you see the Visor and its modem together, you instinctively know how to attach them to one another. Although the two work together seamlessly right from the get-go, after you've used your Visor for a while, some settings may get changed or go awry. Here are the nitty-gritty details about the Handspring Modem in case you get into a pinch.

Setting up your modem

Your Handspring Modem doesn't need much attention. You can set it up in a snap. Here's the routine:

1. **Snap your modem into the back of your Visor.**

   The modem makes a slight clicking sound as it fits snugly into the Springboard slot.

2. **Plug a phone line into the modem.**

   Of course, you need to plug a telephone line into your Visor Modem. A jack is located at the top of the modem — it looks just like the jack on your home telephone. Simply unplug the wire that goes into your telephone and then plug it into your Handspring Modem. The phone line snaps into your modem the same way that it does when you plug it into your phone.

Just feed your modem a new pair of batteries now and again, and you're fine. The batteries fit behind the little door on the lower-front part of your modem case. Just slide the door downward to open the battery compartment.

All phone lines are not alike. Your home phone line is the right type of phone line to use with your modem. It's called an *analog* line, the old-fashioned kind of phone line. Another type of phone line that offices and hotels often use is called a *digital* line. *Do not plug your modem into a digital line!* In some cases plugging your modem into a digital line can damage the modem. Many hotels now have phones with a special jack on the side labeled *modem* or *data* in which you can safely plug your modem. If you're not sure whether a certain line is analog or digital, just ask. You can feel fairly confident that a phone line in a private home is safe. In an office, a phone line attached to a fax machine is also a good bet.

Setting up your Visor to use the modem

After you snap the modem into your Visor and plug in a suitable phone line, you're connected. Just tell your Visor the type of modem that you're attaching and then enter the settings for the kinds of things that you want to do.

International incidentals

Just like your hair dryer or your electric razor, the Visor Modem is designed to be used in the United States and Canada. If you want to connect your Visor modem to telephone systems outside North America, you may need to buy adapters and make special arrangements because the telephone lines and electrical outlets outside North America sometimes don't work with American electronics. I know of one company, called Road Warriors, that specializes in supplying gear to people who travel with computers. Check out the company's Web site at www.warrior.com for details on equipment that enables you to hook up a computer in any country on Earth.

To set up your Visor to work with a Visor Modem, all you really need to do is plug your Visor into the modem. The factory settings on a new Visor enable it to run the Visor Modem quite nicely. If your Visor isn't factory-new, however, the settings may have been changed. To adjust the modem settings (or to make sure that your current settings are correct), follow these steps:

1. **Tap the Applications soft button.**

   The applications list appears, showing icons for all the programs installed on your Visor.

2. **Tap the Prefs icon.**

   The Preferences screen appears.

3. **Tap the pull-down menu in the upper-right corner of the screen.**

   The list of preferences categories appears.

4. **Tap Modem.**

   The Modem Preferences screen appears, as shown in Figure 13-1.

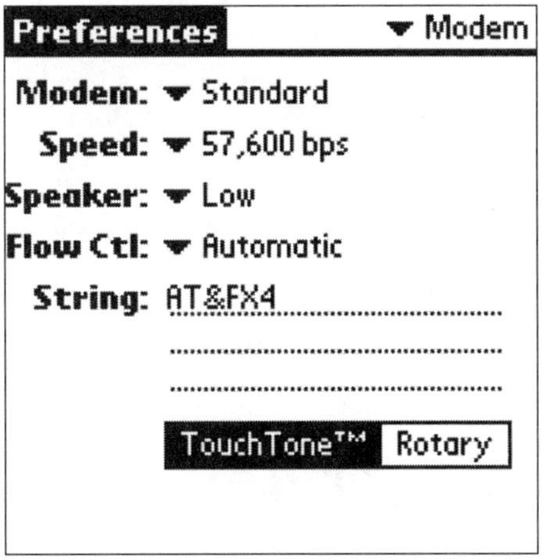

Figure 13-1:
To recon-
figure your
modem, go
to the
Modem
Preferences
screen.

```
Preferences          ▼ Modem
 Modem: ▼ Standard
  Speed: ▼ 57,600 bps
Speaker: ▼ Low
Flow Ctl: ▼ Automatic
 String: AT&FX4 ..............................
          ..............................
          ..............................
          [ TouchTone™  Rotary ]
```

5. **Tap the triangle next to Modem on the first line of the screen.**

   A list of modems that you can use with your Visor appears.

6. **Choose Standard.**

7. **Tap the triangle next to Speed on the second line of the screen.**

   A list of numbers appears, each representing a different modem speed.

8. **Choose 57,600.**

9. **Tap the triangle next to Speaker on the third line of the screen.**

   A choice of speaker volumes appears: Off, Low, Medium, or High.

   None of these settings makes the modem speaker obnoxiously loud, but if you absolutely can't stand the shrill sound of a modem making its connection, you can always turn it off.

10. **Choose the modem speaker volume that you prefer.**

11. **Tap the triangle next to Flow Ctl on the fourth line of the screen.**

    A list appears with the choices Automatic, On, and Off.

12. **Choose Automatic.**

13. **Choose the dialing method that you use for your telephone by tapping either TouchTone or Rotary at the bottom of the screen.**

    You know best which dialing method applies to your phone line. If you dial your phone with buttons, it's TouchTone. If you still have a dial on your phone, choose Rotary and call the Smithsonian. Your phone is a collector's item.

You can fiddle around with your modem settings a little bit without causing big problems in the way that it works, but be careful about changing too much. Modems have a way of getting fussy when you can't call someone for help, so after you get things working, leave the settings alone.

One item that you should definitely leave alone is the crazy characters on the String line, the ones that say something memorable like AT&FX4. That's a set of instructions that tells your modem how to do its work. If you change this string, you may mess up your modem. If you don't know what a modem setup string is, leave it alone.

Setting Up Your Visor for a Modem HotSync

One important purpose of the Handspring Modem is to enable you to HotSync your Visor with your desktop computer via a phone line. To successfully HotSync over the telephone, you need to set up your desktop computer as well as your Visor in advance.

You can't perform a Modem HotSync to a specific desktop computer until you've completed at least one local HotSync with that computer. Doing a local HotSync is important because the HotSync Manager asks you to assign a username to your Visor, and it creates a set of files and folders dedicated to your Visor. After you've completed a local HotSync, the HotSync Manager knows which Visor it's dealing with each time you press the HotSync button, and it knows where to store information about your particular Visor. If you haven't gone through the local HotSync process at least once, the HotSync Manager doesn't know what to do when it picks up the phone. For more on how to HotSync and set up your Visor Desktop program, see Chapter 11.

So, if you plan to take your Visor on your voyage to Venezuela and HotSync from there, you need to run a local HotSync before you go. Also, don't forget your passport and some sensible shoes.

Entering the Modem HotSync phone number

When you perform a Modem HotSync, your Visor calls your desktop computer on the phone and then runs the HotSync program. The most important information that you need to supply is the phone number that your desktop computer answers.

Follow these steps to enter the HotSync phone number:

1. **Tap the Applications soft button.**

   The applications list appears, showing icons for all the programs installed on your Visor.

2. **Tap the HotSync icon.**

   The HotSync screen appears. If you've never entered a HotSync phone number, the box below the Modem Sync icon says Enter Phone #; otherwise, the phone number that you've already entered appears there.

3. **Tap Enter Phone #.**

   The Phone Setup screen appears, as shown in Figure 13-2.

Figure 13-2: HotSync is smart, but you still need to tell it what phone number to call.

Phone Setup

Phone #: 555-5685

☐ **Dial prefix:** 9,
☐ **Disable call waiting:** 1170,
☐ **Use calling card:**

(OK) (Cancel)

4. **Enter the phone number connected to which your desktop computer, by using either the on-screen keyboard or Graffiti (see Chapter 2 for more on entering text).**

   The number that you enter appears on the Phone # line.

5. **If your phone system requires you to dial a prefix before making a call, tap the Dial Prefix check box and enter the prefix.**

   Some offices and hotels require you to dial an 8 or a 9 before making an outside call.

6. **If you're using a calling card, tap the Use Calling Card check box and enter your calling card on the line after the four commas.**

   The four commas make the modem wait a few seconds before dialing the calling card number, just like you do when you dial the calling card number yourself.

7. **Tap OK.**

Disabling call waiting

I don't understand why call waiting is so popular; I hate when people interrupt my phone conversations. Half the time the people interrupting my calls are selling products that I don't want.

Computers hate being interrupted by call waiting even more than I do. They often do crazy things when the little call-waiting beep sounds, but they never buy things from telemarketers. Fortunately, you can program your Visor so that it disables call waiting before beginning a HotSync. Sadly, your Visor can't do much about the telemarketers. Follow these steps just once to tell your Visor to turn off call waiting:

1. **Tap the Applications soft button.**

   The applications list appears, showing icons for all the programs installed on your Visor.

2. **Tap the HotSync icon.**

   The HotSync screen appears. The box below the Modem Sync icon displays either `Enter Phone #` or the last phone number that you entered.

3. **Tap the box below the Modem Sync icon.**

   The Phone Setup dialog box opens.

4. **Tap the box next to Disable Call Waiting.**

   A check mark appears in the box to indicate that you selected it.

To the right of Disable Call Waiting is the number 1170, which is usually the code that you dial to turn off call waiting. If the number used to turn off call waiting in your area is different, select the number that appears on-screen and then enter the number that does the trick in your locale.

5. **Tap OK.**

The Phone Setup dialog box closes.

Setting up Palm Desktop for a Modem HotSync

Doing a HotSync over the telephone has the same result as running a HotSync directly from your desktop computer: It makes the contents of your Visor identical to the contents of your Palm Desktop. If you have e-mail messages on your desktop computer, copies of those messages are transferred to your Visor.

When your Visor performs a Modem HotSync, it dials the phone number of your desktop computer. Your desktop computer then has to answer the phone when the Visor calls. In order to be able to answer that call, your desktop computer must

✔ Have a modem.

✔ Be connected to a phone line.

✔ Be running when you call.

✔ Not be running any other communications program.

✔ Be configured to accept your call.

After that, it's easy! Because there are so many types of computers out there, I can't tell you how to configure yours to accept your call. Refer to your owner's manual for that. But here's how to configure your computer to wait for your Modem HotSync call:

1. **Start Palm Desktop.**

2. **Choose HotSync▷Setup.**

The Setup dialog box opens.

3. **Click the Modem tab.**

The modem settings page appears, as shown in Figure 13-3.

Figure 13-3:
Use the
Modem tab
to tell the
HotSync
Manager
where your
modem is
installed so
that it can
answer the
phone.

4. In the Serial Port list, choose the port assigned to your modem.

You can check which port your modem uses in Windows 95 or 98 by clicking the Start button, choosing Setting⇨Control Panel, and then double-clicking the Modems icon. After the Modems dialog box opens, click the Properties button. The properties page tells you which port your modem uses. The ports are named COM1 through COM4.

5. In the Speed box, choose As Fast As Possible.

I don't know why you'd want to pick anything else. The speed that you choose appears in the Speed box.

6. In the Modem box, choose the type of modem that you're using.

You can check what type of modem you're using in Windows 95 in the Control Panel, just like you checked the port in Step 4. If in doubt, Hayes Standard should work. The modem that you choose appears in the Modem box. The setup string for the modem that you pick automatically appears in the Setup String box. The setup string is the series of commands that your modem uses to configure itself, so don't mess with it.

7. Click OK.

The Setup dialog box closes.

8. Right-click the HotSync Manager icon in the taskbar.

The HotSync Manager icon is the little circle in the lower-right corner of your screen containing a red arrow and a blue arrow pointing in opposite directions. When you right-click the icon, the HotSync Manager pop-up menu appears.

9. If no check mark appears next to Modem, then click Modem.

A check mark appears next to Modem, as shown in Figure 13-4, and then the menu disappears.

Figure 13-4:
Use the
pop-up
menu to tell
the HotSync
Manager to
answer the
phone.

Now just leave your computer on and go your merry way.

The Modem HotSync trick is best for people who call phone numbers that are totally dedicated to taking calls from computers, like the phone numbers that many corporations have. If you need to HotSync by modem frequently, you may want to consider getting an extra phone line.

So, why bother doing a Modem HotSync at all? Because doing a HotSync, anytime, anywhere, backs up your data. After you're completely addicted to your Visor (admit it, you're hooked already), you depend on the collection of information that you've amassed. If your Visor falls from a gondola or gets rammed by a rhino in the course of your adventures, you can replace the Visor with a wave of your credit card; but you could lose months trying to recreate the data.

Using Visor on the Internet

With the Handspring Modem, you can connect to the Internet and do two of the things that make the Internet so popular: exchange e-mail and browse the Web. I won't pretend that the little Visor navigates the Internet as easily or impressively as your mighty desktop computer; the tiny gray screen shows you only so much. But like someone once said about a talking dog, no matter how well the trick is done, it's amazing to see it done at all.

You need some extra software to be able to exchange e-mail messages or browse Web pages, but the foundations are already on your Visor to enable you to access the Internet and take advantage of what it offers. The Visor includes something called TCP/IP, which is the language spoken by all computers connected to the Internet. You never actually see TCP/IP, but if you try to connect a computer to the Internet without TCP/IP, nothing happens.

Setting up your Internet connection

Before you do anything on the Internet, you need to get connected. You'll need something called an *ISP,* or Internet service provider. An ISP is a company like Netcom or CompuServe that gives you a phone number that you dial to connect to the Internet. You may be able to use the same ISP that you use to connect your desktop computer to the Internet; just enter the same information in the Network Preferences program on your Visor, and you're on your way. Check with your ISP to see if you can connect your Visor to the Internet through your ISP's servers.

When you set up your Internet connection, you also need to set up your modem as I describe in "Setting up your Visor to use the modem," earlier in this chapter.

To set up your Visor to dial your ISP, follow these steps:

1. **Tap the Applications soft button.**

   The applications list appears, showing icons for all the programs installed on your Visor.

2. **Tap the Prefs icon.**

   The Preferences screen appears.

3. **Tap the pull-down menu in the upper-right corner of the screen.**

   The list of preferences categories appears.

4. **Tap Network.**

   The Network Preferences screen appears, as shown in Figure 13-5.

Figure 13-5:
Use the
Network
Preferences
screen to
tell your
Visor how to
connect to
the Internet.

5. **Tap the arrow next to Service.**

   Visor displays a list of the available ISPs for connecting your Visor.

6. **Tap the name of the ISP that you use.**

   If your ISP doesn't appear, tap the Menu button and chose Service➪
   New. The line for the name of the service goes blank, allowing you to
   enter the name of the service you want to.

7. **Enter the User Name.**

   If the User Name line is blank, just tap the line and enter your username.
   If temporary text appears on the User Name line, select the text and
   then enter your user name.

8. **Tap the box next to the word Password.**

   The Password dialog box opens, as shown in Figure 13-6.

Figure 13-6:
Enter your
Internet
password
in the
Password
dialog box.

Password
Enter a password:
rutabaga ....
If you do not assign a password, you will be asked for one when you connect.
(OK) (Cancel)

9. **Enter your password.**

10. **Tap OK.**

    The Password dialog box closes.

11. **Tap the box next to Phone.**

    The Phone Setup screen appears.

12. **Enter the phone number of your ISP.**

    The phone number that you enter appears on the Phone # line. You can
    also set up a dial prefix and a calling card number exactly the same way
    as I describe in the "Setting Up Your Visor for a Modem HotSync" section
    earlier in this chapter.

13. **Tap OK.**

    The Phone Setup screen closes.

After you set up your network preferences, you probably won't have to mess with them again except to change the ISP phone number when you're traveling. Of course, many ISPs have toll-free 800 numbers that you can use everywhere. So, you can travel anywhere in North America without changing the phone number.

The Connect button at the bottom of the Network Preferences screen actually makes the modem dial the phone number that you've entered and connects you to the Internet. You don't usually need to tap the Connect button because the e-mail program or the Web browser that you usually use starts up your connection automatically. In a pinch, though, you can return to the Network Preferences screen and tap Connect to force your Visor to connect to the Internet. After you're connected, that same button says Disconnect, so you can tap the Disconnect button to force your Visor to disconnect from the Internet.

Tapping the Details button opens a screen that shows some of the nitty-gritty details that your Visor needs to know to connect to the Internet. I can't think of any reason that you'd change those settings, so leave them alone.

Sending and receiving REAL e-mail

The Palm Mail program, which is pre-installed on every Visor, synchronizes e-mail with the e-mail program on your desktop computer. Unless a message has successfully arrived on your desktop, you can't synchronize it to your Visor.

This setup can be a problem if you plan to use your Visor to get your e-mail while you're on the road, because the HotSync Manager needs to hog your modem 24 hours a day. And if the HotSync Manager ties up your modem all the time while you're travelling, your desktop e-mail program can't dial out to get your messages. So for many people, the Modem HotSync feature keeps everything on their Visors current *except* their e-mail.

One solution to this problem is to set up your Visor to go right to the source and act like a real computer, getting real e-mail from the Internet. If you set up your Visor to connect to the Internet as I describe in the preceding section, you can use a program like HandMail or One-Touch Mail to go out to the Internet and pick up your messages.

Setting up a Visor Internet e-mail program

You can use several e-mail programs to send and receive e-mail through your Visor the same way that a conventional desktop e-mail system does. One option is to use MultiMail Pro, a commercial e-mail program. In this section, I show you how to use this particular program, but most e-mail programs require the same sort of setup routine. The details differ, but the general idea is the same: You need to tell the e-mail program which computer on the Internet holds your e-mail and what username and password enable you to access your mail.

Before you set up an e-mail program to get your messages, you need to install the e-mail program itself. (See Chapter 12 for details on installing programs to your Visor.) You also need to know how your mail system assigns names to itself and to you. Check with your ISP's technical support people.

Of course, if you are a good little Net surfer, you wrote all that information down when you set up your desktop e-mail program, so you may not have to call your ISP. But if you're like me (and who wouldn't want to be like me?), you probably prefer to talk to those friendly people in the middle of nowhere who sit all day and answer phone calls from people like us. Ask 'em if they have a Visor, too! Who knows, you could make a new friend and exchange e-mail on your Visors. Hoo, boy! There's a big time!

Here's how to set up MultiMail Pro (or other program) to get e-mail:

1. **After you've installed the program, tap the Applications soft button.**

   The applications list appears, showing icons for all the programs installed on your Visor.

2. **Tap the icon for the new mail program.**

   The mail program screen appears. Figure 13-7 shows the screen for MultiMail.

Figure 13-7:
MultiMail is one of several e-mail programs that you can use to send and receive Internet e-mail with your Visor.

MMPro	▼ Server 1	▼ Inbox
Subject	Sender	Date
Greetings!	support...	7/23

(New) (Send) (Quick Sync) (Full Sync)

3. **Tap Menu.**

   The menu bar appears.

4. **Choose Options⇨Mail Server.**

   The Mail Server screen appears, as shown in Figure 13-8. Mail servers
   are the kinds of computers on the Internet that hold mail. Your e-mail
   program picks up mail from these computers.

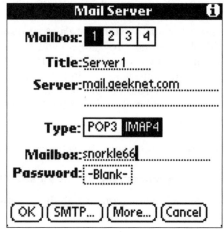

Figure 13-8:
Use the
Mail Server
screen to
tell your
e-mail
program
where to
deliver
your mail.

5. **Tap the number of the mailbox that you want to set up.**

   You can set up more than one mailbox in many e-mail programs.
   MultiMail enables you to set up four mailboxes. If you haven't set up any
   mailboxes yet, tap the number 1.

6. **Enter the name of your mail server on the Server line.**

   You can get this information from the tech support people at your ISP.
   And ask those nice people how the weather is wherever they are.

   If you don't want to wait on hold for an hour with your ISP, another way
   to get this information is to check the settings of your desktop e-mail
   program. Odds are, you entered the same information there that you
   have to enter here.

7. **Enter the name of your mailbox on the Mailbox line.**

   Your mailbox name is usually the part of your e-mail address that comes
   before the @ sign. For example, if your e-mail address is
   snorkle66@dive.com, your mailbox name is probably snorkle66. Check
   with your ISP to be sure.

8. **If** Blank **or** Unassigned **appears on the Password line, tap the text box and then enter your password.**

Again, your tech support gurus know all this stuff, so be nice to them and ask politely.

9. **Tap OK.**

If your tech support people say that's all you need, you're done. Some systems require other settings.

After you set up a mailbox, you're ready to go.

Sending and receiving Visor Internet e-mail

Your Visor isn't always connected to your phone line. Otherwise, you'd have to walk all over town with a really, really, really long phone cord dragging around behind you. You can create or read Visor e-mail anywhere, anytime, but to actually send the messages, you need to make sure that your Visor is plugged into the modem and that the modem is plugged into a phone line. Then give your e-mail program the command to send and receive messages. HandMail requires you to tap Menu, and then choose Mail⇨Send and Retrieve. MultiMail, another popular package, has a Send/Receive button on the main screen.

Browsing the Web

So you can't believe that you can surf the Internet on your Visor? Well, it's true. Granted, most Web sites look pretty poor on that teensy little screen, but you can find a lot of text on the Internet, too, and text looks fine on a little bitty screen.

Visor and AOL mail

As you know, America Online (AOL) is everywhere. As if we haven't seen enough about AOL on movies and TV, now you can even put it on your Visor. In general, AOL is a screaming pain in the neck when it comes to managing e-mail. Most of the terms that I've heard people use to describe AOL's mail system are unfit to put in print here. But sure enough, the AOL mail system is now available for viewing on your Visor. To find out more about exchanging AOL mail on your Visor, point your browser to www.aol.com/anywhere to see what AOL has to say about it.

Not only is reading your e-mail more convenient on a Visor than on a desktop computer, but you don't have to listen to that little troll say, "You've got mail!" That's a plus.

Of course, before you can surf the Web with your Visor, you need two things: an Internet connection and a Web browser. In "Setting up your Internet connection" earlier in this chapter, I show you how to connect to the Internet. You also need to get a Web browser and install it on your Visor.

The Visor Web browser I like best is called ProxiWeb. This program uses something called a *proxy server* along with the software you install on your Visor, which means that ProxiWeb shows you everything on the Web through its computer. ProxiWeb's computer interprets the pages that you request to make them look better on the Visor screen. Although this process makes the pages look better on your Visor, each page takes a while to appear on your screen. ProxiWeb manages to interpret some graphics, but fancy features that many advanced Web sites use, such as frames and animation, just disappear on a Visor Web browser. Visor-friendly Web browsers don't usually let you bookmark pages the way you do in a desktop Web browser. You can save the URL of a Web page by entering it in a list of favorite pages, but you can't really capture the address easily.

Visor Web browsing is very primitive at this point, but I expect rapid progress in the near future.

Sending a Fax with Your Visor

Why would you want to send a fax from a Visor? Because hundreds of millions of fax machines exist in the world. People who don't have e-mail often have a fax machine.

The best fax program for desktop computers is Winfax, from Symantec (www.symantec.com), so it's not surprising that the same company has developed the best fax program for your Visor. Symantec's Mobile Winfax for the Palm Computing Platform enables you to send plain-text faxes from your Visor. Or you can create a fully formatted fax on your desktop computer and send it from your Visor whenever you want, which is great for people who have standard faxable sales materials they like to send to anyone who asks.

Amazingly, the program also enables you to receive faxes on your Visor and view them on the spot. Bear in mind that most faxes are tough to view on that tiny Visor screen, although you can scroll up, down, and sideways to see the whole fax a little at a time. When you HotSync, the faxes you received on your Visor appear on your desktop computer, where they're easier to read and print. My hat's off to the folks at Symantec for putting so much power in such an itty-bitty package.

Part IV

Going "Outside the Box" with Your Visor

The 5th Wave   By Rich Tennant

"OH, WELL SHOOT! MUST BE THAT NEW PAINT PROGRAM ON MY HPC."

In this part . . .

The uses for Palm devices keep growing, and the limits of how you can utilize these functions to assist both your personal and work life are expanding. Read through this part for information on outlining programs, database creation and management, e-books, and career-specific programs.

Chapter 14

Outlining Your Big Ideas

*Y*ou may not think that your little Visor could help you manage big ideas. But remember, big ideas usually comprise many small parts. After you figure out how to keep the small parts straight, making the big ideas happen is a cinch.

Outliners are a popular type of program for the Visor that can help you organize and manage big ideas and all the small details that go into them. In this chapter, I show you how to use a typical outliner to get a handle on lots of details.

Deciding to Use an Outliner

You probably found out about outlines in grade school when old Mrs. Hoover kept telling you that you had to write an outline before you could write your report (and, yes, she really *did* have eyes in the back of her head). Well, Mrs. Hoover turned out to be right (no surprise there): A successful project starts with a well organized outline. Creating an outline helps you map out and keep on top of the essential tasks that need to happen for the project to finish on time. Take a look at the Table of Contents of this book, for example; it's an outline in disguise.

The text in an outline is arranged in a series of levels with lower levels being finer details of the level above them. The broadest idea is on the first level with subsequent levels supporting the top-level idea.

Here's an outline of the U.S government:

- ✔ **The Executive Branch**

    The president

- ✔ **The Legislative Branch**

    The Senate

    The House of Representatives

- ✔ **The Judicial Branch**

    The Supreme Court

    Federal circuit courts

And so on. The item on the top line either includes or depends on the items below. As you think of things that you need to support the top idea, you keep adding them until you have everything you think you need.

The advantage of writing an outline on your Visor is that you can easily change it as your thoughts progress — whenever and wherever that may be. Most people think as long as they're awake, so why throw away some of your best thinking time just because you don't have a computer nearby?

Picking an outliner

Several excellent outlining programs are available for the Visor. Each has its pluses and minuses, as the following list explains:

- ✔ **ThoughtMill** (www.handshigh.com) is the least expensive ($17.95) and most straightforward outlining program for the Palm platform. You can assemble a simple, multilevel outline, rearrange it by dragging items around the screen, and export it to the Memo Pad.

- ✔ **BrainForest** (www.aportis.com) is a bit more sophisticated than ThoughtMill. Priced at $30, it includes things such as due dates and allows you to number your outlines several different ways. BrainForest is probably best for people who need to manage tasks that are too detailed for the built-in To Do List that comes with the Visor.

✔ **InfoSelect** (www.miclog.com) for the Palm platform is an extension of a pretty slick information manager for the PC called InfoSelect. The Palm version of InfoSelect currently comes with a fairly hefty price tag of $69.95 (check the Web site for current pricing information). Although InfoSelect arranges the information you enter into outline format, the program also synchronizes your data to a powerful desktop program that can have some impressive features for managing large amounts of text information. If you do research, write books, or just need to keep a passel of information at your fingertips, InfoSelect can be a big help.

If you plan to do your outlining exclusively on your Visor, you're best off with BrainForest, ThoughtMill, or one of the other Palm-only outliners. If you're collecting data on your Visor and need to manage it on a desktop PC, InfoSelect is your best bet.

I use InfoSelect for all my examples because I believe that it's the most powerful tool available. The outlining features are also fairly similar to the other two organizers, so it's not a stretch to move from InfoSelect to one of the other outliners. Also, I confess: I've been a fan of InfoSelect for many years.

An outlining program helps you organize a series of items and tasks into a cohesive form. You can add, delete, prioritize, and change the order of the outline as your idea takes shape.

Creating a New Topic

Naturally, when you want to think big, you need to start with the big idea first. InfoSelect refers to the biggest ideas as Topics. You don't absolutely have to enter topics, but managing your outline is easier when you start with a topic and work your way down to individual tasks.

To create a new topic in your outline, follow these steps:

1. **Tap the item immediately above the spot where you want your new topic to appear.**

   The spot you tap is highlighted to show that you've selected it.

2. **Tap the New Topic icon at the bottom of the Visor Screen.**

   The New Topic icon looks like a little triangle with an asterisk on the left side. It's the third icon from the right at the bottom of the screen. When you tap the new topic icon, three objects appear: a triangle, a new line, and a blinking bar called the *insertion point* by Those Who Give Names to Computer Thingies (ahem . . . see Figure 14-1).

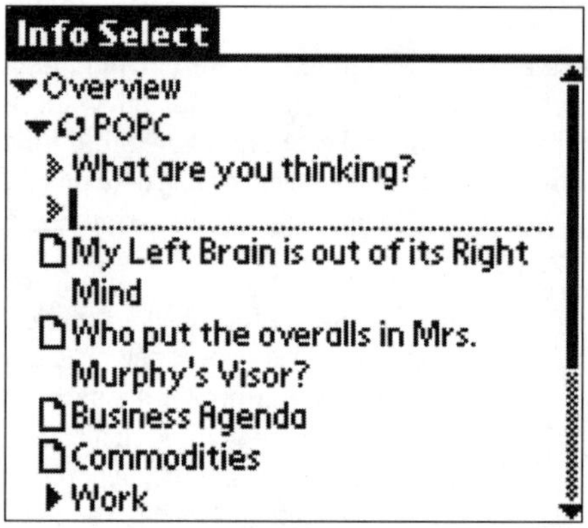

Info Select

▼Overview
 ▼○ POPC
  ▶ What are you thinking?
  ▶|.....................................
  ☐ My Left Brain is out of its Right
    Mind
  ☐ Who put the overalls in Mrs.
    Murphy's Visor?
  ☐ Business Agenda
  ☐ Commodities
  ▶ Work

Figure 14-1:
Pick a
name —
any name —
and assign it
to your note.

3. **Enter the name of your new topic with either the on-screen keyboard or Graffiti.**

   The name you enter appears on your new topic line. See Chapter 2 for more information about entering text.

4. **After you enter the name of your topic, tap any other part of the screen to exit the line.**

   Your new topic is now listed in the outline.

Expanding or Collapsing Topics

Every topic has a little triangle next to it. When the triangle is pointing at the name of the topic, then that topic *collapsed,* meaning subtopics may be hidden below it. You can reveal the hidden subtopics by tapping the triangle.

When you tap a triangle that's pointing sideways, it swivels to become a downward-pointing triangle and shows you everything in the topic (this magic act is called *expanding* the topic). If you tap the downward-pointing triangle next to an expanded topic, the topic collapses and hides its goodies. Think of the old church and steeple game.

If your topic is expanded, then the next item you enter becomes part of that topic. If you create a new item when your topic is collapsed, the new item is separate from your topic.

You can always make an item a part of your topic by dragging it and dropping the item on top of the name of the topic. Then the item you dragged becomes a sub-topic below the topic you dropped it upon.

Entering a New Note

Sometimes you need to enter more than one line of information about a topic. You might need to enter a whole paragraph, or several paragraphs. The place to put a longer piece of text in InfoSelect is called a *note*. A note is just like a topic, it just holds more information. Like a topic, a note has a one-line title, but you can enter more text in a different part of the note called the body.

To create a new note:

1. **Tap the item immediately above the spot where you want your new note to appear.**

   The spot you tap is highlighted to show that you've selected it.

2. **Tap the New Note icon at the bottom of the Visor Screen.**

   The New Note icon looks like a little box with an asterisk in the upper-right corner. It's the second icon from the right at the bottom of the screen. When you tap the New Note icon a new, blank line appears in the display.

3. **Enter the name of your Note with either the on-screen keyboard or Graffiti.**

   The name you enter appears on the new line (see Figure 14-2). See Chapter 2 for more information about entering text.

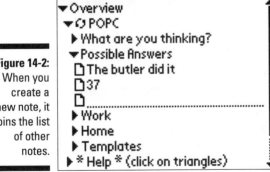

Figure 14-2: When you create a new note, it joins the list of other notes.

4. **If you want to enter text in your note, tap the Note icon at the left side of the screen.**

   The Note Edit screen appears.

5. **Enter the text of your note with either the on-screen keyboard or Graffiti.**

   The text you enter appears in the Note Edit screen.

6. **Tap Done.**

   The Note Edit screen closes and your outline appears.

Your note is only visible when the topic it's connected to is expanded. When you collapse a topic, all the notes connected to that topic are hidden until you expand the topic again. The ability to hide topics and notes allows you to stow away certain parts of your outline so that you can concentrate on others. Because the Visor screen is small, you should hide as much as possible so that you can see everything that you need to see.

Editing the Body of a Note

Notes have both a title and a body (as opposed to topics, which have only titles). When you want to take down a single sentence, you can save it as either a topic or as a note. But when you're saving a whole paragraph or more, only a note will do the trick.

I describe the process of entering the body text of the note in the previous section. But you may want to change the text in the body of a note from time to time. To do so, follow these steps:

1. **Tap the note icon next to the note that you want to edit.**

   The Edit Note screen appears.

2. **Enter the new text that you want to add with either the on-screen keyboard or Graffiti.**

   The text you enter appears, as shown in Figure 14-3. (For more information about entering text, see Chapter 2.)

3. **Tap Done.**

   Your note closes.

Unfortunately, the little icon next to a note doesn't tell you whether or not your note contains body text. You have to open each note to see whether text lurks inside.

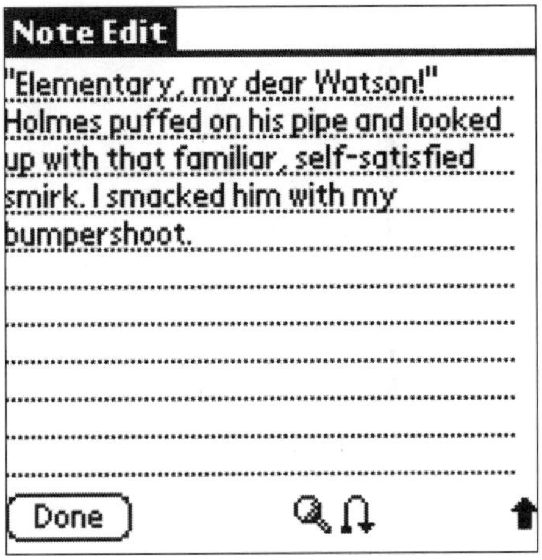

Note Edit

"Elementary, my dear Watson!"
Holmes puffed on his pipe and looked
up with that familiar, self-satisfied
smirk. I smacked him with my
bumpershoot.

Figure 14-3:
You can't
judge a note
by its title;
you have
to put
something
inside.

(Done)   🔍 ↩   ↑

Editing Captions

Seriously, the reason for paying attention to captions is so that you can find items more easily when you need them. A note about Shakespeare will be easier to find if you call it "Shakespeare" rather than if you call it "baboons." But if you start coming across an amazing study about baboons that read Shakespeare, you might want to change the caption to "Shakespearean baboons."

To change a caption, follow these steps:

1. **Tap the caption of the topic or note that you want to change.**

   The item that you tap is highlighted to show that you've selected it.

2. **Tap the same caption again.**

   The second time that you tap a caption, the highlighting disappears, and a blinking line (the *insertion point*) appears (see Figure 14-4).

3. **Enter the caption you want with either the on-screen keyboard or Graffiti (see Chapter 2 to find out about Graffiti).**

   The text you enter appears on the caption line.

4. **Tap any other part of the screen.**

Regardless of how you rename your outline items, it doesn't change what the meaning of the word "is" is. Sorry, Mr. President.

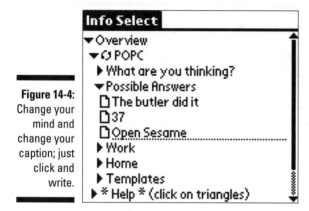

Figure 14-4:
Change your
mind and
change your
caption; just
click and
write.

Searching

Now for the *coup de grace,* the *raison d'etre,* the *mal a la tete,* (whatever you
call it), the whole reason you messed with this product in the first place. How
do you find stuff again after you store it so cleverly? But of course, *Messieurs
et Mesdames,* here is the secret:

1. **Tap the search icon at the bottom of the InfoSelect screen.**

   The InfoSelect search icon is the one above the Graffiti area, not the one
   to the right of it. When you tap the search icon the Search box appears,
   displaying the word "Matches" and a number (see Figure 14-5).

Figure 14-5:
Find what
you're
looking for
with the
InfoSelect
find tool.

2. **Enter the text that you want to search for with either the on-screen keyboard or Graffiti (see Chapter 2, "Going in Stylus," to improve your Graffiti expertise).**

   The text that you enter appears in the Search box. As you enter each letter, the number next to the word Matches changes. When you finish, the number of Matches tells you how many times the text that you want to find appears in your InfoSelect outline.

3. **Tap OK.**

   The screen scrolls to show the first occurrence of the text that you requested.

4. **If the first occurrence isn't the one that you want, tap the Search Again icon.**

   The Search Again icon is the U-turn-shaped arrow at the bottom of the display.

5. **Keep tapping the Search Again icon until the text that you want appears.**

Voila! Okay, so even if you can't pull a rabbit out of a hat, you can find a needle of text in the haystack of information you've stuffed into that tiny Visor.

Moving a Note or Topic

The reason for stashing information in InfoSelect is not merely to store the stuff, but to keep your treasure trove of trivia in some semblance of order. Because there's a place for everything, here's how to put everything in its place:

1. **Tap the note or topic that you want to move one time.**

   The note that you tap is highlighted to show that you've selected it.

2. **Tap the up or down icons at the bottom of the display.**

   The triangles in the bottom-left corner of the display are the up and down icons. The one that points up is the Up icon, and the one that points down — you guessed it — is the Down icon. Each time you tap a triangle, your item moves up or down one line.

3. **Keep tapping until your item resides where you want it.**

A far easier way to move items around the InfoSelect screen is to simply drag them where you want them. However, dragging items on the tiny Visor screen can be tricky because you can't always see where you dropped something off. You may want to tap the icons if you're trying to move an item to a place in the outline that's above or below the area visible on the screen (see Figure 14-6).

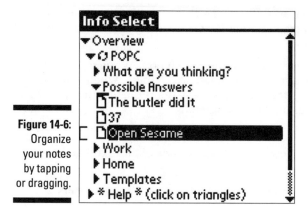

Figure 14-6:
Organize
your notes
by tapping
or dragging.

If you don't want to mess with dragging things around the little bitty Visor screen, you can always rearrange your collection of notes on your desktop version of InfoSelect and do a HotSync to make everything fall into place on your Visor. Sometimes it's easier to manage everything on the desktop computer because the screen is so much larger.

Deleting Notes or Topics

Alas, sometimes your garden of wisdom needs pruning. You can delete a single note or a topic full of notes. If you delete a topic containing a number of notes, the notes disappear along with the topic.

Here's how to cut back on your outline when the time comes:

1. **Tap the note or topic that you want to delete.**

   The item that you tap is highlighted to show that you've selected it.

2. **Tap the delete icon at the bottom of the display.**

   The Delete icon is the big X at the bottom of the screen. When you tap the Delete icon, the Delete Confirmation dialog box appears (see Figure 14-7).

Figure 14-7:
Is that
your final
answer? Be
sure before
you delete.

Delete Confirmation

(?) **Delete item?**

Yes   No

3. **Tap Yes.**

Another one bites the dust.

When you use InfoSelect on the Palm platform, you can see a topic named POPC, which means Palm Organizer PC. Everything under that topic is synchronized between your Visor and your PC. If you want some of your topics or notes to exist only on the Visor, move the topic to the line above POPC on the Visor, and you won't see it on the PC. Likewise, if you move items outside the POPC topic on your desktop computer, they won't show up on your Visor. That's a handy way to unclutter the collection of items you're carrying around on your Visor without discarding your data entirely.

Creating a New Template

Templates are shortcuts for entering information that you use frequently but that only change very little over time. For example, you might create a template for an agenda for a weekly staff meeting. To create a template, set up the meeting items in agenda form; then select the form as a template:

1. **Tap the note or topic that you want to use as a model for your template.**

The item that you tap is highlighted to show that you've selected it.

2. **Tap the Menu soft button and choose Misc⇨Add/Remove Template.**

A second icon appears next to your item, showing that it's a template (see Figure 14-8). The second icon looks like one box behind another box.

Figure 14-8:
When you turn an item into a template, you'll see two icons next to the name of the item.

After you designate an item to serve as a template, any changes you make appear every time you call up the template. You may want to store templates in a separate topic to distinguish them from regular items.

Using a Template

After you create a template, you recall it for use at any time by doing the following:

1. **With Info Select open, tap the Menu soft button.**

   The menu bar appears at the top of the display.

2. **Choose Misc➪Insert Template.**

   The Choose Template dialog box appears (see Figure 14-9).

Figure 14-9: All your templates are listed by name in the Choose Template dialog box.

Choose Template

Meeting Agenda
Passwords
Pricing
Decision

Cancel

3. **Tap the name of the template that you want to use.**

   A new item is created, modeled after your template.

You can change a template at any time by editing an existing template and following these instruction again.

Importing Items

If you've created a bunch of items in the other Visor programs and want to import them to InfoSelect, follow these steps:

1. **With Info Select open, tap the Menu soft button.**

   The menu bar appears at the top of the display.

2. **Choose Misc➪Import.**

   The Import dialog box appears.

3. Tap the scroll-down button (triangle) next to the words Import data
from **and select the source from which you want to import items.**

The source you select, either Memo Pad, To Do List, or Address List,
appears in the Import dialog box (see Figure 14-10).

Figure 14-10:
You can
import from
three of the
standard
Visor
programs
right on
your Visor.

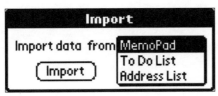

4. Tap Import.

Your imported items appear in the list.

InfoSelect has many advantages over the Memo Pad, such as the ability to
search and replace. There's also one disadvantage to using InfoSelect, you
can't just start writing text and have InfoSelect automatically figure out what
to do with the information; you have to tap either the New Topic icon or the
New Note icon before entering text.

Chapter 15

Database Basics

*T*he word *database* conjures up all sorts of negative images (is Big Brother watching?). But unless you believe in some sort of conspiracy theory, databases are generally harmless. The card catalog at your library is a database as are your phone book and shopping list. A database is a collection of related items organized in manner that allows you to retrieve and sort them. If you compile a Christmas list, what you've built is a database. If you buy all that stuff, the credit-card company compiles a list of your debt. Which brings us back to Big Brother. . . .

Your Visor Address Book is a database, as is the To Do List. In fact, your Visor came straight from the factory chock-full of databases. What if this plethora of information isn't enough? What if you want to keep other lists on your Visor, like favorite movies, shopping items or client contacts? The Palm platform has written many popular databases to satisfy all your information needs.

About Database Management Programs

Using a database is a little like making coffee. A coffeemaker without coffee is useless. Coffee without a coffeemaker is either useless or yucky. You need both parts to get a satisfying result. A Database Management Program is like the coffee maker. A database is like the coffee. Before you can view a database, you need to install a database management program. Here's a list of your choices:

✔ **HanDbase** (www.handbase.com)

✔ **Jfile, MobileDB, or TealInfo** (www.handango.com)

You can download free trial versions of nearly every database management program available for testing purposes. Follow the installation instructions in Chapter 12. I use HanDbase for all my examples because it happens to be my favorite. All of the database management programs have their virtues, but HanDbase makes it easy to create databases right on the Visor without using a desktop program at all. The manufacturer also offers a good set of easy-to-use desktop tools. But if you choose another program, that's okay too. After you get a feel for one program, finding your way around the others is straightforward.

While you're installing HanDbase, download a database of interest. You might want a ready-made database included with the database management program for practice. As an example in this chapter, I use a movie database called *AFI Top 100 Movies*, which comes with HanDbase. *AFI* is the American Film Institute, the people who know more about movies than most people would want to know. They're the kind of people who watch movies without even eating popcorn. Imagine!

Viewing a Database

Check out the Web site at www.memoware. It contains a huge selection of databases for your perusal. Each description includes the database (management) program you'll need to view that particular database. The current crop of database programs for the Visor can't usually read each other's files, so you might need to install more than one database program for reading different database files.

Run the HotSync program to install both the database and the database management program. If you only install a database without the program, the database won't appear on your Visor. Again, it's like coffee without a coffeemaker; yuck!

To view your database:

1. **Tap the HanDbase icon in the application picker.**

   The HanDbase program appears, displaying a list of available databases.

2. **Tap the name of one of the databases.**

   The contents of the database appear, as shown in figure 15-1. (If you're following my example, pick the *AFI Top 100 Movies* database.)

Figure 15-1:
You can
view movies
in the data-
base. Now,
that's enter-
tainment.

Upon opening a database, you can browse, search or enter new items. Every database is unique. Some include elaborate forms, fields and buttons that guide you through the entire process of using the database. Others leave you to muddle through on your own.

Currently, you can only view databases downloaded (or purchased) from the Internet. As I write this, there are no ready-made databases being offered on Springboard cartridges that you can pop into the back of your Visor. It's just a matter of time before cartridges appear on the market.

Finding an Item

Having a database on your Visor allows you to access information instantly anywhere you go. Now, party-related brawls will be a thing of the past because you know *Jaws* came out before *Taxi Driver*. Or did it?

Find out by searching through the downloaded movie database:

1. **Open the database you want to search.**

    The contents of the database appears. In this case, it's a list of movies.

2. **Tap the Find button at the bottom of the display.**

    The Search Database dialog box appears (see Figure 15-2).

Search Database

Search For: TAXI ....

☑ Search All Fields

☐ Case Sensitive
☐ Field Begins with...

(Go)   (Cancel)

Figure 15-2:
Looking for
a Taxi!
Search
here!

3. **Enter the name of the item you want to find using the on-screen keyboard or Graffiti (see Chapter 2 for more about entering text).**

   The name you enter appears on the line that says Search For.

4. **Tap Go.**

   The name you enter will be highlighted in the database list — if it's in the database (see Figure 15-3).

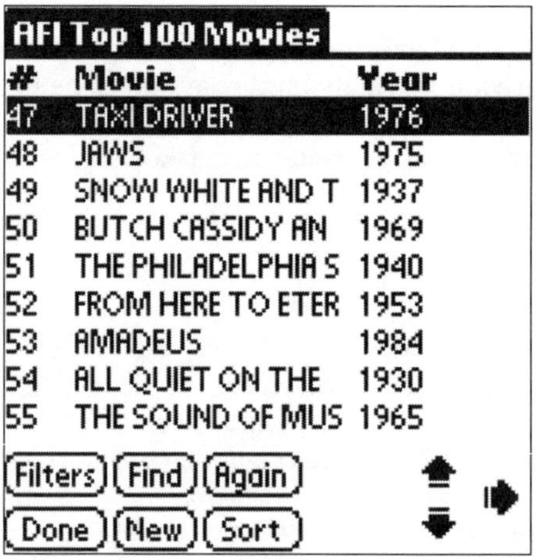

AFI Top 100 Movies

#	Movie	Year
47	TAXI DRIVER	1976
48	JAWS	1975
49	SNOW WHITE AND T	1937
50	BUTCH CASSIDY AN	1969
51	THE PHILADELPHIA S	1940
52	FROM HERE TO ETER	1953
53	AMADEUS	1984
54	ALL QUIET ON THE	1930
55	THE SOUND OF MUS	1965

(Filters)(Find)(Again)
(Done)(New)(Sort)

Figure 15-3:
Just when
you thought
it was safe
in your
pocket . . .
dum DUM
dum DUM!

WARNING!

Database searches can be a bit finicky because they're often case-sensitive. Searches won't locate words in uppercase when you've entered them in lowercase. The movie database, for example, has all the names in uppercase. If you enter *Taxi Driver* in lowercase, the database can't find it unless you uncheck the Case Sensitive box. There's no box that says, "You talkin' to me?"

Sorting a Database

Databases are great for sorting items. You're more likely to see patterns from a sorted list than a random spread of information. Using the AFI movie database, you can sort movies in descending order of popularity. If you're wondering "what was the best year for movies?," you sort the list by year:

1. **Open the database you want to sort.**

   The contents of the database appears.

2. **Tap the Sort button at the bottom of the display.**

   The Sorting screen appears (see Figure 15-4).

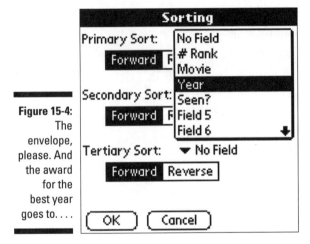

Figure 15-4:
The envelope, please. And the award for the best year goes to. . . .

3. **Pick the field that you want sort by next to the words Primary Sort.**

   In the AFI movie database, the # Rank field appears because that's how the list of movies are sorted. Tap the words # Rank and a drop-down list appears. Tap the word Year to sort the database by year.

4. **Tap OK.**

   The words Sorting Records appear for a second or two, then your database reappears, sorted by year.

And the winner is: 1939 with five top picks, including *Gone with the Wind* and *The Wizard of Oz*.

To get home:

1. **Click your heels together three times.**

2. **Enter** There's no place like home!

Filtering a Database

What if you only want to view specific items, without viewing a screen cluttered temporarily with unimportant ones? Applying a *filter* limits your view of items. If you just want a list of films made between 1970 and 1980, you can filter the AFI list as follows:

1. **Open the database you want to sort.**

   The contents of the database appears.

2. **Tap Filters.**

   The Edit Filters screen appears (see Figure 15-5).

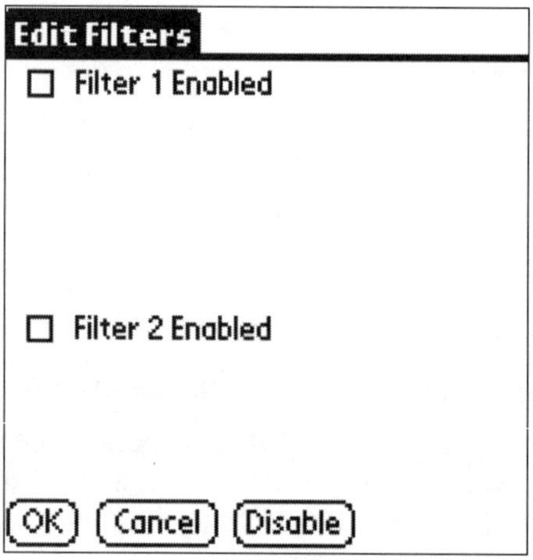

Edit Filters

☐ Filter 1 Enabled

☐ Filter 2 Enabled

(OK) (Cancel) (Disable)

Figure 15-5:
Filter out
the duds
and just see
the hits.

3. **Check the box next to the word Filter 1 enabled.**

   The text Select Field appears.

4. **Tap the scroll-down button (triangle) next to Select Field.**

   A list of fields that you can use as a filter appears (see Figure 15-6).

5. **Tap the name of the field that you want to use as a filter.**

   For this example, tap the Year field. When you do, the program will ask you to enter the criteria for your filter.

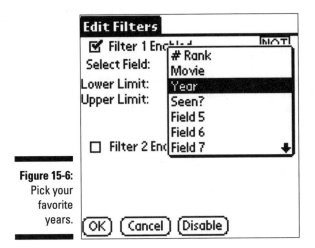

Edit Filters

☑ Filter 1 Enabled   NOT

Select Field:

Lower Limit:

Upper Limit:

☐ Filter 2 End

Rank
Movie
Year
Seen?
Field 5
Field 6
Field 7

(OK) (Cancel) (Disable)

Figure 15-6:
Pick your
favorite
years.

6. **Enter the criteria that you want for your filter.**

   In this example, HanDbase will ask you for a lower limit and an upper limit, so enter 1970 as the lower limit and 1980 as an upper limit.

7. **Tap OK.**

   Your database appears showing only the items that meet your criteria (see Figure 15-7).

AFI Top 100 Movies   Filtered

#	Movie	Year
3	THE GODFATHER	1972
15	STAR WARS	1977
19	CHINATOWN	1974
20	ONE FLEW OVER THE	1975
24	RAGING BULL	1980
28	APOCALYPSE NOW	1979
31	ANNIE HALL	1977
32	THE GODFATHER PA	1974
46	A CLOCKWORK ORA	1971

(Filters) (Find) (Again)

(Done) (New) (Sort)

Figure 15-7:
An offer
your
database
can't refuse.

Ah, the 1970s! Who can forget Rocky's Close Encounter with Annie Hall? Actually, I could, but HanDbase pulled all of 'em together in a jiffy.

You can filter a lot more than movies with a database. Any time you have a list that's too long to manage, filter out the unnecessary stuff so that you can concentrate on what's important.

The results of a filtered view depend on what's in the database. You can't filter for movies starring Barbra Streisand, for instance, because she's been excluded from the AFI list. Babs is very miffed about that. Snubbed again!

Create a New Database

Being portable, the Visor is useful for data collection work, making it unnecessary to write things on notebooks or scraps of paper to end up as pocket lint. This makes it ideal for business trips, for example, where you're collecting information on clients.

If you're creating a fairly simple database, you can probably do the job right on your Visor. By simple, I mean a single list of items with up to maybe five pieces of information per item. For databases bigger than this, consider creating the database on a desktop computer and converting it to load on your Visor (this is discussed later in this chapter).

To create a new database:

1. **Tap the New button at the bottom of the HanDbase screen.**

   The New Database screen appears (see Figure 15-8).

2. **Enter a name for your new database by using the on-screen keyboard or Graffiti.**

   The name you enter appears on the blank line in the dialog box.

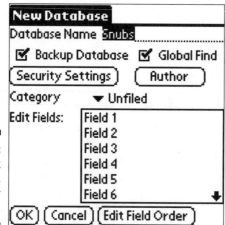

Figure 15-8:
Keep track of anything, no matter how petty.

3. **Tap Field 1.**

   The Edit Field 1 screen appears

4. **Enter the name of the first type of data that you'll want to store.**

   The name you entered appears on the first line. If you're creating a database of your favorite movies, you'll probably start with the title so enter the word **Title**.

5. **Tap the words Not-Used on the Field Type line and choose the type of information that you'll want to enter (see Figure 15-9).**

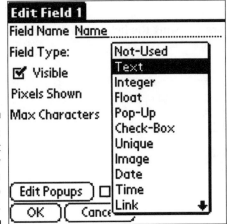

Figure 15-9:
Text is just one of many things you can keep track of.

HanDbase allows you to choose from over a dozen different types of data, including text, date, time, and integer. If in doubt, try text.

6. **Repeat Steps 4 and 5 until you've assigned all the fields that you'll want to use.**

   The names you enter appear on their respective lines on the screen.

7. **Tap Done.**

   The names you've given to the fields in your database appear at the top of the screen.

Some of the items you entered maybe hidden because the database runs off the right edge of the screen. Making the columns narrower allows you to fit more fields on the screen. To narrow a column, tap the Menu button and look for a command that says something about changing column widths.

Add New Items to Your Database

Now that you have a database, how do you add that newly released movie or the client you met last week? Start by looking at the fields in your database and make sure you have information to fill them all.

Add your new items as follows:

1. **Tap the name of the database.**

   The database you selected opens.

2. **Tap the New button.**

   A New Item form appears, showing the fields that you've created in your database (see Figure 15-10).

New Record   —

Snubbed By   Rip Rocknee

Date Snubbed   5/18/00

Personal?   ☑

Avenged   10/31/00

(OK)(Cancel)(Delete)(New)

Figure 15-10:
A short
database is
better than
a long
memory.

3. **Enter the data you want in the first field by using Graffiti or the on-screen keyboard.**

   The data you enter appears in the field you selected.

4. **Tap each field and enter the data that you want.**

   The data that you enter appears in the field you select.

5. **Repeat Steps 3 and 4 until all the data that you want is entered.**

   The data appears where you enter it.

6. **Tap OK.**

   Your new database appears with the new data.

You can view your database in the simple list form you see when the database first opens, or you can tap an individual line in the database to see the contents of that line(or record, as the database people like to say) in full detail.

Converting Desktop Data to Visor Format

Pop quiz: Do you want a large database on your Visor, but the data is larger than a short memo? Is the database so huge you have visions stylus-entry-related hand cramps? What should you do?

Answer: Create a desktop database and convert it for installation onto your Visor (unless, of course, you're the world's fastest Graffiti writer with a lot of spare time). You can install the database like any other Visor program. You can do the same thing if you want to copy data from the Internet or another source, and transfer it to your handheld.

Now I'm going to go out on a limb. Nine out of ten Visor users will never build a database using their desktop, and then download it to their Visor. If you're one of those nine, you can just skip the rest of this chapter and enjoy the cartoons later in the book. If you're that one out of ten:

1. **Choose File⇨Save As.**

   The Save As dialog box appears.

2. **Type a name for your file.**

   The name you type appears in the file name box.

3. **Click the scroll-down button (triangle) at the end of the Save As Type box.**

   The list of file types you can choose appears.

4. **Choose CSV from the list of file types.**

   The Save As Type box now says CSV (see Figure 15-11).

5. **Click Save (or press Enter).**

   Your file is now saved as a CSV file and is ready to be converted.

For more about saving files in Microsoft Excel or other Microsoft Office programs, see *Microsoft Office 2000 9 in 1 For Dummies* (published by IDG Books Worldwide, Inc.).

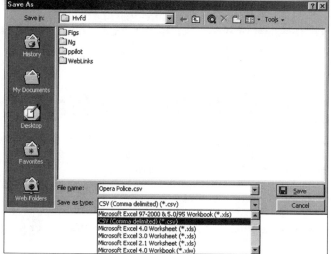

Figure 15-11:
Make CSV
your type
of file.

After you've created a CSV file, fire up the HanDdesk program and set up the CSV file for installation. Here's the routine:

1. **Start the HanDdesk program by finding and double-clicking the file called HanDdesk.exe.**

   If you have trouble locating the HanDdesk program, click the Start button in Windows, choose Find⇨Files or Folders, type **Handdesk.exe** and click Find Now. When HanDdesk appears in the box at the bottom of the Find dialog box, double-click it to start HanDdesk (see Figure 15-12).

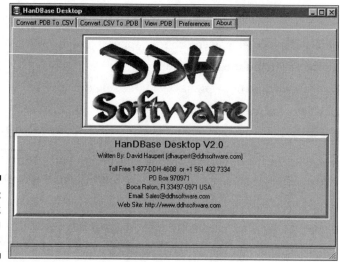

Figure 15-12:
HanDdesk
tabs tell you
what to do.

2. **Click the Convert .CSV to .PDB tab.**

   The Convert .CSV to .PDB page appears (see Figure 15-13).

Figure 15-13:
Open the
file you
just saved.

3. **Click the Browse button next to the Input File box.**

   The Open dialog box appears.

4. **Find and double-click the name of the file you want to convert.**

   The Open dialog box closes, and the name of the file that you double-clicked appears in the Input File box.

5. **Click the check box that says Automatically Install to User.**

   A check mark appears in the box.

6. **Choose your name from the list box next to the words Automatically Install to User.**

   Your name appears in the Automatically Install To User box.

7. **Click the Convert To PDB button at the bottom of the screen.**

   Your file is now converted.

The next time you Hotsync, the database will appear in the list of databases in HanDbase.

Convert HanDbase to Desktop Format

Another reason for keeping a database on your Visor is for collecting information. If you like to keep track of all the exotic butterflies you've seen on your travels or if you keep a record of something practical like how often you put gas in the car, you can record it all in a database, and then generate detailed reports on your desktop when you get home.

1. **Start the HanDdesk program.**

   If you have trouble locating the HanDdesk program, click the Start button in Windows, choose Find➪Files or Folders, type **Handdesk.exe** and click Find Now. When HanDdesk appears in the box at the bottom of the Find dialog box, double-click it to start HanDdesk.

2. **Click the Convert .PDB to .CSV tab.**

   The Convert .PDB to .CSV page appears (see Figure 15-14).

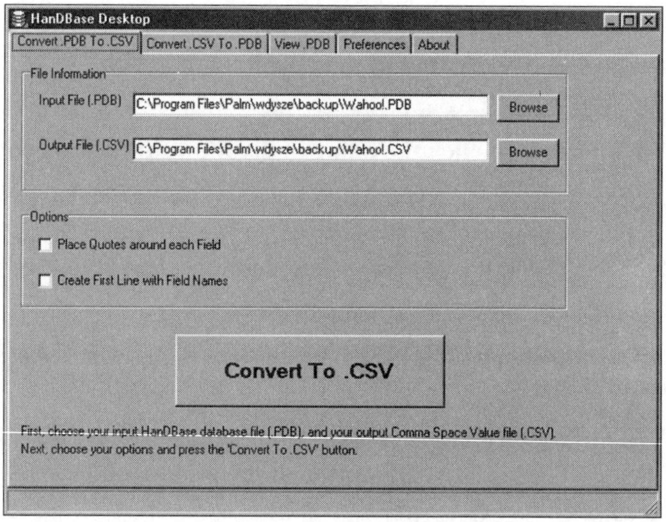

Figure 15-14: PDB files are the Visor version of your database.

HanDBase Desktop
Convert .PDB To .CSV | Convert .CSV To .PDB | View .PDB | Preferences | About
File Information
Input File (.PDB) C:\Program Files\Palm\wdysze\backup\Wahool.PDB   [Browse]
Output File (.CSV) C:\Program Files\Palm\wdysze\backup\Wahool.CSV   [Browse]
Options
☐ Place Quotes around each Field
☐ Create First Line with Field Names
Convert To .CSV
First, choose your input HanDBase database file (.PDB), and your output Comma Space Value file (.CSV). Next, choose your options and press the 'Convert To .CSV' button.

3. **Click the Browse button next to the Input File box.**

   The Select a HanDbase Database File dialog box appears.

4. **Choose your username from the Select a User box.**

   Your username appears in the Select a User box, and the names of all the HanDbase database files that you have on your Visor appear in the list at the bottom of the dialog box (see Figure 15-15).

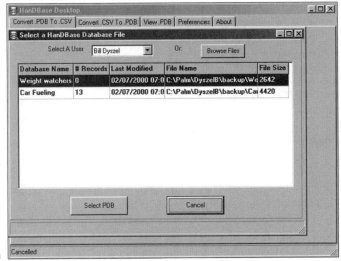

Figure 15-15:
HanDbase
knows what
you've been
watching.

5. Double-click the name of the database you want to convert.

The name of the database that you double-clicked appears in the Input File text box.

6. Click the Convert to .CSV button.

Your file is converted to CSV format.

If you're using Microsoft Excel to manage, you can open the CSV file in Excel and go to work. Excel can open and read a CSV file without making a fuss, and so can most other current spreadsheet programs.

Now that you have a database to retrieve all the facts about the movie *Titanic*, you've probably guessed that I've barely scratched the tip of the iceberg on this subject. Installing database programs on your Visor allows you to travel around with all your essential information.

Chapter 16

A Library in Your Pocket — Visor E-Books

*T*his one short chapter holds the key to all human knowledge.

Truth or fantasy? After reading this chapter, you be the judge.

Soothsayers are predicting that the new wave of handheld technology will replace old-fashioned paperbacks with electronic pulp novels. Because you already have a Visor, you can try out the newest trend today. You didn't know you were on the cutting edge of technology, did you?

Visors give you access to e-books by the world's great geniuses. In some cases, unlimited access can be yours at absolutely no cost (void where prohibited)! You don't even have to send in Wheaties box tops and wait six months for a decoder ring!

Here are several options for getting e-books on your Visor:

▸ **Buy ready-made Springboard modules:** Visor e-books are available in small cartridges called *modules*. Just plug them in and read to your heart's content.

▸ **Download from the Internet:** You can download books onto your Visor from the Internet (follow the installation instructions outlined in Chapter 12). Free programs are available for famous public domain documents, such as the Bible and historical documents. In some cases, you download to your desktop computer and convert it to a Visor-friendly format before sending it. In other cases, you install a program for reading texts on your Visor.

✔ **Write your own book:** You can download a program specifically for writing your own book and admire your work whenever the mood strikes. There's nothing like seeing your own text in living black and green to really make your day.

In this chapter, I'll introduce you to the glorious world of e-books and e-texts for use on your Visor.

Using Store-Bought E-Books

Purchasing a Springboard module is the easiest way to read an e-book. The Springboard connector on the back of your Visor allows you to slide in the module and read without downloading any additional programs. Just pop a Springboard in your Visor the way you'd pop toast in a toaster, and start reading. Although book titles are currently limited, I expect publishers to offer e-books in module format in the near future.

Reading Springboard books

Installing a Peanut Press book from a Springboard module is so simple, you probably don't need these instructions:

1. **Slide your module into the slot on the back of the Visor until it clicks into place.**

   The first page of the reader program is displayed on your screen (see Figure 16-1).

Figure 16-1:
Spring right into an e-book by popping in the module.

ALMA'S GUY

by Bill Dyszel

pg 1

The slot is located on the backside of the Visor at the very top of the casing. You need to slide off the little plastic piece that covers the slot before you can install the module.

2. Read your book.

After reading, you can slide the module out of the Springboard slot, without worrying where you stopped. The program returns you to where you were last reading.

E-Book Options

Books that you buy on Springboard modules work exactly like the books you can download already from the Internet. The only difference between the two types of books is the way that you install them. You can install non-Springboard books just like you install any other piece of software on your Visor, through the Palm Install tool. See Chapter 11 to find out how to use the Palm Install tool. You can also beam books from one Visor to another. Yes, it's just like *Star Trek* (oh, spare me)! Beam yourself over to Chapter 9 for more about beaming.

Whether you're reading a book on a Springboard module or a regular e-book on your Visor, the next part of this chapter shows you how to get the most enjoyment from e-books on your Visor.

Navigating e-books

Moving through electronic books might be harder than flipping novel pages, but e-books have many navigating options.

Scrolling page by page

To scroll through the book, you can do one of the following:

- ✔ **Press the scroll buttons:** Use the up and down scroll buttons to page through the book
- ✔ **Tap the screen directly:** Tapping the bottom half of the screen advances the text one page. Tapping the top half of the display moves you back one page.

Jumping to a specific page

Let your stylus do the walking when you need to go to a specific page. It's faster than tap-tap-tapping your way through all those e-pages.

1. **With your reader program open, tap the Menu soft button.**

   The menu bar appears at the top of the display.

2. **Choose Go⇨Go To Page.**

   The Turn to Page dialog box appears. The number of the page you're currently reading also appears (see Figure 16-2).

Book	**Go**	Options
Find...		✓F
Find Again		✓L
Bookmarks...		✓M
Add Bookmark...		✓A
Annotations...		✓T
Add Annotation...		✓N
Go To Page...		**✓J**
Go To Chapter...		✓H
Go To Beginning		✓B
Go To End		✓E
Back		✓K

Figure 16-2: You can order any page you want right from the menu.

3. **Enter the desired page number with either by using the on-screen keyboard or Graffiti** (see Chapter 2, for more about entering text).

   The number you enter appears on the screen.

4. **Tap OK.**

   The new page appears on the screen.

Peanut Press numbers every tiny screen of text, so even middle-sized books run thousands of pages long. It takes more time to thumb through those pages, but you feel very well read when you're through.

The Peanut Reader gauges how far you've read with a little "gas meter" icon in the lower right corner of the screen. If you want to zoom forward or backward, tap the icon to view a larger meter. Dragging your stylus along the face of the bigger meter permits you to zip through hundreds of pages.

Jumping to a specific chapter

Do you like to read the last page of a mystery novel to see who done it? Cheater! Now, you can do the same thing, electronically:

1. **With your reader program open, tap the Menu soft button.**

   The menu bar appears at the top of the display.

2. **Choose Go⇨Go To Chapter.**

   The book's Table of Contents appears (see Figure 16-3).

Figure 16-3:
Your table of contents gives a preview of the next exciting chapters.

3. **Tap the name of the chapter you want to read.**

   The chapter you tap is highlighted to show that you've selected it.

4. **Tap Go.**

   The chapter you selected appears on the screen.

What do you know? The butler did it.

Annotating

An *annotation* allows you to record notes or comments in an electronic book, just as you might scribble notes in the margin of a paperback.

Adding an annotation

1. **With your reader program open, tap the Menu soft button.**

   The menu bar appears at the top of the display.

2. **Choose Go⇨Add Annotation.**

   The Annotation screen appears (see Figure 16-4).

Annotation Name:

Dyszel's last theorem

Annotation:

I have discovered a truly
remarkable proof of this
theorem, but my batteries are
running out.

(Done)(Go to page)(Delete)   ↑

Figure 16-4:
Add your
own
e-thoughts
to your
e-book by
adding
annotations.
Then let
your
descendants
make sense
of them.

3. **Enter your annotation with either the on-screen keyboard or Graffiti** (see Chapter 2, "Going in Stylus," for more about entering text).

Your comments appear in the annotation screen.

4. **Tap Done.**

The annotation screen closes. A tiny square appears at the bottom of the Visor screen indicating annotation.

Viewing an annotation

After entering annotations in your books, you want to read them again, unless you're entering them for archeologists to see when they dig up your Visor in a million years. Will they mistake your annotated *Star Trek* book for a commentary on society in the 21st century?

1. **With your reader program open, tap the Menu soft button.**

The menu bar appears at the top of the display.

2. **Choose Go⇨Annotations.**

The Annotation list appears (see Figure 16-5).

3. **Tap the name of the annotation you want to view.**

The annotation you tap is highlighted to show that you've selected it.

4. **Tap View.**

The annotation you selected appears.

For a quick peek at that annotation, tap the little square that appears at the bottom of the screen. Changes can be made no matter which method you use to open them.

Figure 16-5:
Record
every
brilliant
insight as an
annotation.

Bookmarking

Let's see, where were you? You can't remember what passage you were reading because searching for Aunt Jane's misplaced purse has driven all logical thought from your head. *Bookmarking* saves your place electronically no matter what the family crisis. Now if you could only find your Visor. . . .

Adding a bookmark

If you've ever stuffed a matchbook or sticky note in your novel to return to a specific passage, you know why you need bookmarks. Fortunately, you can enter as many bookmarks as you want in an electronic book, and they never fall out.

1. **With your reader program open, tap the Menu soft button.**

   The menu bar appears at the top of the display.

2. **Choose Go⇨Add Bookmark.**

   The Bookmark screen appears (see Figure 16-6). The Bookmark screen displays "Bookmark – pg" and the current page number. If you enter a different bookmark name with either the on-screen keyboard or Graffiti, the name you enter will become the bookmark name.

3. **Tap OK.**

   The bookmark screen closes, and a box appears around the page with a little dog-eared corner to show that the page is bookmarked. Isn't that cute!

specific meaning to our people; a
Haydn symphony meant one thing, a
Beethoven sonata meant another, and
so on."
"I had no idea. What did each selection
mean?"
"It varied over time. We changed the
meaning regularly. Sometimes it

Bookmark Name:

Bookmark - pg 122

(OK) (Cancel)   ↑

Figure 16-6:
Mark your
favorite
pages with
bookmarks.

An even quicker way to bookmark a page you're reading is to tap the upper-right corner of the screen where the little "dog-ear" symbol appears. The bookmark screen pops up, and you can name your bookmark right then and there.

Jumping to a bookmark

Why did Hansel and Gretel drop all those breadcrumbs? To find their way back home. You can do the same with bookmarks. Fortunately, bookmarks aren't edible, so you'll always find them again.

1. **With your reader program open, tap the Menu soft button.**

   The menu bar appears at the top of the display.

2. **Choose Go⇨Bookmarks.**

   The Bookmark list appears (see Figure 16-7).

3. **Tap the name of the bookmark you want to see.**

   The bookmark you tap is highlighted to show that you've selected it.

4. **Tap Go.**

   The bookmarked page you selected appears.

Giving each bookmark a unique name isn't necessary, unless you mark your place often and need to distinguish between bookmarks. Naming a bookmark "The secret formula" lets you know why you marked the passage.

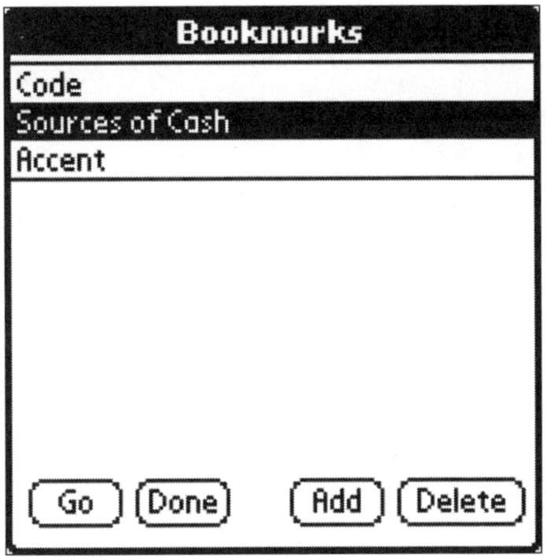

Bookmarks

Code

Sources of Cash

Accent

(Go) (Done)   (Add) (Delete)

Figure 16-7:
Find your
bookmark in
two taps.

Finding text

You can find tidbits of text without hunting page by page in an e-book. Reader programs like Peanut Reader usually include a Find tool for locating key words. Here's how you find a text string:

1. **With your reader program open, tap the Menu soft button.**

   The menu bar appears at the top of the display.

2. **Choose Go⇨Find.**

   The Find Text dialog box appears (see Figure 16-8).

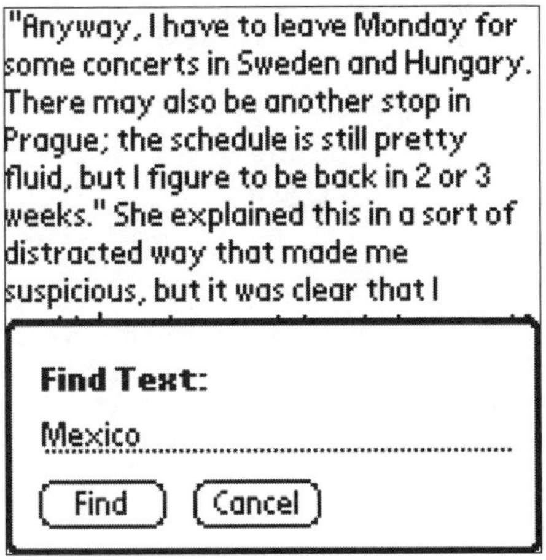

"Anyway, I have to leave Monday for some concerts in Sweden and Hungary. There may also be another stop in Prague; the schedule is still pretty fluid, but I figure to be back in 2 or 3 weeks." She explained this in a sort of distracted way that made me suspicious, but it was clear that I

Find Text:

Mexico

(Find)   (Cancel)

Figure 16-8:
Find the
word like
magic with
the Find
tool. Poof!

3. **Enter the text you want to find with either the on-screen keyboard or Graffiti** (see Chapter 2 for more about entering text).

   The text you enter appears in the Find screen.

4. **Tap Find.**

   The Find Warning screen appears, showing you that the program is finding something. (Duh!)

   The page containing the text you requested appears.

The regular Visor find tool doesn't locate text in a Peanut book. You must to use the Peanut Reader's Find command. If the first occurrence of the word you enter isn't the one that you want, tap the menu button and choose Go⇨Find Again to see the next instance of the word you want.

Finding E-Books and Free-Books on the Web

Because handhelds are a new technology, not many module book titles are available for purchase. This comes as discouraging news to Visor fans, given that modules require no software installation. Until production can keep up with technology, you're limited to downloading the vast majority of e-books with a reader program. The program decodes the e-book format, which squishes the book to fit on the Visor.

Web sites with Doc readers

Not sure where to get a Doc reader for your downloaded Doc files? Here are some options. Doc reader programs range in price from free (CspotRun) to about $30 (Aportis Doc). I prefer iSilo, but all have advantages and disadvantages:

✔ **iSilo** (www.isilo.com)

✔ **Aportis Doc** (www.aportis.com)

✔ **QED** (www.visionary.com)

✔ **TealDoc** (www.tealpoint.com)

✔ **SmartDoc** (www.onetap.com)

✔ **CspotRun** (http://32768.com/cspotrun)

Because new Doc reader programs crop up every few months, you might consider trying different ones until you find the one that suits your needs the best.

There are several options for downloading e-books and readers:

- **Go to Peanut Press Web site** (www.peanutpress.com): You might pay for the books, but the Peanut Reader is free (follow the installation instructions outlined in Chapter 12).

- **Download free Docs files** (www.memoware.com): Literally thousands of books can be downloaded on your Visor at no cost in the popular Doc format. Because the Doc format has been around longer than the Peanut format, you can download many books for free. Once again, you'll have to install a Doc reader to view the Doc files.

- **Project Gutenberg** (http://www.promo.net/pg): Like the song says, the best things in life are free, and so are many of the best books. Since 1971, the University of Illinois has been storing the world's greatest books in electronic form. The archive, named after Johannes Gutenberg, the inventor of the printing press, contains more than 3,300 books and includes every subject from Hans Christian Andersen to Zorba the Greek (see Figure 16-9). The books are all stored in plain-vanilla text files, which you can open in Microsoft Word and convert to Doc format the way I describe earlier in this chapter. Before you go to the trouble of converting Project Gutenberg texts, though, take a look at www.memoware.com, where many of those texts have already been converted to Doc format to save you the trouble.

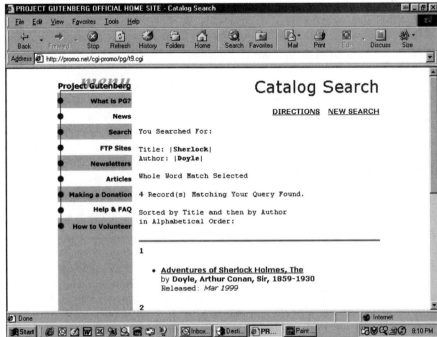

Figure 16-9: You were looking for the key to all human knowledge. It's been here all along.

You can't read Doc files with the Peanut Reader. Likewise, the Doc reader won't read Peanut files. Having both the readers on your Visor presents no problems, so I suggest downloading one of each.

If you need to add a short note for reference (say under 4,000 characters), create a Memo and save it in your Visor Memo pad. Save the Doc format for items that won't fit in a memo (like *War and Peace*).

Creating Your Own E-Books

Several options exist for creating your own literary work:

- ✔ **Create your own books in e-book format:** Free programs are available to crunch regular files down to Peanut Reader's size and style.

- ✔ **Turn any electronic text into a Doc file:** You can carry Doc files everywhere you go. Many of the popular Doc reader programs have an accompanying program for converting regular text files from your computer to the Doc format. Each one works a little differently.

Frankly, I don't recommend creating a book in Peanut format. It's easier to create a book in the popular Doc format. You can create a Doc file with a little tool called PalmDocs. This program plugs itself into Microsoft Word and turns an opened Word document into a Doc file. It also sets it up for Visor installation . You can purchase it at `http://store.yahoo.com/pilotgearsw/allorpiz.html` for $19.95. As long as you can open a document in Word, you can create Doc files with PalmDocs.

If you're not sure about opening files in Word, see the Microsoft Word section of *Microsoft Office 9 in 1 For Dummies* (published by IDG Books Worldwide, Inc.).

To convert a document in Microsoft Word to the Doc format:

1. **Open the document you want in Microsoft Word, after installing PalmDocs.**

   The document you open appears on the screen.

2. **Choose PalmDocs⇨Save PDB and Install from the Menu bar.**

   The Save and Install PDB dialog box appears.

3. **Click the text box labeled "PalmDoc Name" and type a name for your Doc file (see Figure 16-10).**

   The name you type appears in the text box. This will be the name that appears when you look for the document on your Visor.

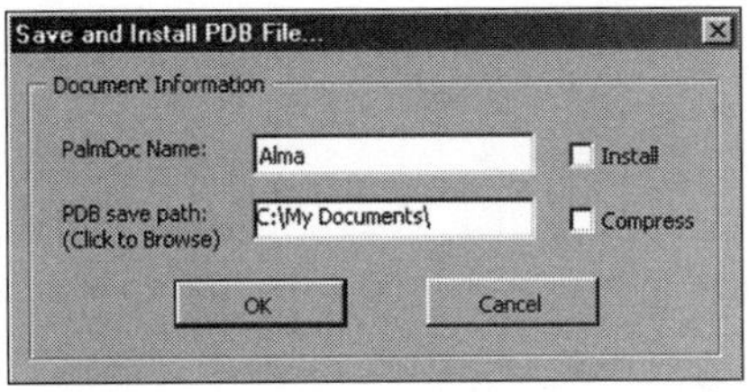

Figure 16-10:
What you
see is what
you get
when you
convert
from Word
to Doc.

Save and Install PDB File...

Document Information

PalmDoc Name: | Alma | ☐ Install

PDB save path: | C:\My Documents\ | ☐ Compress
(Click to Browse)

OK | Cancel

4. Click the check box labeled "Install."

An Install section appears at the bottom of the Save and Install PDB dialog box. Your username should appear in the Install section. If not, choose it from the drop-down list.

5. Click OK.

The Save and Install PDB dialog box closes, and a new box appears saying that your file will be installed the next time you perform a Hotsync.

If you don't want to pay $19.95 for PalmDocs, you can always download a free converter program called Make Doc Windows from http://ourworld. compuserve.com/homepages/Mark_Pierce. You need to fiddle around with the program a bit to do your conversions, but the price is right. There is also a variety of Doc converters for people who use other kinds of computers, such as Mac, Linux, and Amiga. You can find those converters at www.handango.com.

Don't be confused by the fact that Microsoft Word documents all have names ending in .DOC. The Doc files you use on your Visor are different beasts altogether, so you still need to convert from Word's .DOC files to the Visor's Doc format.

Chapter 17

Visor Software by Profession

. . . .

In This Chapter

▶ Finding software to help with your vocation

▶ Sneaking in some software to help with an avocation or two

. . . .

*N*early anyone who can get out of bed in the morning can find some use for a Visor. As long as you need to keep track of people, tasks, or ideas, you can take advantage of the software that's available for PalmPilots and Visors. In this chapter, I list specific professions that can benefit from specially designed Palm software. I know some professionals, however, who rely on their Palm computers without any extra software; a rabbi in New Jersey, actors in Hollywood, and farmers in Mississippi all get something special from the little computers in their pockets.

I apologize if I leave out your profession, but if I do, you can search for Palm and Visor software by checking the list of Web sites and other resources in Appendix A at the back of this book. Several products mentioned here require you to install a product called Jfile first. For more about Jfile, see the manufacturer's Web site at www.land-j.com. The program costs $19.95 to register. You can also use a competing database called MobileDB from Mobile Generation Software at www.mobilegeneration.com.

Some of the software listed in this chapter is free. Some titles are offered as *shareware,* which means that the people who created the program rely on your honor to send in a donation in exchange for the product. Some programs are demos, which work for free for a limited time, and then you have to buy a copy. Quite a few of these programs are real, live, cash-on-the-barrelhead commercial software. I list prices and terms wherever possible, but you may want to check with the manufacturer to confirm the price and find out how to use the program.

Actor

"To be or not to be?" This is the question: If you need to perform a soliloquy from Shakespeare, do you know all the lines? If not, you can get the entire text of all the Bard's greatest hits at `www.memoware.com`. You'll also need a document reader such as iSilo to read your favorite hero's lines from your Visor.

Architect/Building Professional

Putting up a building means putting up with zillions of details. Punch List (`www.punchlist.com`) is a program that helps you track the details of large projects and make sure that everything is done on time and in order. Designed for professionals in the construction industry, Punch List synchronizes with your desktop PC and enables you to maintain lists of tasks that need to be done, along with the names of the people who are supposed to do them.

By using Punch List on your Visor, you collect information at the building site; then when you HotSync to your desktop, the desktop portion of Punch List automatically sends faxes to your subcontractors with task lists and notes about uncompleted tasks. Punch List is commercial software from Strata Systems that costs $179 for each user. You can reach the company by phone at 888-336-3652.

Association Executive

Are you ready to wield a gavel over testy membership meetings? You'll want a copy of *Robert's Rules of Order* on your Visor so that you can zip through your agenda, lickety-split. You can get a free copy of the book at `www.memoware.com`, and I'll second the motion.

Athletic Coach

When Vince Lombardi said, "Winning isn't everything, it's the only thing," nobody dared to say, "That's meaningless, Coach!" Would you? If you're a coach who wants to give your team meaningful information, get a copy of the Athlete's Calculator from Steven's Creek Software (`www.stevenscreek.com`). It's free for one-time use, but you need to pay $14.95 for the registered version. This program enables you to rattle off statistics about time, distance, and pace, and also perform calculations on the spot. Now you can demand 110 percent from your athletes and scream when you only get 109 percent.

Bartender

Every purveyor of potent potables needs a collection of recipes for popular concoctions. Drinks, shown in Figure 17-1, is a collection of 145 recipes for drinks, ranging from an Alabama Slammer to a Zombie. Because Drinks is a Jfile database, you need to install the Jfile program before taking advantage of your newfound repertoire. If you want to customize the collection, you can add recipes for beverages of your own invention. You can download Drinks from www.handango.com and use it for free.

Figure 17-1: When your customers want more than a shot and a beer, look up something more interesting in the Drinks list.

Database Item	◀▶
Name:	Oreo Cookie
Contents:	2 Oreo cookies, 1 oz Creme de Cacoa, 4 oz Vanilla ice cream
AddOns:	various
Type:	Blender
Glass:	various
Notes:	

(OK) (Cancel) (New) (Del)

Comedian

Everybody wants to get into the act, don't they? Stay one punchline ahead of the crowd by keeping an entire joke anthology on your Visor. The Palm Jester, available at www.handango.com, manages your entire collection of quips, jokes and one-liners. Laughs sold separately.

Couch Potato

I won't mention any names, but many people need help in the diet and exercise departments. DietLog from SoftCare Clinical Informatics (www.dietlog.com) is the most popular Visor program for munch-management. Research shows that nothing shocks you into good behavior faster than recalling just how badly you've eaten in the recent past. DietLog helps you track your food intake and set suitable diet goals for your age, sex, height, and weight. You can download a free trial copy of DietLog, which runs for 15 days. If you haven't given up on your diet by then, you can order the full-featured version for $59; just call 800-676-7793. I plan to start using DietLog . . . tomorrow.

Editor

Some people just can't stop themselves from changing what other people wrote. Hey, somebody has to do it, right! When you need to find just the right word, the TrueTerm Thesaurus can find it for you in a variety of languages. You probably want to run TrueTerm on a Visor Deluxe, because it takes up well over 1MB of space, which means it may be too big to fit on a regular 2MB Visor after you've put other stuff on it. You can find out more about TrueTerm at the developer's Web site, www.trueterm.com. It retails for $30.

Electrical Engineer

EE Toolkit can help electrical engineers perform many of the routine calculations involved in building electronic projects. It can calculate the resistance of resistors, the capacity of capacitors, and perform many other useful electronic tasks. You can even draw pictures on a built-in doodle pad. Hey! Even I can handle that! You can download a free, 14-day trial version from the designers' Web site at www.mindspring.com/~jgrand/eetoolkit.htm. If you haven't electrocuted yourself after two weeks, contact Pilot Gear HQ at www.pilotgear.com to buy the $20 high-powered version.

Lawyer

Perry Mason may have spent all his time orating in courtrooms, but real lawyers have to spend time keeping track of documents and tracking their billable hours. For the latest news about new Visor and PalmPilot products for the legal profession, see www.palmlaw.com.

One popular legal application is Amicus Attorney, which is part of a Practice Management system that's designed to help lawyers run their businesses and track their billings accurately on a desktop computer or office network. The program includes a link to your Visor so that you can document billable activities as you perform them. Unless you're the kind of lawyer who works for free, Amicus Attorney can help you stay on top of your business. Contact Gavel & Gown Software at www.amicus.ca.

Mafia Boss

Yeah, yeah, you know your rights! Whaddya, some kinda wise guy? Download the guide to U.S. Police Rights from `www.memoware.com` and carry it on your Visor, along with your machine gun and fake ID. You'll also need a Doc reader program like iSilo to read the thing. And no more wisecracks about cement shoes, okay?

Manager

PalmProject is a simple program that enables you to keep track of tasks that occur in sequence, as shown in Figure 17-2. If you're making a movie, for example, you need to write a script, then hire a director, then cast actors, then shoot the film, and so on. PalmProject enables you to enter up to 99 tasks, each of which can be linked to an earlier task. You can display lists of required resources and milestones and choose either a five-day workweek or a seven-day workweek. If you're a Microsoft Project user, you can also export projects from PalmProject and run them in Microsoft Project, which enables you to create elaborate flowcharts and reports. You can visit `www.pda-ware.com` for a free trial version of PalmProject, or buy the full-featured version for $19.95 at `www.pilotgear.com`.

Figure 17-2: Plan before you act! Good planning can give you a competitive edge.

PalmProject				
No. Task	Start	Dur.	End	Lnk
1 Buy Maps	7/30	1	7/31	0
2 Rent Elephant	7/30	2	8/3	0
3 Cross Alps	8/3	5	8/10	2
4 Beseige Rome	8/10	3	8/13	3
5 Return elepha	8/13	6	8/21	4

(New) (Details) (Done)

Minister

Yes, your Visor even has room for the Good Book. Bible Reader from www.olivetree.com can handle the entire King James Version — your Visor has room for 1.2MB of inspiration. Bible Reader is free, as is the King James Version, and you can buy other versions of the Bible from Olive Tree for $14.95. You can also find devotional text from a variety of religions at the Handango.com Web site and around the Visor Web ring.

Molecular Biologist

OligoCalc is a tool for molecular biologists. According to the Handango.com archive, it's a "calculator for molecular biologists who have to deal with oligonucleotide synthesis and purification. You will get the most common physical characteristics of oligonucleotides — extinction coefficient, molecular weight, etc." Yeah, well, whatever that is, OligoCalc does it for free. Download a copy at www.handango.com.

Musician

Figure 17-3 shows my favorite Visor music program — MiniMusic Note Pad from 5thwall.com. The program enables you to write songs by either playing them on a tiny, on-screen piano keyboard or by entering notes on a regular music staff. After you enter your tune, you can play it back, edit, and save your work for the ages. Even if you're not a composer, MiniMusic is a great tool for learning tunes when you don't have someone around to pound out the notes on a piano. When you win your Grammy, remember me, okay?

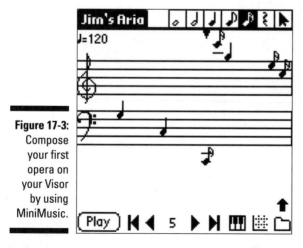

Figure 17-3:
Compose
your first
opera on
your Visor
by using
MiniMusic.

New York City Taxi Driver

Unlike nice, orderly cities, New York City's address numbering system is totally nonsensical. I could give you examples, but why bother when you can make sense of it all with NY CrossTown 1.5 from True North, Inc. (northisup.com). For $12 you can instantly look up the nearest cross street from any avenue address or find the nearest avenue to any street address. If you don't need NY CrossTown because you never visit the Big Apple (or you have a chauffeur), count your blessings.

Parent

Are your kids bugging you to buy a new puppy? Or are they just bugging you? Distract the little darlings with a DigiPet. DigiPet, shown in Figure 17-4, is the Visor version of those popular electronic pet keychains. Your little electronic beast has many of the charming qualities of a real pet, including the need to eat, get sick, demand your attention at all hours, and have "accidents." DigiPet is available in English and Japanese versions. The program was developed by Shuji Fukumoto and is available at www.handango.com. And best of all, it's free.

Figure 17-4: DigiPet can keep you busy for hours, whether you like it or not. Remember, parents, it's only a game. This DigiPet is friendly, but not the brightest beast.

Physician

More Visor medical programs are available than you can shake a scalpel at. To keep up with the latest developments in Palm and Visor programs for physicians, check out the www.pdamd.com Web site.

Several companies offer programs that enable doctors to keep track of patient data and update patients' records from the bedside. Mobile Medical Data at www.medcomsys.com is one of the better-known products for keeping patient records. Another product called Auto Doc (www.auto-doc.com) tracks patient records, and most amazing of all, claims to understand doctors' handwriting 100 percent of the time. That's something I have to see.

Pilot

The fact that Visors are so popular with airplane pilots is no surprise. AirCalc is one of many Visor applications designed to perform the kinds of calculations that airplane pilots need. You can calculate such things as True Altitude (TALT), True Airspeed (TAS), and Mach Number (MN), as shown in Figure 17-5. Unfortunately, AirCalc can't handle frequent flyer miles.

Another favorite program is AvCheck, a simple checklist program that reminds you to complete every step of your preflight preparations so that you don't skip anything essential, such as fuel or parachutes. If you're the type who makes checklists before you go on vacation, you can use AvCheck for that purpose, too, and create your own checklists on your desktop computer by using the AvCheck converter. You also may want to have your little checklist obsession checked out by a shrink. The program is available from www.handango.com. The Personal version costs $29.95, and the Professional version (for flight schools and fleet operators) runs $59.99.

Figure 17-5: AirCalc figures out the more important calculations that you need while flying. Try to make the plane go up quickly and down slowly, please.

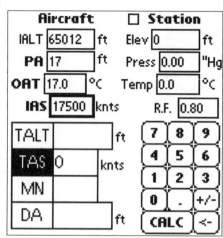

Psychic

Are you a real psychic? If you're really a psychic, you know who you are. Naturally, all psychics who are worth their crystal balls need to play a little Tarot to blow off steam between seances; those cosmic vibrations can get pretty intense. The Tarot Assistant, also available at www.handango.com, deals and interprets pentacles, swords, and cups in a flash, and keeps unsavory psychics from dealing wizards from the bottom of the deck. The program is a text-only offering; sorry, no pictures. Because you're psychic, you know that you can also find the program at the Handango.com Web site. But if you were really a psychic, you wouldn't need to read this because you would already know.

Realtor

Qualify those prospects on the spot with the Pocket Loan Qualifierfrom Information Products (www.infoprod.com). Just enter a few basic pieces of information to find out whether your customers can get the mortgage for the home of their dreams or if they need to settle for that "Handyman Special."

Salesperson

Salespeople are people people, so the standard Visor programs, especially the Address Book, are a must for anyone in sales. But the standard Visor applications lack the powerful contact management and sales automation features that you find in desktop programs like GoldMine and Act! Fortunately, you can set up both of those programs to send their most important information to your Visor. Most of the best sales automation programs include a Visor link, so all you need to do is ask the manufacturer how to use your sales program with a Visor.

Supervisor

Most of the time-and-billing programs for the Visor help you keep track of your own time, but only one that I know of helps you track other people's time, and that's MultiClock from the Kenton Group. You can use MultiClock for tracking the projects of the people you supervise, especially when you have several people doing projects for several different clients.

Teacher

Who says memorization is boring and old-fashioned? Okay, maybe it's old-fashioned, but you can make memorization fun by using one of the flashcard programs available for your Visor. One of the most versatile programs, Flash!, imports lists of text from your Memo Pad and converts them into a system that you can use to drill students on collections of facts. The program even has a quiz mode that automatically generates a multiple-choice test and keeps track of the number of right and wrong answers you choose, as shown in Figure 17-6. You can download a free demo of Flash! from `homunculus.dragonfire.net/flash.html`. Jaime Quinn, the author of Flash!, asks you to send him a voluntary donation of $12.95 or have a meal in his favorite restaurant in Mexico. Another popular memorization program is called JTutor, from Land J Technologies, the same company that offers Jfile. The company's Web site is located at `www.land-j.com`.

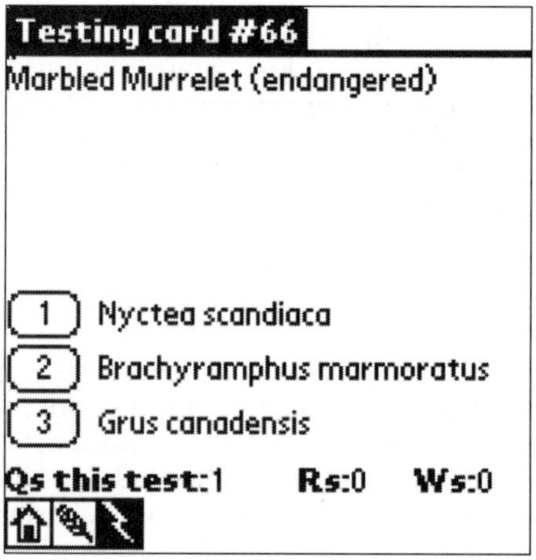

Figure 17-6:
Get ready to
win that big
TV game
show by
drilling trivia
with Flash!
"I'll take
birds for
$100, Alex."

Testing card #66

Marbled Murrelet (endangered)

1 Nyctea scandiaca
2 Brachyramphus marmoratus
3 Grus canadensis

Qs this test:1   **Rs:**0   **Ws:**0

Telemarketer

If you make a lot of phone calls, trying to figure out where you're calling by looking at an unfamiliar area code can be tough. The free Area Codes database at Handango.com can help you figure out where you're calling when your fingers do the walking. The program can't help telemarketers know when to call people in order to catch them during dinner or while they're in the shower, but most telephone salespeople already have that trick down to a science. You need to install Jfile, the Palm and Visor database program, before using the Area Code list.

Travel Agent

You didn't become a travel agent because you like to sit at home; you like to go places — the farther the better. When you travel to a foreign country, you may need to ask for help to find a hotel room, restaurant, or restroom. Small Talk is an electronic phrasebook that helps you get what you need when you don't speak another country's language. I even know of some travel agents who lend (or give) their clients a Visor equipped with the program to keep their customers happy. See Chapter 18 for more about Small Talk, or point your Web browser to www.conceptkitchen.com. The program costs $49.95 for two languages or $79.95 for all five languages. Currently available languages include English, French, Spanish, German, and Italian.

Writer

The Visor is a gift for this writer; I always get my best ideas when I'm farthest from a computer. The most useful program I've ever run across for use as a writer is InfoSelect, shown in Figure 17-7, from MicroLogic (www.miclog.com). InfoSelect is an amazing, triple-jointed information manager that keeps all of the scraps and tidbits of information that you gather up in a huge outline that you can search, arrange, and print nearly any way that you want. The program runs under Windows and includes a Palm version that you can install to your Visor so that you can synchronize information between the Visor and your desktop. The best thing about InfoSelect is that you can find information with it on the desktop almost instantly. I use InfoSelect so often on my handheld that I've reprogrammed the Memo button to run InfoSelect.

Figure 17-7:
Put your thoughts into logical order with InfoSelect. Linear thinking! What a concept!

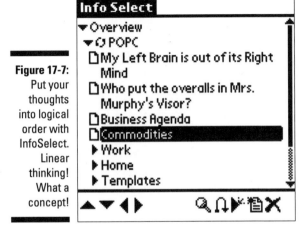

Part V
The Part of Tens

The 5th Wave   By Rich Tennant

"It's a Weber PalmPit Pro handheld barbeque with 24 btu, rechargeable battery pack, and applications for roasting, smoking, and open-flame cooking."

In this part . . .

I've spent an entire book telling you what your Palm device can do; now, I tell you a few of the things it can't do — believe me, it's a short list. In this part, I also tell you about some cool stuff — both software and hardware — that you can add to your Palm device to make it even more productive.

Chapter 18

Ten Things You Can't Do with a Visor . . . Yet

- -

In This Chapter

▶ Running on AC power . . . not

▶ Recharging batteries in the cradle . . . nope

▶ Viewing two programs at the same time . . . I wish

▶ Linking items between programs . . . a pipe dream

▶ Searching and replacing text . . . wouldn't it be nice?

▶ Creating recurring To Do items . . . please, please, please

- -

*Y*ou can make your Visor do a surprising number of tasks for you, considering what a tiny critter it is. But you may expect to be able to do certain things that just aren't on the menu yet. Here, I tell you about ten things that you can't do with a Visor . . . yet. You can be sure that thousands of programmers are toiling away in basements and garages to come up with products that expand the Visor's repertoire, so don't be surprised if many of these gaps are filled in fairly quickly.

Run on AC Power

A Visor can get plenty of use out of a pair of AAA batteries, so you probably wouldn't want to plug the thing into a wall socket . . . unless the batteries die. Murphy's Law guarantees that your batteries will die just when you're farthest from the convenience store. Your best bet: Keep a pair of spare batteries around all the time. Some Visor carrying cases even have room for an extra set of batteries, so don't be caught without juice. If your batteries run down so far that your Visor won't start, leave the old batteries in until you have a new set. A Visor holds its data when the batteries are too low to turn the Visor on, but if you take those batteries out for more than 30 seconds, your data will be lost.

Recharge Batteries in the Cradle

Leaving your Visor in the cradle does *not* recharge the batteries. Rumor has it that batteries drain faster when the Visor is in its cradle than when you're just carrying it around. I won't be surprised if Handspring introduces a Visor someday with a rechargeable battery that actually does recharge in the cradle. But for the moment, only put the Visor in its cradle when you're actually performing a HotSync.

View Two Programs at the Same Time

Visor programs have windows and buttons that remind you a little bit of common Windows or Macintosh programs. However, you can look at two different programs at the same time on a Mac or Windows PC; you can't do anything like that with a Visor. I don't know how you would make sense of what you would see on that tiny screen if you tried to display two programs at once, but I wouldn't mind sometimes seeing my appointments and To Do's at the same time. Right now, it's one at a time, please.

Link Items between Programs

Not only are you limited to seeing one program at a time, but you can't link items in one Visor program to items in another Visor program. I would find it very handy if I could link an appointment in my Date Book with a person in my Address Book. That way, when the reminder for the appointment pops up on my Visor, I could hop right over to the person's address record to jog my memory about who the person is and why we're meeting.

Search and Replace Text

The Memo Pad is just a convenient place to enter and save text; it's not a word processor. You can use the Visor Find program to look up items that contain a certain word, but can't do some of the more clever word-processing tricks, such as search and replace, that you can with popular word processors like Microsoft Word.

Create an Appointment That Spans Two or More Dates

Say you work the graveyard shift in an office, factory, or heaven knows, even a graveyard (I'm not ready to write *Visor For Vampires* just yet). If you plan to hold a meeting that starts at 11:30 p.m. and ends at 1:00 a.m., you're out of luck. Visor appointments can happen only during the span of a single day. You would have to break up your meeting when the clock strikes midnight and start again. And try to finish your meeting before sunrise when the werewolves all go home.

Use Superscripts and Subscripts

If you're the mad-professor type who frequently shouts "Eureka!" and then jots down something like $E=mc^2$, you won't be able to enter the superscript numeral *2* for your formula just yet. You can enter all sorts of foreign accents and special characters, but you can't enter superscript and subscript. Most people don't create footnotes or mathematical formulas on a Visor all that often, but those who do have to wait for a future version of Visor. Then you can really shout, "Eureka!"

Create Recurring To Do Items

You can't create recurring To Do items with your Visor or the Palm Desktop program, but you can synchronize your Visor with another desktop program that lets you create *recurring tasks,* which are To Do items that repeat at regular intervals. The task of filing your quarterly tax payment is an example of a recurring task. If you enter that kind of task in your Visor, you can't just enter the task once and then tell your Visor to make it recurring. Your only choice is to enter the task in January, April, July, and October. Fortunately, if you enter the task in a different desktop program that allows recurring tasks, the Visor automatically repeats what it sees on the desktop.

Assign Multiple Categories to One Item

If you have items that could fit into more than one category, you'll have to pick just one. For example, if you have a Key Customer category and a Business category, you might want a name to appear in both categories. Sorry, no can do.

Categorizing Dates

Do you want to categorize your appointments just like you categorize the Tasks in your To Do List? Sorry! No can do! Some desktop organizers, such as Microsoft Outlook, can do the job for you, but the category information doesn't show up on the Visor. Visor developers plan to add this feature in the future.

Other Things a Visor Can't Do

There are quite a few things I wish a Visor could help me do, but sadly, I'm on my own. Here are a few problems that nobody even pretends a Visor can solve, although I believe I've heard of other products that are supposed to fit the bill:

- ✔ Kill the Germs That Cause Bad Breath
- ✔ Wipe Out Soap Scum
- ✔ End the Embarrassment of Palm Sweat
- ✔ Cure Toe Fungus
- ✔ Predict the Stock Market
- ✔ Awaken Your Inner Wizard
- ✔ Attack Plaque
- ✔ Take the *Jeopardy* Challenge
- ✔ Change TV Forever
- ✔ Put a Tiger in Your Tank

Chapter 19

Ten Nifty Visor Accessories

*A*s usual, there's good news and bad news on the Visor accessory front. The bad news is that most of the really cool accessories that the Visor was designed to work with weren't available at the time I wrote this book. The good news is that by the time you read this, there'll probably be scads of great accessories to add to your Visor. Having something to look forward to is great, isn't it? At the moment, here's what I've seen that I like.

The Stowaway Folding Keyboard

Right now, the hottest accessory for handheld computing is the Stowaway folding keyboard from ThinkOutside. An astonishingly well-crafted gadget, the Stowaway looks like something straight out of a James Bond movie. But you don't only want a Stowaway to make you look cool; you want to be more creative and productive. A Palm/Stowaway combination can improve your productivity because you can get things done any time, anywhere. You'll be more creative, too, if you're like me and always get your best ideas when you're nowhere near a computer. You can buy the Stowaway from the retailer who sold your Visor for about $99 or you can check www.targus.com.

Canon BJC-50 Printer

Canon makes several portable, battery-powered printers with an IR port just like on your Visor. If you use printing software on your Visor (such as PalmPrint or IR Print) you can print memos, appointments, or any number of things you've created on your Visor. My favorite printer model is the tiny Canon BJC-50, which is smaller than a carton of cigarettes (and much better for your health). You can also connect the Canon BJC-50 to your regular computer with a cable and use it just like any other printer.

8MB Flash Module

If you store really huge amounts of data on your Visor, you may want an extra 8MB of storage space that plugs right into that springboard plug on the back of the Visor case. You can't run programs from the flash module, but you can store oodles of e-books, databases, and other things you want to store for safekeeping. You can get the module from the Handspring Web site for $79.95.

Backup Module

Like your mother said, brush your teeth and back up your data. Well, maybe mothers don't say anything about backing up data yet, but they will, soon enough. For $39.95, you can back up the data on your Visor at the touch of a button with the backup module. That way, if your Visor is stolen by pirates or abducted by aliens you can just get a new Visor, pop in the backup module, and poof! You're back in business.

E-Holster

Do you harbor secret fantasies of being an FBI agent? Do you dream of packing "heat" under a cheap sportcoat while snooping around unsavory neighbor-hoods? Your dreams are answered; the E-Holster lets you conceal a Visor and cell phone the way Joe Friday packed a 38-caliber. A sharp looking all-leather shoulder holster, the E-Holster is armed with two elastic pockets that are just right for your Visor and one other small electronic device. Find out more at www.eholster.com. And remember, you have the right to remain silent.

PDA Survival Kit

Because your Visor has virtually no moving parts, it has almost nothing that can wear out except the screen itself. After you've scribbled a few million words of Graffiti, the plastic screen can take quite a beating. A company named Concept Kitchen offers a collection of accessories, the PDA Survival Kit, for keeping the screen of your Visor sparkling. The kit includes WriteRights, small layers of plastic you can add to your PalmPilot screen to reduce wear and tear. Some people stick plain old transparent adhesive tape to the Graffiti area — a perfectly adequate solution, although the tape can be tricky to remove.

The kit also includes Brain Wash, a screen-cleaning system for getting the grime off your Visor screen without using any nasty abrasives or chemicals that could scratch or cloud your screen. Brain Wash consists of two items: a moist towelette and a dry towelette. Karma Cloth, another product cooked up by Concept Kitchen, is perfect for giving your screen a quick buffing; the cloth can even remove minor scratches. Karma Cloth contains some protective substances that make your Visor screen clearer and smoother and, therefore, easier to use. And, of course, a Karma Cloth can bring you good luck if you rub your screen just right.

Extra Styluses

You can find scads of new and improved styluses (or is that styli?) for your Visor, many of them made by the same folks who make fancy and expensive writing pens. If you want a stylus that displays your taste, class, and distinction, check out the better office supply stores. The nice people who made the Cross pen you got as a graduation present also make a fancy stylus that you'll treasure all summer.

Card Scanner

Corex Technologies makes two products for entering business card data into your PalmPilot: software for scanning business cards from any scanner (called CardScan 5.0) and a special scanner that's perfectly sized for business card scanning (called CardScan Plus 500). If you travel to attend trade shows or conferences regularly and need to get business card info entered into your Visor and desktop contact manager in a hurry, the Corex card scanner can help you. The scanner doesn't attach directly to your Visor; you attach the scanner to the desktop or laptop computer that you use as the host for your Visor. Scan your collection of business cards into the host computer first. When all the cards are entered into the host computer, put your Visor in its cradle and do a HotSync.

UniMount

For those who frequently use a Visor in the car, Revolv Design Company makes a special device called the UniMount to keep your Visor easy to see and use on the road. Now, I don't recommend using your Visor while driving, but when you're stopped, you might want to consult your Visor for the address of the person you're going to see, or his phone number if you plan to call from your car phone. And speaking of telephones, you can also attach your cell phone to the UniMount right next to your Visor to make a little mobile office for yourself. All you need now is a water cooler.

Extra Cradles

If you use your Visor at work and at home, you may want to synchronize with both computers every day. That's why Handspring sells extra cradles for your Visor. Check out the company's Web site at www.handspring.com.

Chapter 20

Ten Ultracool Commercial Software Programs for the Visor

● ●

In This Chapter

▶ QuickSheet

▶ Forms programs

▶ CardScan

▶ Small Talk

▶ WinFax Mobile

▶ Synchronization programs

▶ Docs-to-Go

▶ Pocket Quicken

▶ Pocket Journal

▶ Franklin Planner

● ●

*B*ehind the friendly face of a Visor is a real computer waiting to take on the work you want to do. All you need to add is the right software.

Many of the better Palm computing programs aren't available as shareware; you have to buy the programs up front. In this chapter, I give you a sampling of the commercial, pay-before-you-play programs I consider worth paying for. You can find many more than the ones in this chapter; software companies release new programs every day, but I put these programs at the top of the class.

QuickSheet

Spreadsheets were the first highly popular programs for desktop personal computers back in the darkest days of DOS. QuickSheet (from Cutting Edge Software) is the first really useable spreadsheet for Palm devices like the Visor. You can get a shareware spreadsheet named TinySheet that costs only a few bucks, but if you do any serious work with spreadsheets and you want to do any of that work on your Visor, spending the money for QuickSheet instead is worth it. You can synchronize QuickSheet with an Excel 5.0 or later spreadsheet on your desktop computer to take advantage of the collection of work you've amassed over the years. You don't find the kind of power in QuickSheet that you do in major desktop programs like Excel. QuickSheet doesn't have nearly as many automated functions, and it has no autofill or drag-and-drop copying, but if you ever need to carry around and update a tiny version of your most important spreadsheet, QuickSheet gives you a way to do it for only $39.95.

Forms Programs

The more you do with your Visor, the more you want to do. If, sooner or later, the standard Palm computing applications don't do it for you anymore, you may have to resort to a do-it-yourself solution. If you're not ready to turn into a programmer (I'm certainly not), you can use other programs to create simple forms for entering and managing data on your Visor. Although you need to create your forms on a PC running Windows 95 or later, you can install on the Visor the forms you create.

Pendragon Forms (from Pendragon Software) is the simplest and least expensive of the forms programs available. You can choose from a limited assortment of predesigned forms (for an example, see Figure 20-1) and link those forms to a file on your PC or to a Microsoft Access database. If you want to make your fortune writing slick programs you can sell to other Palm device users, Pendragon Forms probably isn't for you. If you just need a quick way to catalog your collection of rare tulip bulbs, Pendragon Forms can get you there easily.

Another important forms program is Satellite Forms from Puma Technology. A step up from the price and performance ladder of Pendragon Forms, Satellite Forms enables you to build your own forms from scratch and write real programs (see Figure 20-2) that you can install as separate programs that show up as icons on your Visor applications list. Don't expect to master Satellite Forms in a single sitting; the program comes with two thick manuals to tell you how to create applications. Still, if you have ambitious ideas about creating programs for the Visor but you're not ambitious enough to become a master programmer, Satellite Forms is for you.

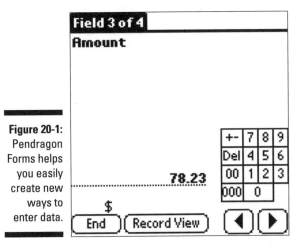

Figure 20-1:
Pendragon
Forms helps
you easily
create new
ways to
enter data.

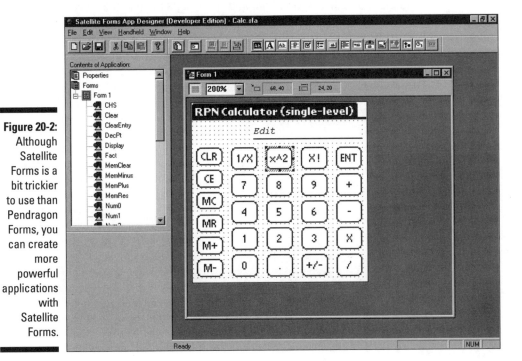

Figure 20-2:
Although
Satellite
Forms is a
bit trickier
to use than
Pendragon
Forms, you
can create
more
powerful
applications
with
Satellite
Forms.

CardScan

Face the facts: Some people still don't own a Visor or any kind of Palm organizer. That means that when you go to conferences or trade shows, most
people give you conventional business cards rather than beam their cards to
your Visor. Until that unfortunate problem is fixed, you need a quick way to

enter business cards in your Visor. The CardScan software (from Corex Technologies Corporation), which you can buy for $49 or get for free when you buy a CardScan Plus 500 business card scanner, reads the text on all those business cards and creates contact records in your favorite personal information manager. Unfortunately, you have no way to connect the scanner directly to the Visor and cut out the middleman; however, you can use the Corex software with any scanner you want.

Small Talk

Small Talk (from Concept Kitchen) is an interactive electronic language translator for people who travel frequently. I call Small Talk a phrase book rather than a translator because it translates only a handful of sentences that cover the most common situations a traveler might encounter, such as checking in to a hotel, finding transportation, and ordering a meal (see Figure 20-3). You can't use Small Talk to translate today's Parisian newspapers, although you can use it to help order *escargots*.

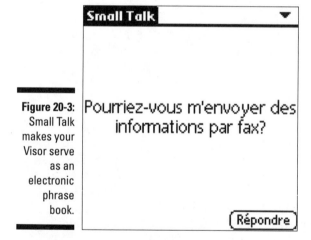

Figure 20-3: Small Talk makes your Visor serve as an electronic phrase book.

WinFax Mobile

If you have the Handspring Modem, you can turn your Visor into a pocket-size fax machine with WinFax Mobile, from Symantec (www.symantec.com). Fax any item from the Memo Pad to any standard fax machine, and include your own cover page. You don't even have to remember the recipient's fax number; just look up the number in the Address Book.

Synchronization Programs

The folks who invented the Visor were smart enough to make it work with the programs you already have on your Windows PC. You may already have a PIM (personal information manager) you're attached to (or stuck with) for good reasons. As Palm devices have caught on, more and more companies that make PIMs are offering ways to link those PIMs to the Palm devices like the Visor. Other companies are making their fortunes by creating ways to connect your Visor to programs from companies that don't want to support Palm devices (yes, Microsoft — how did you know?).

The Palm Desktop program that comes with your Visor talks directly to your Visor every time you hit the HotSync button (for more info about HotSyncing, see Chapter 11). Because the Visor was made to talk to the Palm Desktop, you don't need another program to act as a go-between. If you're already using a different program for your PIM, though, such as Microsoft Outlook or ACT!, you need a program to translate and move information between your Windows PC and your Visor. Several programs, called *conduits* or *synchronizing tools,* can do the job for Windows users.

Windows users can choose between three well-known conduit programs. These programs all do a similar job, but each offers a slightly different set of features at a different price:

- **PocketMirror for Outlook, from Chapura:** The least expensive synchronization program; in fact, you get a copy of the program for free with the purchase of your Visor. If you buy your own copy of PocketMirror, it runs $39.95. PocketMirror can synchronize your Visor only with Microsoft Outlook, and it offers relatively few of the more advanced features that competitors offer; but because many people don't use the more advanced features, PocketMirror is a perfectly good choice. If you had Microsoft Outlook installed before you installed your Visor software, PocketMirror should have installed itself. You may never see it, but it's right there connecting your Visor to Outlook. Isn't that thoughtful?

- **Desktop To Go, from DataViz, Inc.:** For about $49.95, synchronizes a Palm device to only Microsoft Outlook and Schedule+, but enables you to do a couple of fancy things when you synchronize that you can't do with PocketMirror (such as tell Outlook to send information from your Outlook custom fields to certain fields on your Visor). Because almost nobody uses more than one type of PIM, Desktop To Go does a fine job of synchronizing your Visor. You can also use Desktop To Go to synchronize a limited date range in the Date Book so that you spend less time waiting for your Visor to finish synchronizing. For example, if you have 100 appointments in your schedule, spread out over the next year, a HotSync takes longer than if you have only a few appointments scheduled in the next week. Although the Visor is pretty zippy about finishing up a HotSync over the USB line it uses, you still may want to tell the conduit to synchronize only the appointments for the next week to speed up the HotSync process even more. After all, time is money.

✔ **IntelliSync, from PumaTech:** The most powerful and best-known conduit available for the Palm device; also costs the most. At $69.95, IntelliSync enables your Palm device to trade information with just about every major personal information manager out there, including GoldMine, Ecco, and Lotus Organizer. If you're an Outlook user, IntelliSync also lets you synchronize your Palm device to any Outlook folders you choose, and it retains the categories you assign to your items in Outlook when those items turn up on your Palm device. IntelliSync is overkill if you use Outlook in only the simplest way, but if you're an Outlook power user or you use organizers other than Outlook, IntelliSync is indispensable. You can also find IntelliSync products for synchronizing handheld computers with Web sites, laptop computers with desktop computers, and heaven knows what else. If they made a product that synchronized your VCR with your popcorn popper, I wouldn't be surprised.

For more information about Microsoft Outlook, check out *Microsoft Outlook 2000 For Dummies,* written by yours truly and published by IDG Books Worldwide, Inc.

Before you rush out and buy a special program to synchronize your Visor with your PIM, check with the people who make your PIM to see whether you can get a free conduit for the program you use. For example, the people who make ACT! offer a special program to link their product with Palm devices. In fact, ACT! 4.0)includes with the program a Palm link right on the CD.

Unfortunately, I can't cover in this book how to use your other PIM; this book is about the Visor, after all. Don't fret, though: If you work with another PIM and want to know more about it, try to find a *For Dummies* book on the subject. Odds are that one exists.

The three most popular PIMs have books devoted to them. I wrote a book about Microsoft Outlook, cleverly titled *Microsoft Outlook 2000 For Dummies,* which, as you might guess, I highly recommend. For ACT! users, Jeffrey J. Mayer has written a great book just for you: *ACT! 4 For Windows For Dummies*. And Lotus Organizer, which remains popular after years as one of the top PIMs, is covered in *Lotus SmartSuite Millennium Edition For Dummies,* by Michael Meadhra and Jan Weingarten. (All these books are published by IDG Books Worldwide, Inc.)

Documents To Go

The same people who make the Desktop To Go synchronization program I already mentioned also make a program that lets you carry around copies of your Microsoft Office documents on your Visor and view them at any time.

Although you can't edit documents, you can admire your skillful formatting and brilliant analysis. Documents To Go also synchronizes the documents on your Visor with the desktop versions every time you HotSync. That way, you can carry around the latest information.

Pocket Quicken

It was only a matter of time before someone said, "Gee, I'd sure like to have a copy of Quicken on my Visor." The nice people from Landware worked with the people who make Quicken to produce Pocket Quicken, a convenient way to keep your most important financial data on a Palm organizer. It synchronizes with Quicken 99 to help you keep track of your current balances and lets you make entries to Quicken 99 from your Visor while you're roaming around.

Pocket Journal

Outlook users have a module named the Journal that isn't included on the Visor. The Outlook Journal from Chapura (www.chapura.com) is a pretty good place to record phone calls and other daily transactions with other people just for your records. Pocket Journal creates a version of your Outlook Journal on your Visor and synchronizes itself with your desktop version of Outlook. Pocket Journal also offers check boxes for checking off phone calls you've returned, unlike the desktop Outlook Journal. In many ways, Pocket Journal is more useful than the desktop version.

Franklin Planner

Stephen Covey, the man who wrote *The Seven Habits of Highly Effective People* (1989, Simon & Schuster) teaches courses in time management that involve using a Palm organizer. Using a Visor or other Palm product is obviously a highly effective thing to do. His company also sells software for your Visor to make you still more effective. I know that you don't miss a trick, so you'll probably check it out on the Web, at www.franklincovey.com.

Internet Resources for the Visor

•••

*T*ime flies quickly in the technology business! Every few weeks, a smashing new program for the Palm platform turns up from some emerging software genius. Every so often, the geniuses at Handspring release a whole new Visor. How can you possibly keep up? Your best bet for staying abreast of the latest developments, is to turn to the Internet. You can find thousands of sources of information on the Internet; this appendix lists some of my favorites.

PalmPilot Web Ring

This is the place to start. If I were to give you a list of all the Web sites devoted to the PalmPilot and Visor, the list would number in the hundreds, but it would be out of date by the time you read it. A great place to begin your Internet search for Visor Web sites is the PalmPilot Web Ring — you can access this site at www.handango.com. The PalmPilot Web Ring is a chain of hundreds of Web sites that advise Visor and PalmPilot users on how to get the most from their handheld computer. If you explore the Web Ring long enough, you'll encounter all the other sites that I mention in this appendix.

Jiffylearn

I'm such a Web junkie. Every time I see an Internet URL in a book or magazine article, I want to click right on the page to visit the site. Sadly, that doesn't work yet. I decided to give my readers the next best thing by posting all the Web links I list in this appendix (as well as links in some other parts of the book) to my personal Web site at www.jiffylearn.com/booklinks.htm. I also add links to other sites I find interesting as time goes along.

Handspring

www.handspring.com

If you want good information, you might as well go right to the horse's mouth. At the Handspring Web site, you can find out about the latest products and accessories for your Visor and even buy a new Visor or accessories. The site is also an excellent place to look for technical support.

InSync Online

www.insync-palm.com

The "Palm people" at 3Com run an Internet mailing list called InSync Online that sends regular messages describing tips, tricks, and special offers for PalmPilot users. Most of the tips and tricks that work on a PalmPilot work just as well on a Visor. You can sign up at the InSync Web site.

Handango

www.handango.com

Handango is my favorite source for the latest, greatest, and strangest software available for PalmPilot. The site offers downloadable copies of every kind of Visor and PalmPilot software, from scientific calculators to a database of the birthdays of every Beanie Baby.

Visorcentral.com

www.visorcentral.com

A useful Web site and news archive, Visorcentral.com includes reviews of products and software carefully organized into categories. You can also find a list of PalmPilot programs that are not compatible with your Visor.

PalmPilot Newsgroups

```
comp.sys.palmtops.pilot
```

```
alt.comp.sys.palmpilot
```

Gee, what funny-looking Web site addresses. Well, they aren't Web addresses —
they're the addresses for two PalmPilot newsgroups. The Internet has thousands of online discussion forums called *newsgroups,* in which people post and
reply to questions, opinions, and announcements on nearly every conceivable
topic. You can read any newsgroup through a news-reading program, such as
Microsoft Outlook Express, or by pointing your browser at `www.dejanews.com`
and searching for PalmPilot.

PalmPower Magazine

```
www.palmpower.com
```

I read *PalmPower Magazine* daily. Every morning, *PalmPower* lists up to a half-
dozen stories of interest to Visor and PalmPilot users around the Web. Also,
the editors prepare monthly features about technology and reviews of new
Palm and Visor accessories. If you want to stay updated in the Palm universe,
PalmPower is an important resource.

Smaller.com

```
www.smaller.com
```

Good things come in small packages, right? So it figures that better things
come in smaller packages. And really, super, duper great things come in
itsy-bitsy, teeny-weeny. . . . Anyway, smaller.com is devoted to the latest
news about itty-bitty computers like the Visor and PalmPilot. Smaller.com
discusses the Visor and Psion palmtop computers, Rex personal organizers,
Windows CE products, and the late Apple Newton.

PalmGear

www.palmgear.com

Part newspaper, part online store, PalmGear is the place to find information about accessories that you can buy for your Visor or PalmPilot. The folks at PalmGear gladly take your credit card number over the phone or the Web and sell you anything from a modem cable to a doohickey that lets you hang your Visor around your neck.

PDA Geek

www.ugeek.com/pdageek

Some people call Visor a PDA, short for *Personal Digital Assistant*, not the *Public Display of Affection* that earned you two weeks of detention in high school (if you were lucky). PDA Geek is for people who may be a tad more enthusiastic about Visor than a normal person would be. But if you want to learn inside info about using your Visor, check out this site.

Palm.com

www.Palm.com

Before Handspring, there was Palm, and it's still out there, going strong. Even though the Palm.com Web site pretends that Visor doesn't exist, if you point your browser to the PalmPilot manufacturer's Web site, you can read the official word on PalmPilot products, upgrades, and links. Not all of the information is applicable to Visor owners, but a lot of it is. You can find a complete collection of articles, Web site links, and the latest versions of all the software that you need to keep Visor or PalmPilot in tip-top condition. The Palm.com Web site also features links to the Web sites of other companies that manufacture software and accessories for the PalmPilot, many of which also serve Visor owners.

Index

• **C** •

• *H* •

• *I* •

• N •

• P •

• Q •

QED Doc reader program, 274
Quicken, 307
Quicklist category, 78
QuickSheet (Cutting Edge Software), 302
Quinn, Jamie, 288

• R •

realtor, Visor programs for, 287
Recent Calculations option, 21
Record Completion Date check box, 101
Record menu
  Attach Note, 74, 128
  Beam Category, 148
  Beam Event, 146
  Beam Item, 94
  Beam Memo, 116
  Create Template, 142
  Delete Address, 79
  Delete Event, 131
  Delete Item, 34, 98
  Delete Memo, 113
  Delete Note, 80, 99
  New Floating Event, 138
  New Journal Entry, 141
  New To Do, 139
  Purge, 103, 134
  Select Business Card, 77
  Undelete from Archive, 142
recovering deleted names, 80
recurring tasks, 295
Remember Last Category box, 82
Remind Me box, 133
remote control, Visor use as, 152
Remote HotSync option, 166
Remove Category dialog box, 93
Rename Category dialog box, 195
Rename Custom Fields dialog box, 82
Rename Custom Fields option, 82
renaming categories, 93, 94
Repeat box, 129
Reply Options dialog box, 158, 159

replying to mail messages, 158, 159
reset button, 14
restoring data, 212
Retrieve All High Priority check box, 167
Retrieve Only Messages Containing
    option, 167
return character, Graffiti, 31
Revolv Design Company, 300
Road Warriors, 218
Robert's Rules of Order, 280
Run option, 174

• S •

salesperson, Visor programs for, 287
Satellite Forms (Puma Technology), 302
Save an Archive Copy on PC option,
    98, 103
Save and Install PDB dialog box, 276, 277
Save Archive Copy on PC box, 113, 131
Save As command, 259
Save As Type box, 259
Save Draft dialog box, 162
scanner, card, 299, 303
schedule
  changing appointment time, 64
  views, types of, 63
Schedule+, 305
screen
  cleaning, 299
  display area, 15, 16
  overview, 14
  protection, 299
  scratches, 28, 62
  smudging with fingers, 62
  soft buttons, 16, 17, 19
scroll bar, 16
scroll buttons, 12, 13
  Date Book, 63, 120, 122, 123
  hard reset use of, 14
  To Do List, 87
scrolling e-books, 267
Search Again icon, 243
search and replace text, 294

• U •

• V •

• W •

• Y •

SPECIAL OFFER FOR IDG BOOKS READERS

FREE GIFT!

FREE

IDG Books/PC WORLD CD Wallet

and a Sample Issue of

PC WORLD

THE #1 MONTHLY COMPUTER MAGAZINE

How to order your sample issue and FREE CD Wallet:

✉ Cut and mail the coupon today!

☎ Call us at 1-800-395-5763
Fax us at 1-415-882-0936

☛ Order online at
www.pcworld.com/subscribe/idgbooks

ORDER TODAY!

FREE GIFT/SAMPLE ISSUE COUPON

Cut coupon and mail to: PC World, 501 Second Street, San Francisco, CA 94107

YES! Please rush my FREE CD wallet and my FREE sample issue of PC WORLD! If I like PC WORLD, I'll honor your invoice and receive 11 more issues (12 in all) for just $19.97—that's 72% off the newsstand rate.

NO COST EXAMINATION GUARANTEE.
If I decide PC WORLD is not for me, I'll write "cancel" on the invoice and owe nothing. The sample issue and CD wallet are mine to keep, no matter what.

PC WORLD

Name

Company

Address

City _____ State _____ Zip _____

Email

Offer valid in the U.S. only. Mexican orders please send $39.97 USD. Canadian orders send $39.97, plus 7% GST (#R124669680). Other countries send $65.97. Savings based on annual newsstand rate of $71.88 .

SPECIAL OFFER FOR IDG BOOKS READERS

Get the Most from Your PC!

Every issue of PC World is packed with the latest information to help you make the most of your PC.

- Top 100 PC and Product Ratings
- Hot PC News
- How Tos, Tips, & Tricks
- Buyers' Guides
- Consumer Watch
- Hardware and Software Previews
- Internet & Multimedia Special Reports
- Upgrade Guides
- Monthly @Home Section

YOUR FREE GIFT!

As a special bonus with your order, you will receive the IDG Books/ PC WORLD CD wallet, perfect for transporting and protecting your CD collection.

SEND TODAY

for your sample issue
and FREE IDG Books/PC WORLD CD Wallet!

How to order your sample issue and FREE CD Wallet:

✉ Cut and mail the coupon today!
Mail to: PC World, 501 Second Street, San Francisco, CA 94107

☎ Call us at 1-800-395-5763
Fax us at 1-415-882-0936

☞ Order online at www.pcworld.com/subscribe/idgbooks

PC WORLD

YOUR
ONLINE
RESOURCE

WWW.DUMMIES.COM

Discover Dummies Online!

The Dummies Web Site is your fun and friendly online resource for the latest information about *For Dummies®* books and your favorite topics. The Web site is the place to communicate with us, exchange ideas with other *For Dummies* readers, chat with authors, and have fun!

Ten Fun and Useful Things You Can Do at www.dummies.com

1. Win free *For Dummies* books and more!
2. Register your book and be entered in a prize drawing.
3. Meet your favorite authors through the IDG Books Worldwide Author Chat Series.
4. Exchange helpful information with other *For Dummies* readers.
5. Discover other great *For Dummies* books you must have!
6. Purchase Dummieswear® exclusively from our Web site.
7. Buy *For Dummies* books online.
8. Talk to us. Make comments, ask questions, get answers!
9. Download free software.
10. Find additional useful resources from authors.

Link directly to these ten fun and useful things at
http://www.dummies.com/10useful

For other technology titles from IDG Books Worldwide, go to
www.idgbooks.com

Not on the Web yet? It's easy to get started with *Dummies 101®: The Internet For Windows® 98* or *The Internet For Dummies®* at local retailers everywhere.

Find other *For Dummies* books on these topics:
Business • Career • Databases • Food & Beverage • Games • Gardening • Graphics • Hardware
Health & Fitness • Internet and the World Wide Web • Networking • Office Suites
Operating Systems • Personal Finance • Pets • Programming • Recreation • Sports
Spreadsheets • Teacher Resources • Test Prep • Word Processing

The IDG Books Worldwide logo is a registered trademark under exclusive license to IDG Books Worldwide, Inc., from International Data Group, Inc. Dummies.com and the ...For Dummies logo are trademarks, and Dummies Man, For Dummies, Dummieswear, and Dummies 101 are registered trademarks of IDG Books Worldwide, Inc. All other trademarks are the property of their respective owners.

IDG BOOKS WORLDWIDE BOOK REGISTRATION

We want to hear from you!

Visit **http://my2cents.dummies.com** to register this book and tell us how you liked it!

- ✔ Get entered in our monthly prize giveaway.

- ✔ Give us feedback about this book — tell us what you like best, what you like least, or maybe what you'd like to ask the author and us to change!

- ✔ Let us know any other *For Dummies®* topics that interest you.

Your feedback helps us determine what books to publish, tells us what coverage to add as we revise our books, and lets us know whether we're meeting your needs as a *For Dummies* reader. You're our most valuable resource, and what you have to say is important to us!

Not on the Web yet? It's easy to get started with *Dummies 101®: The Internet For Windows® 98* or *The Internet For Dummies®* at local retailers everywhere.

Or let us know what you think by sending us a letter at the following address:

For Dummies Book Registration
Dummies Press
10475 Crosspoint Blvd.
Indianapolis, IN 46256

BESTSELLING
BOOK SERIES